SPY SAGA

SPY SAGA

LEE HARVEY OSWALD AND U.S. INTELLIGENCE

PHILIP H. MELANSON

PRAEGER

New York
Westport, Connecticut
London

Library of Congress Cataloging-in-Publication Data

Melanson, Philip H.
    Spy saga : Lee Harvey Oswald and U.S. intelligence / Philip H.
Melanson.
        p.   cm.
    Includes bibliographical references.
    ISBN 0-275-93571-X
    1. Oswald, Lee Harvey. 2. Intelligence service—United States.
3. United States—Central Intelligence Agency. 4. Kennedy, John F.
(John Fitzgerald), 1917–1963—Assassination. I. Title.
E842.9.M44   1990
327.12'092—dc20   90-7237

Library of Congress Catalog Card Number: 90-7237
ISBN: 0-275-93571-X

First published in 1990

Praeger Publishers, One Madison Avenue, New York, NY 10010
An imprint of Greenwood Publishing Group, Inc.

Printed in the United States of America

The paper used in this book complies with the
Permanent Paper Standard issued by the National
Information Standards Organization (Z39.48–1984).

10 9 8 7 6 5 4 3 2 1

To Dorothy Edwards Hart

In 1978 former CIA Director Richard Helms exited from his executive-session testimony before the House Select Committee on Assassinations. He paused to talk with the press. *Washington Post* reporter George Lardner, Jr. described the encounter in his paper's August 10 edition:

> Helms told reporters during a break that no one would ever know who or what Lee Harvey Oswald, named by the Warren Commission as Kennedy's assassin, represented. Asked whether the CIA knew of any ties Oswald had with either the KGB or the CIA, Helms paused and with a laugh said, "I don't remember." Pressed on the point, he told a reporter, "Your questions are almost as dumb as the Committee's."

Contents

Photographs follow page 90.

Acknowledgments

The author gratefully acknowledges the support and assistance provided during this lengthy project by persons too numerous to mention here. Over the past decade, students at Southeastern Massachusetts University in my course on Political Assassinations in America and in my research seminars have offered questions and insights and served as a stimulus to my research—especially Brian Bennett. My colleagues in the political science department have given professional and intellectual support, particularly John Carroll who served as both reader and gadfly, pressing me to bring this project to fruition. Two research grants from my university helped fund the extensive time required at Washington, DC research facilities. Our department secretary Liz Tucker was helpful, as always, typing much of the extensive correspondence. Ron Quintin and Jennifer Tavares helped as my research assistants.

Ms. Helen Neer and her staff at the FBI reading room in Washington, DC were efficient and accommodating during my numerous visits. The CIA employees who babysat me in the tiny reading room in Roslyn, Virginia were always courteous and their curiosity about my work was a welcome break from the routine. The staff of the National Archives in Washington, DC—and the now-retired curator of the Warren Commission papers and exhibits, Marion Johnson—processed all my requests for reading and copying with speed and accuracy. The U.S. Secret Service was—in the author's extensive experience with Freedom of Information Act requests to federal agencies—a model of responsive public disclosure in locating the last of their unreleased case files, as was the National Archives which processed the documents for release.

Without implying anyone's endorsement or agreement with this analysis, I wish to acknowledge the valuable contributions made by competent and energetic researchers over the past 27 years. The best of this work constitutes a cumulative historical record that is more accurate and enlightening than the body of official governmental reports. Without the leaps of understanding and ground-breaking research generated by previous efforts, this project would not have been possible. The late Sylvia Meagher set a standard for meticulous, probing analysis that serves as a beacon for all responsible students of this case. Her landmark book *Accessories After the Fact* remains the most perceptive general work on the case despite its early origin in 1967. Among those who have studied intelligence-related aspects of the case, I have benefitted most from the detailed, enlightening analyses of Professor Peter Dale Scott, University of California, Berkeley, and the pioneering investigative work of British journalist Anthony Summers, who also generously shared with me some of his private papers. I wish to thank Paul Hoch, generally regarded as one of the sharpest, most careful researchers, for his unselfish sharing of data and his thoughts and criticisms concerning the manuscript.

Special thanks are due my friend and colleague Lauriston R. King, of Texas A & M University. He served as reader and clinician and provided steadfast encouragement regarding the importance and viability of the project. My friend and former departmental colleague Jack Fyock gave me a critical analysis of the manuscript, intellectual encouragement, and (as my office-mate) was willing to digress from his own work to discuss my research at length. Thanks to Peggy Adler Robohm for her critical reading of portions of the manuscript and for her insights and sharing of data.

Larry Schlossman has been a major influence on my research. His ideas, sources, and contacts were extremely valuable, as was his support. His 1983 nationally syndicated radio documentary on the case served as a primary catalyst for this project. He interviewed dozens of researchers and spent many dozens of hours on the telephone, sharing what could be shared while keeping everyone's confidences. He collated a great deal of data and stimulated further research. All of this has been enormously enriching to my work.

Much thanks to Mary Glenn, my editor at Praeger, for her guidance and support and her attentiveness to the project.

My extended family (especially my Mom) and friends too numerous to mention generously listened to my monologues and gave moral support throughout the project. My sons Brett and Jess have been willing to listen to progress reports and were understanding of the pressures on my time created by the workload.

As always, I owe my greatest debt to my wife Judith. She typed and edited the various drafts, and was a source of sound advice and unwavering support and encouragement throughout all phases of this sometimes difficult enterprise.

For all this, I am extremely grateful.

Introduction

Everybody will know who I am.

Lee Harvey Oswald, Nov. 22, 1963[1]

The above comment was generally interpreted as a smug self-certification of Oswald's own infamy, his assured place in history as the President's assassin. As years passed, skepticism concerning the Warren Commission's findings about Oswald's background and his role in the assassination reached majoritarian levels. Researchers hypothesized a different meaning: namely, that Oswald was a complex young man playing roles and affecting political postures, and that these were about to be stripped away by the legal process as he sought to defend himself against charges of murder. Oswald was silenced by Jack Ruby before he could participate in the process, and before he could tell us who he really was. That task has been left to others, who must follow the rich and mysterious trail of events and artifacts he left behind.

As we approach the third decade since Oswald's death, nothing approximating historical clarity has been achieved. The question "Who was Lee Harvey Oswald?" remains unanswered. He has been portrayed by official investigators, journalists, or researchers as a disgruntled loner and muddled leftist, a Russian spy, a pro-Castroite or pawn of the Castro government, a low-level Mafia pawn, and a U.S. intelligence agent. These images have been dismissed by some as the product of conspiracy mentalities or of the psychological need to portray the President's assassin as complex and larger than life. This need, it is argued, results from an unwillingness to believe that a lone nut with a cheap rifle can so profoundly alter our political history. He must be someone special, the embodiment of dark, powerful forces. The mystique of Camelot and the lure of conspiracy-think have undeniably combined to distort various facets of this case. But the fact is that Oswald actually lends himself to all of these divergent portraits, although to some much better than to others. He is by far the most fascinating and complex assassin (alleged or actual) in U.S. history. Despite three major national-level investigations and hundreds of file drawers full of documents, despite the work of hundreds of journalists and researchers, there is no agreement about who this man was.

This analysis seeks to provide the answer to this question by presenting the best known evidence in systematic, detailed form. That Lee Harvey Oswald was some sort of U.S. intelligence agent has always been one of the options. The author will place the available data about Oswald's activities and associations—some of the data old, some new—within the context of the perspectives, programs, and people that were operative in the U.S. intelligence community (primarily the CIA) in Oswald's era. In doing so, this book hopes to elevate what was formerly one option to the status of the correct answer: Lee Harvey Oswald spent nearly all of his adult life working for U.S. intelligence—most likely for the CIA— as an agent-provocateur. He did so in both the domestic and international arenas, right up to his involvement in the assassination.

As Warren Commission member Allen Dulles told his commission colleagues, it is difficult to prove a negative: proving that Oswald was *not* a CIA operative would be nearly impossible, Dulles warned. Similarly, the other options for Oswald (Mafia soldier, communist spy, crazed loner) cannot be disproved here. However, presenting the evidence that he was a U.S. intelligence agent goes a long way toward establishing what he was not, through mutual exclusivity.

What follows is a dossier on Oswald-the-spy. The reader is invited to review it as an FBI counterintelligence officer would: Is he a spy? For whom? How consistent and cross-corroborative is the data? Oswald is too often misperceived as an infamous assassin whose name and face are so familiar that we know everything about him.

This is not primarily a psychological profile, except implicitly as we describe his patterns of behavior and reactions to crucial situations. This study eschews many of the controversies that the author credits as valid and important: Did Oswald kill the President? What was his precise role? The failure to understand who he really was has severely inhibited all official attempts to resolve the issues attending this crime. We will take a micro look at Oswald through the lens of tradecraft, of espionage. Hopefully, the clarity provided by this view will help bring into focus the unresolved questions and controversies that still plague the assassination of our thirty-fifth president after nearly 30 years.

Oswald is the most complicated individual ever to be charged in a major political assassination case in the United States. Valid questions have been raised about Sirhan Sirhan's motive and mental state, about James Earl Ray's officially ascribed modus operandi. But their lives are relatively simple and explicable, even uneventful, compared to Oswald's. We know who they are in terms of the major dimensions of their lives. While this in no way precludes unanswered questions, mysteries, or even conspiracies, it presents a more solid baseline from which to seek valid conclusions.

Oswald is enigmatic partly because he spent so much of his life in the shadowy, compartmentalized world of U.S. intelligence, where deception is more the norm than the exception, where valid data is difficult to unearth. As we shall see, he maintained a façade of leftism by his politically charged letters and solo public performances. In contrast, his associations and contacts were decidedly right-wing and anti-communist. Moreover, as we shall see, false information was purposely created about Oswald, blurring further the truth about his political identity and his activities.

In spite of all this confusion there is still a dominant image of Oswald. It is the one put forth by the Warren Commission in 1963 and shared by the House of Representatives Select Committee on Assassinations in 1978, the one so pervasive among mainstream historians and journalists. Lee Harvey Oswald—a hot-headed, violence-prone, confused leftist who could not find his political niche, a "loner" who couldn't hold a job, frustrated and "unstable." The Warren Commission described him as a man who

> was perpetually discontent with the world around him. Long before the assassination he expressed a hatred for American society and acted in protest against it. Oswald searched for what he conceived to be the perfect society and was doomed from the start. He sought for himself a place in history— a role as the "great man" who would be recognized as having been in advance of his times. His commitment to Marxism and communism appears to have been another important factor in his motivation.[2]

This public perception was shaped more by the media than the Commission's report, but the image was consistent. The February 21, 1964 issue of *Life* magazine had Oswald on the cover, the infamous photo of him dressed in black, holding a rifle and leftist literature, wearing a pistol strapped to his waist. An editorial proudly touts the massive investigative effort that produced "our study of Lee Harvey Oswald." The huge spread (12 pages of pictures and text) traces his life from early childhood to the assassination. It is titled "The Evolution of an Assassin, A Clinical Study of Lee Harvey Oswald." There are quotes from teachers, family members, Marine Corps associates, and neighbors. There is not one hint of intrigue or mystery. There is no mention of the shadowy characters portrayed here (David Ferrie, George de Mohrenschildt), characters central to the Oswald enigma. For *Life* and its readers there was no enigma—only the depressing banality of a psychological misfit, an awkward, struggling loner who could never find himself:

- A neighbor said he shouted at his wife, "I am the commander!"
- A truant officer claimed that Oswald told him that "most of all he liked to be by himself and do things by himself."
- "He never came to squadron parties," said a Marine.
- "He looked like he was just lost," said a teacher.

Life's Oswald was summed up vividly by a psychiatrist who had once examined him when he was thirteen. Said Dr. Renatus Hartogs:

Psychologically, he had all the qualifications of being a potential assassin. Such a criminal is usually a person with paranoid ideas of grandiosity who can get satisfactory self-vindication only by shocking the entire world. He had to show the world he was not unknown, that he was someone with whom the world had to reckon.[3]

You are about to meet a very different young man: a poised, rather resourceful political manipulator who surely lived one of the most eventful, intrigue-filled lives imaginable—albeit a very short one. His life was spent within the shadow, if not the networks, of U.S. intelligence. Whatever ethical judgment one might render about his activities, he was, it would seem, good at what he did—successfully posing as a defector and spying in the Soviet Union, functioning as a low- to mid-level agent-provocateur in the United States.

From the time he was an eighteen-year-old Marine until his murder at twenty-four, he lived a secret life. We will follow it from the Marines to Moscow to New Orleans to Mexico City to the Texas School Book

Depository in Dallas. He might have become an infamous character apart from President Kennedy's assassination. He could easily have been portrayed as the traitor who gave the Soviets the information needed to shoot down our U–2 spy plane, an incident that created a diplomatic crisis and caused a loss of military intelligence secrets that was unparalleled in the previous decade. Oswald had access to the U–2 while in the Marines; he had defected to the Soviet Union, offering to reveal military secrets, and was still in the USSR when the spy plane was shot down in May 1960. As we shall see, the fact that he was not cast as a notorious traitor is one of the key factors to unravelling the Oswald mystery.

Ironically, although none of the agencies involved would admit it, young Oswald probably had one of the longest government paper trails of any person his age in the entire nation in terms of the number and volume of files. The destruction or suppression of some of this material, especially CIA and military intelligence files, contributes substantially to the historical confusion. This data would be dwarfed by the mountain of post-assassination paper. Still, not many twenty-four-year-old Americans could claim to have been a subject of interest to the U.S. State Department, CIA, FBI, military intelligence, passport office, KGB, MVD (the Soviet equivalent of our FBI), and unofficial dossiers kept by a variety of anti-Castro groups and interests in the United States.

This analysis will reach a conclusion about a conspiracy in John F. Kennedy's assassination, although it does not seek to establish Oswald's innocence or the existence of a second gun. Instead, it will demonstrate that Oswald's movements were still being choreographed by his handlers in U.S. intelligence—however fringe or renegade they may have been— at the time of the assassination. Whatever his role in the crime, persons who knew his background were fabricating not only his image as a hot-headed communist but also evidence of his guilt in the assassination. Such activity—if clearly and deliberately connected to the impending crime, as some of it definitely was—constitutes conspiracy. The legal definition of conspiracy is knowingly attempting to further the success of a crime at any phase of its commission.

In any assassination investigation, authorities check on the background and associations of the accused. They attempt to discover if he or she was part of any group or interest that might be behind the crime, either directly (by providing assistance) or more indirectly (by encouraging or manipulating the alleged assassin). If so, authorities have found a conspiracy. For example, the FBI investigated Sirhan Sirhan to see if he was part of, or backed by, any Middle Eastern organization or terrorist group,

since he was Palestinian in origin and Robert F. Kennedy strongly supported Israel. No such connection was found. In Oswald's case, the
conclusion that he was a U.S. intelligence agent is not a footnote to the
crime of the century but rather a window onto the conspiracy behind
President John F. Kennedy's assassination.

1

Agent Oswald:
Setting the Framework

> . . . suspicions that Oswald served as an intelligence operative—and,
> in any such case, there is great disagreement over *whom* he might
> have been working for—arise from examinations of his activities by
> observers dedicated to the study of the world of spies.
> Henry Hurt, Reasonable Doubt[1]

To the Warren Commission, Lee Harvey Oswald was simply a disgruntled
Marxist. The political highlights of his life that were used by the Commission to sketch a tableau of leftism included: his defection to the Soviet
Union, his founding of a New Orleans chapter of the pro-Castro Fair
Play for Cuba Committee (FPCC) and his public demonstrations on its
behalf, and his attempt to return to Russia (via Cuba) the month before
the assassination. Still, these major events were surrounded by intrigues,
mysteries, and anomalies sufficient to force the Commission to worry
about "the dirty rumor" that Oswald was connected to U.S. intelligence.
In the final analysis the Commission officially concluded that Oswald
was not anyone's agent. In 1978 the House Select Committee on Assassinations (HSCA, also commonly referred to as the House Assassinations
Committee) concluded that he was not a CIA agent:

> The results of this investigation confirmed the Warren Commission tes-
> timony of [CIA Directors] McCone and Helms. There was no indication
> in Oswald's CIA file that he had ever had contact with the Agency. Finally,
> taken in their entirety, the items of circumstantial evidence that the Com-

mittee had selected for investigation as possibly indicative of an intelligence association did not support the allegation that Oswald had an intelligence agency relationship.[2]

Setting aside the quaint notion that if Oswald were linked to the Agency, proof would reside in the CIA files revealed to the Committee, there is extensive circumstantial evidence that Oswald was in fact an agent. The Committee examined only some of it, sometimes superficially. Before presenting this evidence, it is useful to examine some general propositions for interpreting Oswald's case history.

To conclude, as the Commission and the House Committee did, that Oswald was not an intelligence agent of any kind is to believe that his life was structured by endless coincidences and heavy doses of good and bad luck, that the pattern of mysteries and anomalies that dominated his adult existence were random and innocent. It is to believe that the incongruity between his actions and his alleged beliefs, and between his public and private behavior, had no significance beyond manifesting his alleged mental instability. It forces the conclusion that his frequent and unusual interactions with government agencies lacked any overarching significance. In sum, the circumstantial evidence is so rich that to explain it away as coincidence or happenstance strains credulity. There are simply too many shadows of the unseen hand cast on Oswald's short but eventful life.

Whose agent was Oswald—ours or theirs? To hold that he was recruited as a Soviet spy, one must posit that virtually all of the agencies of U.S. intelligence and law enforcement were so completely ineffective when it came to Oswald that they must be imagined to be not just incompetent but comatose. Any government, any agency can be fooled. Spies do penetrate the other side, sometimes at the highest levels. But the opportunities of the U.S. government to discover Oswald-the-Soviet-spy were so numerous, and his interaction with U.S. agencies so extensive, that it requires too elastic a notion of U.S. bad luck (and Soviet good luck) to imagine that the Soviets slipped him past U.S. intelligence. As will be demonstrated, the notion that Oswald was a Russian spy requires the suspension of belief concerning a great deal of very good evidence.

A CIA memo written one month after the assassination makes a key point: "Longstanding KGB practice generally forbids agents serving outside the U.S.S.R. to have any contact with domestic communist parties or with Soviet embassies or consultants [deletion]. Yet Oswald blazed a trail to the Soviets which was a mile wide."[3]

Another theory, offered by British author Michael Eddowes, is that the Soviets pulled a switch while Oswald was in Russia, substituting a KGB agent who proceeded to assassinate the President on Moscow's orders. It is not the James Bond-like flavor to Eddowes's scenario that one balks at, for this is one arena in which truth is indeed stranger than fiction. Eddowes's contention rests primarily on alleged discrepancies in records of Oswald's height and appearance.[4] For example, official records describe the Oswald who returned from Russia as shorter than the Oswald who enlisted in the Marines years before defecting to Russia. One difficulty with the scenario is that it assumes Oswald's mother and brother were fooled by an impostor, which seems extremely unlikely. In 1981, under a court order obtained by Eddowes and Oswald's widow Marina, the badly decomposed body was exhumed and positively identified as the real Oswald.

The other foreign-agent theory ties Oswald to the Cuban government or its agents. Beyond the flimsy assertion that he had contact with people at the Cuban consulate in Mexico who paid him money just before the assassination (assertions emanating from the CIA itself or from anti-Castro sympathizers), there is no convincing circumstantial evidence that he had such ties. As this analysis will show, one flaw in this scenario is the assumption that Oswald's pro-Castro involvements were real rather than deceptive. It would be feckless for Cuban intelligence to employ an assassin so publicly identified with Castro's cause. Moreover, as will later be discussed, someone was controlling Oswald's movements in a manner that made him appear increasingly pro-Castro and pro-communist in the months preceding the assassination. Someone was also fabricating embellishments on a leftist image for Oswald—hardly a smart move for Castro's agents. The notion that Oswald was linked to Cuban intelligence but committed the assassination on his own still requires that he be a genuine pro-Castroite (when, in fact, he was just the opposite).

The assertion that Oswald belonged to U.S. and not Soviet intelligence only partially answers the question, "Whose agent was he?" FBI? CIA? National Security Agency? Defense Intelligence Agency? Army or Navy intelligence? Robert Sam Anson is correct when he cautions that "Oswald's having been an agent does not necessarily mean he was a CIA man. Part of the common misunderstanding of the nature of intelligence derives from the assumption that all spies work for the CIA."[5] Not only do other U.S. intelligence organizations have their own spies, but the CIA by no means had exclusive turf rights to the various intelligence contexts in which Oswald appeared. Military intelligence had been in-

volved in the arena of Soviet espionage; the FBI and military intelligence
were very active in Cuban-exile politics and espionage within the United
States.

What can be said is that Oswald's links to CIA-related persons, projects,
and contexts appear far stronger than do those to any other U.S. intelligence agency, although the FBI and military intelligence run a distant
second and third. Oswald's two spookiest known associates, George de
Mohrenschildt and David Ferrie, seemed more firmly linked to the CIA
than to any other intelligence organization.

Another frequently encountered misconception is that U.S. intelligence agencies are monolithic, either as an entire community or as
individual organizations. In fact, secrecy and turf rivalry significantly
compartmentalize them from each other and within themselves. It is thus
possible that one CIA office in Langley, Virginia was earnestly studying
Oswald to see if he was a Russian spy (as in the previously mentioned
CIA memo), while someone in another section was running him as a
U.S. agent.

As former CIA Director Allen Dulles indicated to his colleagues on
the Warren Commission, proving or disproving that Oswald worked for
the Agency would be very difficult given the nature of the organization.[6]

> *Allen Dulles*: There is a terribly hard thing to disprove, you know. How
> do you disprove a fellow was not your agent? How do you disprove it?
>
> *Congressman Hale Boggs (Dem., LA)*: You could disprove it, couldn't
> you?
>
> *Dulles*: No. . . .
>
> *Boggs*: . . . Did you have agents about whom you had no record what-
> soever?
>
> *Dulles*: The record might not be on paper. But on paper would have
> hieroglyphics that only two people knew what they meant, and nobody
> outside of the agency would know and you could say this meant the agent
> and somebody else could say this meant another agent. . . .
>
> *Boggs*: . . . Let's say [U-2 pilot Francis Gary] Powers did not have a signed
> contract, but he was recruited by someone in CIA. The man who recruited
> him would know, wouldn't he?
>
> *Dulles*: Yes, but he wouldn't tell.
>
> *Chief Justice Earl Warren*: Wouldn't tell it under oath?
>
> *Dulles*: I wouldn't think he would tell it under oath, no.
>
> *Warren*: Why?

Dulles: He ought not tell it under oath. Maybe not tell it to his own government, but wouldn't tell it any other way.

Commissioner John McCloy: Wouldn't he tell it to his own chief?

Dulles: He might or might not. If he was a bad one, then he wouldn't.

Direct proof that Oswald worked for the CIA is probably impossible to come by without Agency cooperation. The evidence will be circumstantial, but this does not mean that a valid conclusion cannot be reached. In counterintelligence work, U.S. agencies must constantly reach decisions about which employees might be spying for a foreign government, which defectors are real and which are planted spies. Since the KGB and other adversary organizations will not provide accurate data, conclusions must be reached by assessing the weight, consistency, and validity of accumulated circumstantial evidence. Was the case in question treated unusually or suspiciously by a foreign government? Who are the suspect's associates? Did the suspect do or know something that tends to indicate that their story is a fabrication? Is there a discernible pattern to their actions and linkages, a pattern whose individual components may seem benign but whose cumulative image is clearly one of espionage? The same paradigm through which the CIA seeks out moles in its headquarters, double agents in its field offices, and foreign spies who have pretended to defect is what we will apply to Oswald to determine if he worked for U.S. intelligence (and, more specifically, the CIA).

It should also be noted that not all CIA agents operate at the level or in the sophisticated style of James Bond. As former deep-cover agent Philip Agee reminds us:

> There are many different types of agents in the CIA parlance. Many operations are structured under the leadership of a single agent to whom other agents respond either as a group working together or in separate, compartmented activities. The single agent who runs the operation under station direction is known as the *principal agent* and the others as *secondary* or *sub-agents*. . . . An *action agent* is a person who actually provides secret information, e.g. a spy in a communist party, whereas a *support agent* performs tasks related to an operation but is not the source of intelligence.[7]

There are agents who work for an organization on a full-time basis throughout their entire careers. There are also contract agents who are hired to perform assigned tasks of variable duration—from weeks to decades—to fly secret missions, produce phony documents, perform assassinations.

Such men are not all cut from the same mold. Some could pass as mild-mannered accountants or college professors while others display the bravado of cowboy heroes or an ideological zealousness bordering on derangement. Former Warren Commission Counsel David Belin said of Oswald, "There is nothing in CIA files to give even the slightest hint that he was a CIA agent. Moreover, it is relatively obvious that a man of Oswald's background and emotions is not the kind of person the CIA would entrust with anything."[8]

Belin neglects the fact that the U.S. intelligence community has been populated by some of the most emotionally volatile characters imaginable, persons who at times are so unstable that even their handlers are at a loss to control them. In a subsequent chapter we will meet Oswald's associate David Ferrie, who was unstable by almost any conventional measure. Still, he found work as a pilot and as a soldier in the CIA's war against Castro. Released CIA documents indicate that two CIA contract killers here in the early 1960s were flamboyant types who became involved in narcotics, in freelance assassination, and in serious trouble with the law while under Agency employ. One of the hired guns was described in a Senate hearing as an "unguided missile." It is only in the world of fiction that intelligence-employed assassins are ice-cool, unflappable professionals like Frederick Forsythe's Jackal.

In a Warren Commission executive session, commissioners briefly discussed this very point behind closed doors.

> *John J. McCloy (Rep. IN):* Well, I can't say that I have run into a fellow comparable to Oswald, but I have run into some very limited mentalities in the CIA and FBI.
>
> *Chief Justice Earl Warren:* Under agents, the regular agents, I think that would be all right, but they and all the other agencies do employ undercover men who are of terrible character.
>
> *Allen Dulles:* Terribly bad characters.
>
> *Senator Richard B. Russell (Dem., GA):* Limited intelligence, even the city police departments do it.
>
> *Warren:* It almost takes that kind of man to do a lot of this intelligence work.[9]

Oswald's odyssey in the grip of U.S. intelligence would take him to Russia and back, then to New Orleans, Dallas, and historical infamy. But it began while he was a nineteen-year-old Marine.

2

The Pinko Marine

It was almost as if he [Oswald] was trying to bait the consul into taking adverse action against him. He mentioned that he knew certain classified things in connection with having been, I think, a radar operator in the Marine Corps and that he was going to turn this information over to the Soviet authorities. And, of course, we didn't know how much he knew or anything like that. . . .

U.S. Embassy official John McVickar[1]

In October of 1956, seventeen-year-old Lee Harvey Oswald joined the Marine Corps. By 1957 he had been trained in radar techniques and air traffic control. He finished seventh in his class and was certified as an aviation electronics operator. According to the official Marine Corps records, he was given a "confidential" clearance.[2] That same year he was assigned to the MACS–1 Marine Air Control Squadron at Atsugi Air Force Base, Japan.

Atsugi was no ordinary base. In clandestine parlance, "black" means secret. Atsugi was one of the blackest bases anywhere in the world. Among other things, it was the home of what the Soviets called "the black lady of espionage"—the U–2 spy plane.[3] The aircraft's primary mission was to gather photographic intelligence over the Soviet Union and China. The plane's lofty cameras ferreted out missile sites, airfields, aircraft, missile-testing and training activities, special weapons storage, submarine construction, and even atomic production.[4] The U–2 accounted for no less than 90 percent of America's hard data on Soviet military and defense activities. It is easy to understand why the black lady was the KGB's highest-priority target. The problem for the Soviets was that it flew so high (80,000 to 90,000 feet) that nothing could find it, much less shoot it down, or so it was assumed by the United States.

Inside the radar "bubble" at Atsugi (the control room from which friendly and unfriendly aircraft were monitored as they flew through a vast chunk of Pacific air space) the U–2 was easily identified. The world altitude record was then 65,889 feet; the U–2 pilots would ask the bubble such things as, "Request winds aloft at 90,000 angels" (90,000 feet). According to some of the Marines who worked in the bubble, one of their colleagues showed an extraordinary interest in the flight paths of the conspicuously high-flying blip.[5] His name was Lee Harvey Oswald. He worked inside the bubble directing air traffic and scouting for incoming aircraft.[6]

Even the lowliest Marine stationed at Atsugi knew that the Utility Plane (U–2) was something special. The hangar that housed it was ringed with machine-gun-toting guards. Oswald's squadron kept its gear in this hangar.[7] All data on the plane, including its altitude, were ultrasecret. Official Marine records state that Oswald's clearance was only "confidential." According to one of the Marines who worked in the bubble and who testified before the Warren Commission, minimum clearance for the men in the bubble was "secret."[8]

Outside the bubble, Oswald saw the U–2s being taxied out of their hangars for take-off. So interested was he that he discussed the plane with the officer in charge of his unit.[9] He was also seen strolling around the base taking pictures.[10] Whether Oswald violated regulations and photographed the U–2 is not known, but he did take pictures of other aircraft and military bases while in the service.[11]

Top secrecy concerning the aircraft was essential because any technical information could be of potential help to the frustrated Soviets in their attempts to catch the black lady. Any data on altitude and flight patterns, which the men in the bubble had witnessed firsthand, would certainly have been of help to the Soviets, who presumably could not even track the U–2. Whatever Oswald's security clearance, his presence in the bubble ensured that he would possess information useful to the Soviets.

Atsugi had another claim to black fame: it was one of the largest CIA bases in the world.[12] Two dozen buildings, euphemistically called the Joint Technical Advisory Group, comprised the nerve center of the CIA's pervasive covert operations in Asia.[13] It was from Atsugi that the CIA flew Chinese Nationalist agents to be parachuted into Communist China.[14]

It was only fitting that the black lady lived here, since she belonged not to the Air Force but to the CIA. The plane was developed by Richard M. Bissell, Allen Dulles's deputy. Bissell worked in concert with experts from the Air Force and from Lockheed Aircraft, which built the planes.[15] He was an urbane, six-foot-four former professor of economics, but he was no ivory-tower type. He was a key member of the Agency's clandestine elite and directed some of its most secret operations.[16] Bissell's clandestine career, like Oswald's, was to span both of what were then the CIA's most important arenas—the U–2/Soviet sphere and Cuba. Bissell was in charge of planning the ill-fated Bay of Pigs invasion in which the Agency attempted to use an army of Cuban exiles to overthrow Castro.[17]

The U–2 was the Agency's most prized toy. From the time it became operational in 1956 until it was shot down in 1960, it was considered the most spectacular technical achievement in the history of U.S. intelligence. Its capabilities and its success were without peer.[18] Twenty-two of the planes were built. They represented dramatic advances in aircraft technology and design as well as in photographic technology.[19] When the Soviets finally shot down pilot Francis Gary Powers's U–2, they did more than stop surveillance: they came into possession of wreckage that provided clues to spectacular U.S. advances in several realms of technology.

Powers was shot down in May 1960, while Oswald was in the Soviet Union. His plane was equipped with self-destructive charges that were supposed to be activated after the pilot had ejected during trouble. It is possible that Powers, knowing the mentality of his employers, suspected that the explosive charges might be designed to terminate the pilot as well as the plane, in case he were to become squeamish about following the order to poison himself before being captured.[20] Whatever the cause, both Powers and his aircraft fell into Soviet hands.

Oswald's Asian activities, like Atsugi itself, are shrouded in mystery. In September 1958 his Marine unit was transferred from Atsugi to Taiwan. The Department of Defense told the House Assassinations Committee that its data indicate that Oswald stayed behind at Atsugi when his unit moved out.[21] However, one of Oswald's officers, Lieutenant Charles Rhodes, remembered that Oswald *was* in Taiwan but was abruptly flown back to Atsugi by military aircraft. Rhodes was told that Oswald was going back for "medical treatment." Marine Corps files indicate that Oswald had a very mild case of venereal disease.[22] The question arises as to why a mild disease which is not known to preclude a regular work routine would cause Oswald to be flown across the China Sea back to Japan. One possibility is that the disease was a cover to allow Oswald to leave his military duties to pursue some other assignment for a while. In actuality, the sickness ploy is an intelligence cover frequently used for getting military personnel out of circulation to receive special training.[23]

When Oswald's tour of duty in Asia was finished, he returned stateside. In late 1958 he was assigned to El Toro Air Station in California. Again official records indicate that he had only "confidential" clearance.[24] Lieutenant Charles Donovan, the officer in charge of Oswald's El Toro radar unit, told the Warren Commission that he "must have had 'secret' clearance to work in the radar center, because that was the minimum requirement for all of us."[25] A Marine who served with Oswald testified that "we all had access to classified information," which the Marine believed to be classified as "secret."[26] Marine Kerry Thornley said of Oswald's El Toro rating, "I believe that he at one time worked at the security files. . . . [P]robably a 'secret' clearance would be required."[27] The Marine Corps's then director of personnel wrote to the Warren Commission that Oswald may have had a secret clearance while performing certain duties.[28]

His access to sensitive—most likely, secret—information while at El Toro is important because of his strange behavior there. His duties were never changed and his access was not restricted even though he became conspicuously leftist—a Russophile.[29] The young Marine studied the Russian language, an endeavor he had begun while in Asia. He played Russian records so loudly that they could be heard throughout his barracks; he read Russian books, hour after hour; he subscribed to a Russian-language periodical. He openly discussed Soviet politics. Oswald blathered Russian at his fellow Marines, who could not begin to understand him.

It was all extremely conspicuous. His Marine peers humorously dubbed him "Oswaldskovich." In return, he addressed them as "comrade."[30] It was not all language and literature: there was a decidedly pro-Soviet flavor to Oswald's Russian interests. He touted Soviet communism as "the best system in the world."[31]

This behavior occurred in 1958, when Cold-War tensions were high. The House Un-American Activities Committee was active; blacklisting was declining but still in evidence. It had been only four years since Senator Joseph McCarthy's witchhunts for alleged communists in the government exploited the national paranoia about subversion. It was an era of extreme tension and distrust between the United States and the Soviet Union. This young Marine, who had access to a wealth of radar information relevant to U.S. forces in the Pacific and who had served at one of his nation's most sensitive foreign bases, could have been in deep trouble. The Marine Corps is not renowned as a bastion of liberal tolerance and free thinking, but it acted in Oswald's case as if it were. There was no reaction at all to Oswald's "pinko" inclinations—at least, not in any records or in the recollections of military personnel involved.

If Oswald was a foreign spy at this point in his life, he certainly had a novel approach to building a cover—flaunting his communist tendencies in the midst of America's most conservative military subculture. If so, the tactic worked: the Marines ignored him. Mailroom personnel dutifully reported the leftist nature of Oswald's mail.[32] Nothing came of it. One officer who attempted to discuss Oswald's Russophile behavior with him remembers the young man replied that he was "trying to indoctrinate himself in Russian theory in conformance with Marine Corps policy."[33] Evidently this putative policy superseded any worries the Corps might have had concerning some of its other policies, such as loyalty and the protection of secrets (unless someone in authority knew that there was nothing to fear from Oswaldskovich).

Oswald made a crash effort to master Russian language as well as theory. In February 1959 he failed a Marine Corps proficiency test in Russian. Six months later he had made remarkable progress. It seems likely that Oswald received special training from the government, as part of the preparation for his forthcoming espionage mission to the Soviet Union. One of his Marine friends arranged for him to meet an aunt who was also studying Russian. The aunt, Rosaleen Quinn, spoke Russian with Oswald for over two hours during supper. She was preparing to take a State Department exam and had worked with a tutor for more than a year. According to Quinn, Oswald spoke Russian better and more confidently than she did.

When Oswald failed his Russian test in February, he had scored a "−5" in understanding spoken Russian. By the time of his summertime encounter with Quinn, he not only understood it but spoke it with considerable fluency. Neither Quinn nor, supposedly, anyone else had tutored him. His explanation for this progress was that it resulted from listening to Radio Moscow. Not only would that be a hard way to learn a language, since Radio Moscow is not noted for talking slowly, but Russian is a difficult language for an American to master.

I consulted Dr. James Weeks, a professor of modern languages at Southeastern Massachusetts University who teaches Russian and who himself underwent language training while in the military.[34] He cited statistics to indicate that attaining Russian fluency requires more than twice as many hours as did Spanish or French—1,100 hours or more, including instruction. Weeks opined that the kind of progress described in Oswald's case would be exceedingly difficult if not impossible to attain in such a short time by using only the radio and self-study props. Such progress would require instructors, Weeks asserted, or, at a minimum, persons proficient in the language who would be willing to converse extensively with the student. Oswald supposedly had no access to either formal or informal tutors.

In 1974 a transcript of an executive session of the Warren Commission was released after a prolonged legal battle by researcher-author Harold Weisberg.[35] Classified as "Top Secret" until its release, it contains a reference by Chief Counsel J. Lee Rankin to the Commission's efforts "to find out what he [Oswald] studied at the Monterey School of the Army in the way of languages."[36] There is no know official record of Oswald having studied there. The Monterey School (the Defense Language Institute), located in California, was operational in 1959. It was and still is the linguistic West Point for U.S. military and intelligence personnel who need to learn a language thoroughly and quickly. If Oswald studied there, it would explain his phenomenal progress.

The Monterey School is not a self-improvement institution offering courses to anyone who is interested. In 1959 it was a school for serious training relating to government work, not to the academic whims of military or intelligence personnel. Only those with a certain level of aptitude were admitted, and training was conducted in a language selected for the student by the government, according to needs or assignments.[37] If Oswald went there, it would also explain why he was not seen as a threat to Marine Corps security: he was indeed being trained in Russian in conformance with someone's policy—most likely, U.S. intelligence.

In September 1959 Oswald left the Marine Corps—three months ahead of his scheduled discharge.[38] In the first of what was to be a long series of quick and favorable treatment by various government agencies, he was given a dependency discharge because of an injury to his mother.[39] The speed of his release surprised his Marine peers.[40] But the Marine Corps was duped, or so it appears; the discharge was obtained on false grounds. Oswald's mother's injury consisted of a jar falling on her toe while at work. She stayed home for a week, but when she returned she did not mention the injury at all, much less describe it as a continuing problem. This incident took place the year before Oswald's dependency discharge.[41]

Perhaps Oswald was in a hurry to get out of the Marines because he had other things to do. In October 1959—one month after his early discharge—he was on his way to Moscow to defect. As with most aspects of his defection and his return, his journey to Russia is enigmatic.

First, there is the problem of financing. The trip cost at least $1,500. The Warren Commission decided that Oswald, being frugal, saved the money out of his Marine Corps pay.[42] Before his departure for Moscow his bank account contained only $203. He could have squirreled away $1,300 in cash and carried it around with him to pay for his trip (awkward, but by no means impossible); alternatively, his trip could have been subsidized by someone. Friends and relatives claim not to have given him any money during this period, but perhaps someone else did.

Second, there is the problem of Oswald's itinerary. He arrived in England on October 9 and left October 10, according to his passport, stamped at the London airport.[43] His next destination was Helsinki, en route to Moscow. He arrived there on October 11. But there was no available commercial flight that would have gotten him there that soon.[44] Either his nest egg of cash was bigger than anyone imagined—enough to hire private air transport—or he was flown to Helsinki by noncommercial aircraft, private or military.

After arriving in Moscow in October 1959, he told Soviet officials of his desire for Soviet citizenship. The officials were unimpressed and probably more than a bit suspicious. They rejected his request for citizenship and ordered him to leave Moscow within two hours.[45] Oswald's alleged response to this rejection was to slit his left wrist. He was rushed to a hospital by a Soviet Intourist guide who found him bleeding in his hotel room. He was then confined to a psychiatric hospital while the Soviets decided his fate. Certainly they must have debated whether Oswald was an authentic defector or a spy. This was an era in which the United States and the Soviet Union were playing extensive spy games with ostensible defectors.[46]

After waiting several days for the Soviets to make up their mind, Oswald decided to take action. He went to the U.S. Embassy in Moscow where he denounced the United States, praised the Soviet Union, and stated that he wanted to renounce his U.S. citizenship.[47] He also made another, very dramatic announcement: he stated that he had offered to give the Soviets radar secrets that he had learned in the Marines. He added ominously that he "might know something of special interest," an obvious reference to the U–2.[48]

This action seems counterproductive on Oswald's part. To make such threats to the U.S. Embassy might cause officials to panic, to employ extraordinary means to stop the young Marine from spilling secrets. If the U.S. Embassy did not previously know of Oswald's access to secret materials, it did now. If Oswald's real goal was to become a Soviet citizen, taunting U.S. officials with thinly veiled threats about the ultrasecret U–2 might have caused them to devise some Cold-War caper to silence Oswald and thus eliminate risk to the U–2. In addition to U–2 data, Oswald had access to a wealth of secrets concerning radio communications codes, radar installations, and aircraft deployment in the western United States.

Still, nothing happened. U.S. officials listened to Oswald's threats with tranquility. Perhaps he knew that they would not try to stop him; perhaps he wasn't even talking to them, but to the Soviets. In the late 1950s, the U.S. Embassy was one of the best places in Moscow to get the ear of Kremlin intelligence officers. The bugging of our embassy there was common Soviet practice, as was our bugging of their embassy in Washington. Oswald's statement may well have been advertisements to the wavering Soviets, not threats to the U.S. officials.

The Soviets remained unconvinced. Oswald languished for weeks in a Moscow hotel, writing pro-communist letters to his family back in the United States and explaining at length the reasons for his defection. Since it would have been a safe assumption that the Soviets would open and read his mail, these too may have constituted self-advertisements for Soviet citizenship.[49]

Finally Oswald's frantic efforts to be accepted paid off. The Russians took him and, presumably, his store of radar secrets, although they would later claim that they had had no interest in Oswald and had never debriefed him.[50]

It is interesting to note that the CIA expressed extreme skepticism concerning the Soviets' professed disinterest in Oswald. It did not seem logical, given Oswald's radar knowledge, that the Kremlin would not even talk with him. Yet the CIA wanted everyone to believe that *its* claims of disinterest in Oswald upon his return from Russia were perfectly logical, that there was no reason why they would want to discuss with Oswald just what and how much he told the Soviets.

The Warren Commission's vision of Oswald is one of a hot-headed ideologue whose political passions compelled him to do everything from slashing his wrist to shooting the President. The vice-consul of the U.S. Embassy in Moscow has an interesting recollection about Oswald's defection speech. John A. McVickar told the Warren Commission that the young defector seemed to be following some "pattern of behavior in which he had been tutored by person or persons unknown, that he had been in contact with others before or during his Marine Corps tour who had guided him and encouraged him in his actions."[51]

McVickar was not alone in his perception that Oswald was a cool and purposeful young man. A New Orleans radio host who interviewed him about his pro-Castro activities said, "He seemed to be very conscious about all of his words, all of his movements, sort of very deliberate . . . and he struck me as being rather articulate. He was the type of person you would say inspired confidence."[52] Fifteen years after the assassination, Dallas Police Chief Jesse Curry and Assistant District Attorney William Alexander were still haunted by the eerie demeanor of their most famous prisoner. Curry said he thought Oswald "had been trained in interrogation techniques and resisting interrogation techniques."[53] Said Alexander, "I was amazed that a person so young would have had the self-control he had. It was almost as if he had been rehearsed, or programmed, to meet the situation that he found himself in."[54]

A New Orleans policeman who interviewed Oswald following his arrest for a street fight that ensued from his pro-Castro leafletting described him as "answering questions in a mechanical manner, much like a machine that could be turned on and off."[55]

The other embassy official who dealt with Oswald, besides John A. McVickar, tried to talk Oswald out of defecting. After conversing with him for about an hour, the official told the young Marine to return in two days to formally renounce his U.S. citizenship.[56] This official was Richard Snyder, a man alleged by some Warren Commission critics to have been working for the CIA under diplomatic cover.[57]

In 1977 the House Assassinations Committee was attempting to sort out the CIA's possible interaction with Oswald. The CIA and Snyder denied that he worked for the Agency while in Moscow, although admitting that he had worked for it briefly at an earlier time. The Committee discovered that his CIA file had been "red flagged" and specially segregated. In attempting to find out why, the Committee found the CIA's innocent explanation unsatisfactory. HSCA termed the matter of Synder's file "extremely troubling."[58] However, based on Snyder's testimony, a review of his file, and statements from his former State Department personnel officer, the Committee concluded that "a finding that he was in contact with Oswald on behalf of the CIA was not warranted."

HSCA was told by a former State Department official who was "familiar with State Department procedures regarding CIA employees" that "at no time from 1959 to 1963 did the CIA use the State Department's overseas consular positions as cover for CIA intelligence officers." But in his 1980 book *Wilderness of Mirrors*, David C. Martin alleges that in November 1962 Hugh Montgomery was "a CIA officer under diplomatic cover in the embassy [U.S. Embassy in Moscow]," as was Richard Jacobs, "another CIA officer serving under diplomatic cover." Martin's book is based in part on interviews with retired CIA officers.

Snyder, who was the embassy's second secretary, listened to Oswald's threats to reveal secrets but apparently took no action to stop him beyond trying to talk him out of it. While the author has no knowledge of what standard procedure would be in such cases, this reaction appears rather casual, given that no one at the embassy could have known the magnitude of secrets Oswald might spill.[59]

Snyder was in charge of Oswald's handling by the embassy. In a confidential State Department memorandum he stated, "I was the sole officer handling the Oswald case."[60] In addition to this chore, Snyder described himself in a Yale alumni book as having been "in charge of the Gary Powers-U2 trial matters," when Powers's U–2 was shot down by the Soviets.

The defection of this radar operator who dealt with secret codes and files in California, and who worked in the bubble that monitored U–2 flights, brought a mixed reaction from the U.S. military. At El Toro Air Base in California, Oswald's last assignment before leaving the Marines, there was a flurry of activity when local commanders learned of his defection. According to Oswald's former commanding officer there, the defection precipitated wholesale changes in codes, frequencies for radio transmission and for radar, and aircraft call numbers—changes designed to repair any leaked secrets.[61] Marine Lt. John Donovan told the Warren Commission that Oswald had a wealth of knowledge about West Coast air bases, including "all radio frequencies for all squadrons, all tactical call signs, the relative strengths of all squadrons, number and type of aircraft in a squadron, . . . the authentication code for entering and exiting [the air defense zone], . . . the range of surrounding units' radio and radar."[62] At the higher levels of military bureaucracy in Washington, however, there was scarcely a ripple.

According to Colonel Thomas Fox, former head of counterintelligence for the Defense Intelligence Agency, it was standard operating procedure to conduct a "net damage assessment" for defectors.[63] The assessment was an analysis of the secret information that a defector might have had access to in order to discern what operations might be compromised. In the cases of the only two U.S. enlisted men who defected to communist countries before Oswald, damage assessments were conducted; in the cases of at least two of those who defected after Oswald, assessments were conducted.[64] There was none for Oswald.

It is not that he had no secrets or could cause no damage. It would seem that with El Toro, Atsugi, and the U–2 there was plenty of potential damage to assess. It is not that there were so many defectors flocking to Russia that our bureaucracy couldn't keep up with them, so that Oswald slipped through the cracks. Neither is it that U.S. officials had no warning that Oswald was going to divulge secrets. Is it that the "damage" had already been precisely calculated when designing Oswald's cover as a defector?

If Oswald had been a genuine defector instead of a spy, U.S. intelligence could well have taken the view that his was one of the most damaging defections in history. The sequence of events surrounding his threats to divulge secrets could have rendered Oswald the traitor of the decade. As Sherlock Holmes told Dr. Watson in *Silver Blaze*, the key to the mystery lies in why the dog did not bark.

On May 1, 1960, six months after Oswald defected, broadcasting that he "might know something of special interest," the CIA's black lady came crashing to Russian soil outside the city of Sverdlovsk. The diplomatic fallout was immense. At first, Washington claimed that the downed craft was a weather plane that had innocently drifted into Russian air space from Turkey, because the pilot became oxygen-deprived and lost his sense of direction.[65] Moscow waited 48 hours, allowing plenty of time for the U.S. cover story to circulate, before blowing it out of the water. Then the Soviets revealed that they had both the plane and pilot. President Eisenhower was probably advised by the CIA that the U–2 had been blown up per standard procedure. Eisenhower paid dearly for the Agency's unfounded optimism—with his own credibility. The State Department admitted the craft was a spy plane but said the flight was not authorized in Washington. Two days later this fallback position crumbled: Eisenhower finally assumed responsibility for the U–2. The other casualty of the affair, in addition to administration credibility, was the upcoming four-power summit conference, which collapsed in the wake of the spy flight.

How did the Soviet Union catch the black lady? Colonel Fletcher Prouty, who was liaison officer between the Air Force and the CIA for the U–2 project, believes that the plane must have been flying at an abnormally low altitude when it was shot down.[66] Another qualified source, U–2 pilot Francis Gary Powers, opined that technical data supplied to the Soviets by Lee Harvey Oswald may have been U–2's downfall. Powers voiced the suspicion that Oswald's knowledge of the plane's operational altitude and of the radar techniques used during its flight provided what the Soviets needed in order to target their missiles more accurately and at a much higher altitude than was previously possible.[67] Commenting on Oswald, Powers said, "He had access to all our equipment. He knew the altitudes we flew at, how long we stayed out on any mission, and in which direction we went."[68]

Whether Prouty or Powers is correct, or neither is correct, it would seem that the CIA should have had an intense interest in discovering just what role Oswald may have had in the fate of the U–2—especially since the spy planes continued to fly after the Soviets brought Powers down. The Agency claims it had no interest in Oswald and never debriefed him upon his return from Russia. Was the CIA so simple-minded that it saw no possible connection between Oswald and the U–2? Did it see one but forget to follow up on it by debriefing him? Or did it already know precisely what Oswald had told the Soviets?

Powers was eventually returned to the United States in February 1962 in exchange for Soviet spymaster Rudolf Abel. This exchange occurred while Oswald was still in the Soviet Union. If Powers told his CIA employers the same story he would later tell, the Agency's interest in Oswald should have been piqued, to say the least. According to Powers, his Soviet interrogators were surprisingly knowledgeable about certain matters.[69] The Agency should have entertained the notion that Oswald had provided the information, unless it knew better.

Powers lied to his captors about the spy plane's altitude, insisting that he flew at 68,000 feet (much lower than the U–2's actual capability). He believed that since the aircraft could fly higher than the Soviets could monitor, they would be ignorant of the actual altitude. Not only did they correctly state his altitude, but they also showed him his actual flight path; these are data to which Oswald had access.

Powers also claimed that he was questioned extensively about Atsugi air base. He denied ever being there (even though that is where the U–2 flights originated and Oswald's Atsugi squadron commander recalled that Powers was at the base). But he asserted that the questions put to him by the Soviets reflected considerable knowledge about U–2 flights from Atsugi.

After Powers's return to the United States, Oswald should have been high on the mail-surveillance list of U.S. intelligence. He wrote to his brother Robert in February 1962 (after Powers's return), commenting that Powers "seemed to be a nice bright American type fellow when I saw him in Moscow."[70] Oswald never explained when or how he had seen Powers. He had moved from Moscow to Minsk by the time the U–2 was downed. His "diary," allegedly chronicling his Soviet sojourn, states that he was attending a party in Minsk on May 1, 1960, when Powers was captured. Back in the United States, however, Oswald would tell a co-worker that he had been in Moscow for the big May Day celebration honoring the Communist revolution. Of the three May Days Oswald spent in Russia, he was accounted for as being out of Moscow on the other two. We have only an entry in his diary—a suspicious artifact in its own right, as will be discussed later—to preclude his being in Moscow when Powers was shot down. This should have alerted the CIA to the possibility that Oswald played some U–2 role after the plane was downed as well as possibly having a hand in its demise. He was, after all, presumably the only person in the Soviet Union who had first-hand knowledge of the spy plane and its base, besides the prisoner who was being interrogated.

In February 1961, after nearly two and a half years n Russia, Oswald had a wife (the former Marina Prusakova), a baby daughter, and a yen to return to the United States. Our embassy in Moscow responded to the latter request with expeditiousness and generosity. Oswald wrote the embassy and asked for guarantees against prosecution upon his return to the United States. At the request of Richard Snyder, the State Department officer who had handled Oswald's defection, Lee and Marina traveled to Moscow and appeared at the embassy.[71] There Oswald recanted, saying that he had learned his lesson the hard way, that he had been "completely relieved of his illusions about the Soviet Union."[72] Snyder returned Oswald's passport to him and recommended to Washington that it agree to Marina's application for a visa.[73]

While at the embassy, Marina was given a physical exam by the embassy doctor, Air Force Captain Alexis Davison.[74] Davison was evidently so moved by Oswald's recantation that he went out of his way to befriend the former Marine. He suggested that Oswald might contact Davison's mother if Oswald ever got to Atlanta. There is no evidence that Oswald ever saw Mrs. Davison, but he did go out of his way to go to Atlanta. The plane that he took from New York to Dallas after returning from the Soviet Union stopped briefly in Atlanta to exchange passengers. There were direct flights to Dallas, but Oswald chose one that stopped in Atlanta.[75] Inexplicably, the Oswalds started for Texas with five suitcases and arrived in Dallas with only two; the three missing suitcases are unaccounted for.[76] Could Oswald have been performing some sort of courier function for materials originating in the Soviet Union?

When arrested in Dallas following the assassination, he had the name of Captain Davison's mother listed in his notebook.[77] Oswald's Dallas patron George de Mohrenschildt made a cryptic, unexplained comment in an unpublished manuscript concerning "Lee's activities in Atlanta, New Orleans, and Mexico City."[78] Oswald had no known activities in or visits to Atlanta, except the brief stopover.

Captain Alexis Davison was declared persona non grata by the Soviet Union in May 1963 in connection with his alleged involvement in the sensational Penkovsky spy case. Colonel Oleg Penkovsky was a Soviet spy for the West. He revealed secrets that turned out to be of crucial importance to the United States during the subsequent Cuban missile crisis.[79] The Soviets claimed that Captain Davison's phone number was found on Penkovsky when he was arrested for spying. Penkovsky was executed after a swift trial. The Soviets named eight foreigners as his spy contacts, of which Davison was one.[80]

After the assassination Davison told the Secret Service that he did not remember the Oswalds, but he subsequently recalled the embassy meeting quite clearly when talking with the FBI. He also admitted that he had not provided his mother's address to anyone else going to the United States besides Oswald.[81]

Davison told the House Assassinations Committee that his only involvement with intelligence work was the activity for which he was kicked out of the Soviet Union. The CIA asserted that his involvement in the Penkovsky affair was a "one shot" deal. Davison flatly denied any intelligence-related link to Oswald.[82]

It seems that the U.S. Embassy in Moscow (or some of its officials, at least) could not get Oswald back home quickly enough. Richard Snyder returned the former defector's passport to him several months ahead of his scheduled departure, although the embassy had been specifically instructed, in writing, not to do so. The Passport Office in Washington had ordered that Oswald's passport be returned to him only after his travel plans were finalized, to prevent the document from being used in the interim by the Soviets as part of some espionage scheme.[83] Snyder and the embassy were either very careless, very trusting of the Soviets, or very trusting of Oswald. The best explanation for his favorable treatment is that he was finishing one mission for U.S. intelligence and was about to be debriefed before undertaking other assignments.

On the recommendation of the U.S. Embassy in Moscow, Marina was exempted from the usual immigration quotas and allowed to come to the United States with her husband.[84] The Immigration Service objected, but the State Department made a "strong case" on Marina's behalf; the Service acquiesced.[85]

The State Department loaned Oswald $435 to help him get home. On receiving the loan, the State Department file should have been flagged with a "lookout card" posted by the Passport Office until the loan was repaid. No lookout card was ever placed in his file. The State Department told the Warren Commission that this resulted from human error.[86]

Oswald's interactions with the State Department and the Passport Office produced not one but a series of alleged errors or coincidences.

According to standard procedure, a lookout card should also have been posted at the time of Oswald's defection to the Soviet Union.[87] The purpose of this procedure was to alert all U.S. embassies and passport offices not to issue the defector a new passport. No such card was posted for Oswald. There was another chance, according to standard operating procedure, to post a lookout card. By March 1960 the embassy in Moscow had lost track of Oswald's whereabouts. The State Department in Washington typed up a refusal sheet, as it was bound by law to do in such cases. This sheet was the first bureaucratic step toward the posting of a lookout card. Once again, because of alleged human error, the lookout card never appeared. Three chances were missed—defection, unknown whereabouts, and outstanding loan—to flag the file of the U–2 defector.

Human error and coincidence continued to shape Oswald's interactions with the Passport Office even after his return to the United States. When he applied for a new passport with which to go back to the Soviet Union in New Orleans in 1963, he got it without a hitch within 24 hours.[88] He wrote on his application that his destination was the Soviet Union, and he virtually red-flagged his status as a former defector by referring to a previous "cancellation" of his passport.[89]

His fast, favorable treatment is all the more unusual given the organizational subculture of the Passport Office during that era. It was headed by Miss Francis Knight, whose strident anti-communism was legendary with the Washington bureaucracy. One of her assistants, Otto Otepka, was a zealous red-hunter.[90] Knight and Otepka were known to challenge the loyalty of ordinary citizens, but they managed to allow the Soviet defector to slip through their bureaucratic net three times.[91]

The State Department was so anxious to have Marina admitted to the United States that it disregarded or failed to notice aspects of her case that normally would have caused great concern. She had spent the previous few years of her life living with her uncle, who was an MVD (Soviet secret police) colonel. In her youth, she had been a member of the Komsomol, the youth apparatus of the Communist Party. The U.S. government was so concerned about being infiltrated by Soviet Communists that the visa application form specifically asked entering Russians if they were or had been a member of the Komsomol. Marina Oswald solved that problem by simply answering "no."[92] In keeping with the general pattern of good will or incompetence that marked the response of government agencies to her defector husband, Marina was admitted without any problem concerning the information on her visa application.

As we would by this time expect, the Oswalds' return trip manifested its own mysteries. According to the Warren Commission, Lee and Marina crossed the Soviet border at Jelmstedt, one of the most sensitive and security-conscious checkpoints along the iron-curtain border between East and West Berlin.[93] Marina's passport stamp reflects that crossing; her husband's does not.[94] How did Oswald pass from East to West? Was it that his very presence somehow caused any government bureaucracy he came in contact with to suddenly become *non compos mentis*, so that his passport was not stamped? Or did he cross somewhere else?

The Oswalds made an unexplained stop in Amsterdam. As Warren Commission Chief Counsel Rankin noted in an executive session, "When they came back, they went to Amsterdam and were there for, I think it was two days, before they went to Rotterdam to take a boat, and it is unexplained why they happened to go there to stay, and got a place to live, some little apartment, and what they were doing in the interim."[95]

The mysterious stopover, in a private apartment rather than a public hotel, is viewed by some researchers as the opportunity for Oswald to have been debriefed by U.S. intelligence, perhaps in a CIA "safe house."

The Oswalds departed the Soviet Union on June 2, 1962, and finally arrived in the United States on June 13. Lee Harvey Oswald was not met by the CIA, the FBI, military intelligence, or a Marine Corps representative, any or all of whom might be expected to have an interest in him. Instead, he was met by a man the Warren Commission described as "a representative of a travelers' aid society which had been contacted by the Department of State."[96] It may have been a welcome-home gesture on the part of a very hospitable State Department, but the greeter had odd credentials for the role. Spas Raikin was a former secretary of the American Friends of Anti-Bolshevik Nations, an anti-communist lobby with extensive ties to U.S. intelligence agencies.[97]

By far the most suspicious and significant element of Oswald's return is that the CIA claims never to have debriefed him. He should logically have been of prime interest to the Agency. During this same period, the CIA saw fit to debrief U.S. tourists who had been anywhere behind the iron curtain. Eastern European émigrés were extensively debriefed as prime sources of information concerning communist bloc countries.[98] Yet CIA Director William Colby would insist in 1975 that "We had no contact with Mr. Oswald. . . . No contact with him before he went to the Soviet Union, no contact with him after he returned from the Soviet Union, no contact with him while he was in the Soviet Union."[99]

Why not? One of the first answers floated unofficially by defenders of the Warren Commission's conclusions was that the Agency did not want to further embarrass the United States by focusing attention on someone who had defected to the Soviets. Needless to say, that did not quell suspicions about the handling of Oswald's case. In 1975 CBS-TV correspondent Dan Rather put the question of debriefing directly to Colby. Rather reported that "Mr. Colby indicated that the CIA might have passed up Oswald because the FBI interviewed him."[100] While it is true that the FBI did interview him upon his return, Colby's claim of CIA lethargy still rings hollow.

First, the FBI did not interview Oswald until he had been in the United States for three weeks.[101] The CIA's U–2s continued to soar through unfriendly skies while the U–2 defector sat in Texas without being debriefed. Second, the Bureau's interest in Oswald was to check him out as a possible subversive threat (that is, to determine whether the Soviets sent him back here to spy or commit acts of sabotage). The Bureau had no technical competence by which to discern what, if anything, Oswald may have told the Soviets about U–2. The FBI agents who interviewed him did not get into detailed, technical interrogation.[102] They found him to be "cold, arrogant, and difficult to interview."[103] But he did deny that he gave radar secrets to the Soviets.[104] Perhaps this blanket assurance was all the CIA needed to hear, second-hand, in order to allay its fears about the fate of its spy planes around the world.

Three years after Colby's comment about "passing up" Oswald because of the FBI, the House Select Committee on Assassinations came up with the explanation that the CIA did not debrief returning defectors: "It appeared to the Committee that, in fact, the CIA did not contact returning defectors as a matter of standard operating procedure. For this reason, the absence of contact with Oswald on his return from the Soviet Union could not be considered unusual."[105] In fact, the CIA is known to have debriefed at least three defectors—an Air Force man, a soldier who deserted in Germany, and a Rand Development Corporation employee.[106] It is difficult to imagine that these three men were of more significance to the Agency than the man who might have spilled numerous Atsugi-related secrets.

Even putting aside the U–2 and radar secrets, there was another very important intelligence dimension in which the Agency should have had a burning interest: Oswald was a walking data bank regarding Soviet techniques of debriefing and handling defectors. After all, the Agency claimed that it did not believe for a moment the KGB's assertion that it was not interested in Oswald. After the assassination the Agency claimed to harbor suspicions that Oswald was a Soviet spy. It is beyond credulity

that in 1962, with all the double-agent machinations involving "defectors," the CIA would not be suspicious of his ideological change of heart
until after he had assassinated a president of the United States. CIA
counterintelligence is not noted for either its sanguine attitude toward
the Soviets or its willingness to simply sit back and let the FBI handle
important cases. The Agency was known to view the Bureau's competence
in such matters as less than adequate. [107]

In 1948, only a year after the CIA's creation, it negotiated a "delim-
itation agreement" with the FBI. The pact sought to codify the domestic
responsibilities of the two organizations, and it gave the Agency specific
rights to deal with defectors. [108] Moreover, the CIA has never been shy
about pursuing intelligence wherever and with whomever it deems necessary, even in the absence of specific authorization, and sometimes in
the presence of laws and policies to the contrary (as in its illegal domestic
surveillance activities during the 1970s).

Regarding Oswald's case, a senior State Department official wrote in
March 1961 that the "risk" involved in his returning would be more than
compensated for by "the opportunity provided the United States to obtain
information from Mr. Oswald concerning his activities in the Soviet
Union."[109] Yet the Agency continues to steadfastly assert that it had no
interest in him as a source, a risk, or anything else. As recently as 1976,
the illogical and tortured explanations concerning the CIA's alleged disinterest were still being embellished. In preparation for a television appearance, former CIA Director Colby was provided with an Agency
briefing paper to help him answer some difficult questions. Of the failure
to debrief Oswald, the paper stated that if he had come to the attention
of the Agency's DCD (Domestic Contacts Division) he would easily have
been bypassed: "he did not have the kind of information that this division
was seeking."[110]

The paper went on to claim that there was so much tourist traffic to
and from communist countries in 1962 that the Agency simply could
not talk to all of the tourists. [111] One is led to wonder what kind of
information did catch the fancy of the CIA's DCD during this period, if
a man who spent nearly two and a half years in the Soviet Union was
presumed not to have relevant information. The Agency would have us
believe that its efforts were so casual and ineffective that a defector was
viewed as no more important than a tourist and was simply lost in the
crowd of travelers to communist countries.

In the three decades before the 1960s there were only two U.S. defectors
to the Soviet Union. [112] The year before Oswald showed up there was a
bumper crop—four in all. Two more followed close behind Oswald. [113]

Eventually six of the seven had a change of ideological priorities and returned home.[114] Most of this group followed the same route of entry into the Soviet Union as did Oswald.[115]

One of these was Robert Webster, a plastics expert who worked for the Rand Development Corporation. Rand Development's offices were located in New York City just across the street from the supposedly separate, more famous Rand Corporation (a think tank that had the CIA as a client).[116] Rand Development Corporation itself held several contracts with the Agency.[117] Its president, Henry Rand, had been a senior officer in the Office of Strategic Services (OSS), the CIA's predecessor organization of which so many CIA officers were alumni.[118] Another of Rand Development's top executives was also a former OSS man; the corporation's onetime Washington representative had been a CIA agent.[119]

While Robert Webster was in Moscow representing Rand Development at a plastics exhibition, he went to the U.S. Embassy and announced his intention to defect. Like Oswald, he did so in the presence of Richard Snyder, the CIA-linked State Department official who handled Oswald's Soviet entrance and exit.[120] When Oswald was arranging to return to the United States he was heard to inquire about the fate of another young man who had come to the Soviet Union shortly before he did—Robert Webster.[121]

Colonel Fletcher Prouty, who served as "focal point officer" (liaison) between the Pentagon and the CIA during the period of Oswald's Marine Corps service and defection, revealed in 1979 his first-hand knowledge of CIA agents using military cover.[122] Prouty asserted that an agent would be given a regular Marine file created by fabricating duty assignments and inserting the usual personnel reviews and promotions. Prouty said his office would tend to those records in concert with CIA.

An internal CIA memo released in 1976 reveals that there was evidently another Marine enlisted man (a technician like Oswald) who was in Russia in 1958 and 1959. The man's identity is blanked out. Whoever he was, the memo reveals that he lived in the city of Minsk (as did Oswald), departed the Soviet Union before Oswald, and was debriefed by the Agency in Copenhagen on his way home (calling to mind Oswald's unexplained stop in Amsterdam).[123]

A former chief security officer for the State Department, Otto Otepka, claims that in 1963 his office undertook a study of U.S. defectors to determine which were real and which were spies. The study was necessitated by the fact that neither the CIA nor military intelligence would tell the State Department which defectors were genuine. One of the cases under study was Oswald's. According to the security officer, only months before the assassination the State Department was still pondering whether his defection was real or only a cover.[124]

It had been suggested that Oswald was simply too young and volatile to be recruited as a U.S. spy, or perhaps not smart enough. Yet we have heard officials from Moscow to Dallas take note of what a cool customer Oswald was. Moreover, his records from school and the Marines indicate that he was far from intellectually deficient. At age thirteen he had registered an IQ of 118 on the Wechsler Intelligence Scale for children, a score described as being "in the upper range of bright, normal intelligence". He was three years ahead of his class in several subjects. His general intelligence had been noted by his Marine Corps superiors. All of this is less relevant than the composure he seemed to manifest in difficult situations from Moscow to New Orleans to Dallas.

In October 1962 Oswald took a series of tests offered by the Texas State Employment Commission. Helen P. Cunningham, a counselor with the Employment Commission's Dallas office, described the nature and results of the tests to the Warren Commission. These were not IQ or personality tests but ones seeking to discover an "occupational aptitude pattern." By noting which of 23 areas applicants tested well in, counselors offered career advice. Oswald met the minimum standard in twenty areas, failing to qualify in only three.[125] His "G" score (general ability) was 127; 50 percent of those taking this test scored less than 100. He also scored "quite high" on verbal and clerical tests. According to Cunningham,

> there are some things in it [his test results] that would tend to say that he could do college work. . . . If I recall correctly, 100 is thought to be sufficient to do junior college or possibly in some [people] a four-year course, that 125 is required on the G score for professional schools, and 110 is quite good for finishing a four-year college.

The counselor concluded, "In general I would say that his tests indicate potential for quite a broad number and range of semi-skilled or skilled occupations." He demonstrated "outstanding verbal and clerical potential," according to a 1962 test designed for the position of insurance claims adjuster. In addition, it is relevant to his scholastic potential to note that he became very fluent in Russian in a short period of time while in the Marine Corps (as previously described).

We have it from former CIA director Allen Dulles that agents are not required to have formidable intellects but only to be smart enough to navigate within the operational context of their assignments. As for Oswald's youth, one presumes that youthful ideological zeal may have been an important element in his cover. The Soviets, who were being bombarded with "defectors" at the time, almost decided to reject Oswald. Had he been a thirty-year-old Marine or a Marine officer, they might have been even more suspicious and probed his cover more intensely.

Oswald proved himself to be a rather keen observer of the things around him. Back in Dallas a fellow worker remembers his commenting that the Soviet disbursement of military units was different from the U.S. pattern: the Soviets did not intermingle their armor and infantry divisions, and they would have all of their aircraft in one location and all of their infantry in another.[126] These are curious interests for a befuddled young ideologue. With an eye for detail like that it is indeed a shame that the CIA missed talking to him.

But perhaps such data were communicated to U.S. intelligence by Oswald. Among his effects found in Dallas after the assassination was a Russian novel that he had apparently brought back from the Soviet Union. On page 152 of the book, seven letters had been cut out from different locations. The National Security Agency analyzed the book but reached no conclusion about the status of the missing letters. The excising of letters from printed pages is one of the classic techniques used in espionage coding. The excisions refer to broader, more complex codes, perhaps involving the page number or line or work in which the excision occurs. Thus one excision could cue a number of additional references to a prearranged code. The missing letters were never found.[127]

Once back in the States, Oswald settled in Dallas under the wing of George de Mohrenschildt, the right-wing Russian with CIA ties. The Marine Corps, which could have court-martialed Oswald by calling him back to duty to face charges of disclosing secrets, did not do so.[128] The Marines gave him an undesirable, rather than dishonorable, discharge. Oswald wrote to then Texas Governor John Connally to protest that his discharge was a "gross mistake or injustice."[129] Perhaps it was: U.S. Health, Education and Welfare Department records in Dallas casually asserted that Oswald went to Russia "with State Department approval" to work as a radar technician.[130] For a year after his defection, military records failed to reflect his new status as a traitor. Was the bureaucracy just slow, or was there an impression somewhere in its data systems that Oswald was still in government service?

Even the FBI seems to have entertained this second possibility. A post-assassination memo explaining why the Bureau did not order Oswald's passport to be segregated by the State Department after his defection asserts, "We did not know definitely whether or not he had any intelligence assignments at that time."[131]

It is extremely difficult to analyze accurately a distant espionage situation, which is what makes counterintelligence work so challenging. Still, some logical speculation is possible based on the conclusion that Oswald was not a genuine defector but a spy, which would explain why he was not punished as a traitor for revealing secrets to the Soviets. Certainly he would be extensively debriefed upon his return but not through normal, overt channels: a cover of feigned disinterest would be appropriate. But it is likely that the mysterious stopover in Amsterdam allowed for debriefing at a CIA safe house. Oswald had much to tell. His observations about the deployment patterns of the Soviet military would, by themselves, justify such a stop.

The CIA would not have sacrificed its prized U–2 just to provide a cover for a fake defector. Either Oswald told the Soviets other, more expendable radar secrets, or he managed to give the Soviets whatever they already had on the plane, or he gave them disinformation. If he had turned around on his U.S. handlers and given the Soviets the data needed to catch the U–2, he would not have been treated so favorably. Neither would he have continued in a domestic-spying role for the CIA on his return to the United States (as will be described later), or would he continue to have CIA contacts. The only way that Oswald could be accepted as *not* being the traitor who downed the spy plane is if the Agency had precise control over the content and number of the "secrets" he delivered to the KGB. Back in the United States, Oswald launched himself into another leftist political context as an ardent supporter of Castro's Cuba—or so it appeared.

3

Oswald in New Orleans: Marxist or Mole?

Was his [Oswald] public identification with the left a cover for a connection with the anti-Castro right?
Senator Gary Hart, Senate Intelligence Committee, 1976[1]

To the Warren Commission, Oswald's pro-Castro activities in New Orleans were further evidence of his leftist mentality. They helped to form what appeared to be a consistent pattern of anti-American, pro-communist political beliefs. Behind the façade of Oswald's pro-Castro involvements was another very consistent pattern of extensive links with CIA-related activities, organizations, and people, including anti-Castro activities in which the Agency had a proprietary interest.

The main elements of Oswald's pro-Castro activities in New Orleans took place from April to August 1963.[2] He founded a chapter of the Fair Play For Cuba Committee (FPCC), a pro-Castro organization head-quartered in New York. He printed up some pro-Castro leaflets and handed them out to sailors from the *U.S.S. Wasp* before police ordered him off of the dock. He again handed out his leaflets, this time on a downtown street. There he got into a scuffle with some anti-Castro activists and was hauled off to jail. The third time he passed out leaflets, near the New Orleans Trade Mart, the local TV news cameras were

Note: In intelligence jargon, a "mole" is an agent who penetrates an organization or context while under cover, in order to spy and/or perform covert missions.

there. He engaged in a radio debate in which he upheld the pro-Castro
position against two anti-communists. As with most of Oswald's life,
none of these events were what they appeared to be.

First, Oswald was the only member of the New Orleans Fair Play for
Cuba Committee.[3] He founded the chapter in spite of the cautions given
by the FPCC national director in New York, who wrote Oswald that
New Orleans' right-wing political culture was not hospitable ground on
which to start a chapter. The director warned him not to create "un-
necessary incidents which frighten any prospective supporters."[4]

Oswald disregarded the advice. He was so outrageously provocative
that he created precisely these kinds of incidents. He walked into the lair
of the enemy, visiting Carlos Bringuier, a militant anti-Castro activist.[5]
According to Bringuier and his associates, Oswald showed up unan-
nounced at Bringuier's store and started talking. He portrayed himself as
a compatriot of these anti-Castro exiles and boasted that he could train
men to fight against Castro. He returned the next day and left behind
an old Marine Corps manual as proof of his ability to help in the fight
against Castro.

What was Oswald up to? Was he that determined to taunt the anti-
Castro Cubans? Was he really trying to infiltrate them in order to advance
his pro-Castro cause, or was he simply a political schizophrenic?

Only three days after he had made his overtures to the anti-Castro
group, he was in downtown New Orleans handing out pro-Castro leaflets.
Most intriguingly, Bringuier was tipped off by a "friend" that Oswald was
doing this.[6] Infuriated by Oswald's apparent double-dealing, Bringuier
searched him out and found him. Bringuier then began to yell to passersby
that Oswald-the-communist had tried to join in the fight against Castro.
A crowd gathered. Bringuier continued his harangue and proceeded to
lose his temper. A scuffle ensued. Oswald, Bringuier, and a couple of
Bringuier's associates were arrested.[7]

It would be interesting to know the ultimate source of the alleged tip
that brought Bringuier into a confrontation with Oswald. Where did
Bringuier's "friend," alleged by Bringuier to have been Celso Hernandez,
get the information? Bringuier and his associates were extensively involved
with the CIA. He was the New Orleans head of the *Directorio Revolucionario Estudiantil*, an outgrowth of a militant anti-Castro student group
that was heavily involved with the Agency during the Bay of Pigs invasion
and received CIA funding long after the invasion.[8] At the time of the
incident with Oswald, Bringuier was the publisher of a right-wing New
Orleans newsletter. It was funded by the Crusade to Free Cuba Committee, yet another CIA-funded, anti-Castro organization.[9]

Were Oswald's appearances at Bringuier's store, followed by the tip, calculated to set up an incident that would provide Oswald with a crisp pro-Castro image? One of the New Orleans policemen who broke up the scuffle had the distinct impression that Oswald had things intentionally "set up to create an incident."[10]

Upon his arrest, Oswald did another very strange thing: he requested that an FBI agent come to visit him in jail. A local agent came to his cell, whereupon Oswald spun a wildly fictitious story (according to the FBI report, he had apparently told the New Orleans police that he had been born in Cuba). He described himself to the FBI agent as having a long history in the pro-Castro movement.[11] Why would Oswald go out of his way to lie to the FBI? One explanation is that he was salting the Bureau's files as part of establishing his pro-Castro cover, which he needed in order to pursue certain intelligence activities (to be described in the next chapter). He made sure that the FBI man left with samples of the FPCC leaflets.[12]

Oswald pleaded guilty to disturbing the peace, paid a ten dollar fine, and was back on the street. One week after he left jail, he put together another pro-Castro incident. Not demanding that his recruits possess ideological fervor, FPCC chapter president Oswald went to the waiting room of the Louisiana State Unemployment Office in order to recruit demonstrators. This visit was necessitated by the fact that he was president of an organization that had no members. He offered money to anyone who would help him pass out leaflets for a few minutes. His two-dollar offer had only one taker. As advertised, the job lasted but a few minutes: he and his lone helper passed out leaflets just long enough to be photographed by a mobile unit from a local TV station.[13]

Oswald's foray into Cuban politics was shortlived; it ended in August 1963 after beginning in the spring of that year. Once he left New Orleans in late August, he would never again engage in public activities on behalf of Castro's Cuba.

As the data presented here will seek to demonstrate, the events in New Orleans were designed to establish Oswald's pro-Castro credentials, the immediate purpose of which seems to have been to allow him to spy on and/or discredit the Fair Play For Cuba Committee. The FPCC national director's warning to Oswald about not creating embarrassing incidents was well founded; the FPCC was having more troubles than even its unpopular stance could generate, courtesy of the U.S. intelligence agencies that had targeted it for surveillance and disruption.

In 1976 the Senate Intelligence Committee's investigations revealed that in the early 1960s the CIA's domestic spying in general and domestic spying on Cubans in particular underwent a dramatic escalation.[14] Although much still remains secret, we now know that the CIA had extensive spy networks in the Cuban exile community, especially in Miami but elsewhere as well. At the time of President Kennedy's assassination, the Agency's efforts in Miami may have outstripped those of the FBI:[15] by 1963 the CIA actually had more domestic agents there than did the Bureau.[16]

This key fact was unknown to the Warren Commission. It asked the FBI to investigate Cuban political groups (including the FPCC) as part of the general check on Oswald's background, but it neglected to ask the CIA for any information concerning these groups.[17] FBI Director J. Edgar Hoover implicitly acknowledged the CIA role when he wrote the Commission that the Agency may have "pertinent information concerning these organizations."[18] Another FBI document, not given to the Warren Commission but discovered by the Senate Intelligence Committee in 1976, notes that army intelligence and the CIA had "operational interests" in Cuban political groups, including the FPCC.[19] The Senate Committee defined these operational interests as using groups or individuals for "intelligence collection or covert operations."[20]

The CIA had specifically targeted the FPCC for covert activity. Moreover, the timing of Oswald's pro-Castro activities precisely coincided with their targeting.

Behind Oswald's pro-Castro façade lay numerous linkages to the Byzantine world of the anti-Castro movement. The war against Castro was a massive, although primarily covert one. It involved a bizarre coalition of interests united by an opposition to Cuban communism that seemed at times to border on fanaticism. Elements of the FBI, army intelligence, organized crime, Cuban exiles, and right-wing businessmen were, to varying degrees, involved in the efforts to overthrow Castro. By far, however, the broadest, most intense involvement was that of the CIA—the prime mover in anti-Castro politics.

The literature that Oswald distributed in New Orleans included a pamphlet entitled *The Crime Against Cuba*. This rather moderate exposition against U.S. policy was hardly noteworthy, except for the address stamped inside the back cover: FPCC, 544 Camp Street, New Orleans, LA.[21] Additional copies of the pamphlet, bearing the same address, were found among Oswald's possessions in Dallas after the assassination.[22] In his correspondence to the national director of the FPCC, Oswald proposed setting up an office for the local chapter, then wrote implying that he had done so.[23]

The address 544 Camp Street was an odd choice for a pro-Castro organization. On the ground floor of this shabby, elongated, three-story wooden structure located in a blighted section of New Orleans were the offices of Guy Banister.[24] He was a former FBI agent whose career had included a role in the capture of John Dillinger, the notorious public enemy number one. He served with naval intelligence during World War II. Banister rose to become the head of the Bureau's Chicago office. He left the FBI and went to New Orleans in the early 1950s; the mayor had asked him to serve as deputy police chief. His sudden retirement from the force at age fifty-eight came shortly after he allegedly threatened a waiter with a pistol during a dispute in a New Orleans restaurant.

Banister's superpatriotism led him to take up a personal campaign against communism upon his relatively early retirement from law enforcement work. He was a leading figure in the local John Birch Society. He joined the Minutemen, a paramilitary anti-communist organization, and founded the Anti-Communist League of the Caribbean. Banister was a virulent racist, an alcoholic who was prone to violence (he reportedly pistol-whipped the head of a man who drew his ire).[25] This volatile combination did not prevent him from being a pivotal figure in the shadowy world of New Orleans anti-Castroism.

He set up his own "detective agency," Guy Banister Associates, located on the ground floor of 544 Camp Street. Banister was a very active anti-Castro organizer. He helped to establish the CIA-backed Cuban Revolutionary Democratic Front.[26] He was also one of the founders of an organization called the Friends of a Democratic Cuba, yet another CIA-backed group. It was this group that in 1961 obtained a bid from a New Orleans Ford dealer for the purchase of ten trucks, just before the Bay of Pigs invasion. After the assassination two employees of the Bolton Ford Company told the FBI that one of the Cuban Revolutionary Democratic Front representatives called himself "Lee Oswald." The form for the bid bore the printed name "Oswald," yet the real Oswald was in the Soviet Union at the time.[27] Perhaps Banister knew Oswald, or knew of him, even before he arrived back in the United States and came to New Orleans. After Banister's death, some of Oswald's FPCC leaflets were found among his effects.[28]

One of Banister's roles seems to have been that of arms supplier. Members of his detective agency staff recall that during the time Oswald was in New Orleans the Camp Street offices were strewn with guns of all kinds.[29]

No wonder that a group called the Cuban Revolutionary Council (CRC) had its headquarters in the same building as Banister's "detective agency." The CRC was a CIA-supported anti-Castro group, and a very key one at that. The Agency urged its creation and then gave it millions of dollars. Its original purpose was to recruit young Cuban exiles in Florida and along the Gulf Coast and train them as soldiers in the war on Castro, under the direction of such CIA agents as E. Howard Hunt of Watergate fame. CRC served as the Agency's main front organization for the Bay of Pigs invasion.[30]

New Orleans was the CRC's second most important base (Miami was the first). The organization rented 544 Camp Street—the same address as on Oswald's pamphlets—as its New Orleans headquarters. The group rented the office before Oswald came to New Orleans.[31] Although the CRC had theoretically vacated the office by the time Oswald arrived in New Orleans—the group was no longer paying rent—CRC members continued to use the office during the entire summer of Oswald's stay in New Orleans, throughout all of his FPCC activities.[32]

Was Oswald again manifesting a penchant to confront the enemy, as with his visit to Carlos Bringuier's store? Or was the real Lee Harvey Oswald right at home in the anti-Castro enclave that was 544 Camp Street? If pro-Castroite Oswald was looking for unfriendly turf, he could not have done better than Camp Street. The area was a veritable Disneyland of anti-Castroism. The New Orleans offices of the FBI and the CIA were nearby. In addition to the CRC and Banister's offices, there was the Reily Coffee Company located around the corner. William Reily, the company's owner, was a patron of the anti-Castro Free Cuba Committee,[33] a fundraising group for the Cuban Revolutionary Council located at 544 Camp Street.[34]

The Reily Coffee Company is notable for another reason: it employed Lee Harvey Oswald shortly after he arrived in New Orleans.[35] He greased the coffee machines. Oswald's first public pro-Castro activity, passing out literature near the *U.S.S. Wasp*, occurred in mid-June while he was still employed at Reily.

Guy Banister died, reportedly from a heart attack, seven months after the assassination. He was never officially questioned about Oswald or the assassination. His former secretary, Delphine Roberts, said that her boss had access to a large amount of money in 1963; she believed that he received money from the CIA.[36] She remembers that a variety of anti-Castro types visited Banister's office.[37] One was Sergio Arcacha Smith, a prominent figure in the CRC. Smith told a friend that Camp Street was a "Grand Central Station" for exiles.[38] He also claimed privately that he was controlled by the CIA.[39] Another CRC member, Frank Bartes, was an associate of Carlos Bringuier and had witnessed Oswald's appearance in court after the street scuffle.[40]

The Camp Street locale was not only a hotbed of anti-Castroism but also, consequently, of hatred toward President Kennedy. Cuban exiles and many of their CIA sponsors felt betrayed by the President. After approving the April 15, 1961 invasion of Cuba by the Agency's exile army, Kennedy had cancelled an air strike by U.S. planes, fearing the diplomatic and military consequences of overt U.S. involvement. The strike had been designed to knock out Castro's planes and tanks before the invaders hit the beaches. Pinned down in salt marshes without effective air cover, the exiles were defeated, incurring heavy casualties. Several hundred were taken prisoner. The reaction against Kennedy was exceedingly bitter and longlasting. For example, Mario Kohly, whose father claimed to be Cuba's president in exile, said that Kennedy was "a traitor" and "a communist."[41] In October 1963 at a Dallas meeting, a surviving Bay of Pigs veteran lashed out at Kennedy, "Get him out? . . . I wouldn't even call him President. He stinks? We are waiting for Kennedy the 22nd [November], buddy. We are going to see him, in one way or the other. We're going to give him the works when he gets in Dallas."[42] And earlier, in April 1963 a flyer circulated within the exile community in Miami stating, "Only through one development will you Cuban patriots ever live again in your homeland as free men. . . . [Only] if an inspired act of God should place in the White House within weeks a Texan known to be a friend of all Latin Americans."[43]

A list of index cards obtained from Banister's office files by New Orleans District Attorney Jim Garrison provides some insight into the nature of Banister's operations.[44] Garrison did not obtain the files themselves, only the titles and classification numbers:

American Central Intelligence Agency	20–10
Ammunition and Arms	32–1
Anti-Soviet Underground	25–1
B–70 Manned Bomber Force	15–16
Civil Rights Program of JFK	8–41
Dismantling of Ballistic Missile System	15–16
Dismantling of Defenses, U.S.	15–16
Fair Play For Cuba Committee	23–7
International Trade Mart	23–14
Italy, U.S. Bases Dismantled in General Assembly of the United Nations	15–16
Latin America	23–1
Missile Bases Dismantled—Turkey and Italy	15–16

Banister's secretary also claims to have seen Oswald visit Banister at Camp Street.[45] Her daughter, who used a room above Banister's office as a photo studio, claims that she too saw Oswald visiting Banister.[46]

A notebook found on Oswald by the Dallas police the day of the assassination contained some mysterious addresses. Listed on the same page as Carlos Bringuier (the anti-Castro Cuban who was involved in the street scuffle with Oswald) were three addresses with no names attached: 117 Camp, 107 Decatur, 1032 Canal.[47] At first glance the listings seem to be nonsensical: 117 Camp was the address of a dress shop; 107 Decatur did not exist. But by juggling the numbers, assassinologist Harold Weisberg and others found that two of the listings were significant.[48]

The address of 107 Camp belonged to Ronnie Caire, a prominent anti-Castroite and a leader of the Free Cuba Committee (the group patronized by Oswald's employer, William Reily).[49] And 117 Decatur was the address of Orest Pena, a prominent Cuban exile and anti-Castroite.[50] The significance of the Canal Street listing remains unknown.

The scrambled addresses could have been the product of careless writing or a defective memory (although Oswald was not known for the latter); or they could have been a crude form of coding. In any case, they are consistent with Oswald's entire New Orleans experience: behind a façade of pro-Castro sentiments lies a pattern of linkages with anti-Castro groups and individuals directly or indirectly involved with the Central Intelligence Agency.

Again, the CIA's failure to monitor Oswald—or, at minimum, to generate file data on him—is nearly impossible to imagine from the perspective that he was a Russian defector engaging in pro-Castro activism. However, it is easily explained by his working for the Agency. The CIA's extensive network of spies within the Cuban political sphere had as one of its prime targets the FPCC, yet the Agency claims never to have noticed Oswald. So pervasive was CIA spying that Cuban exiles spied on their neighbors and reported to the Agency. As one Cuban described it: "As far as I know they haven't discovered a single Castro spy here, but they made many detailed reports, including gossip, about personal lives of prominent Cubans, if anything usurping the functions of the FBI."[51] Yet when a potential left-wing spy walked right into the nerve center of anti-Castroism in New Orleans and tried to pass himself off as an pro-Castro activist, the network supposedly missed him completely. It is not as if Oswald didn't give the Agency a fair chance: he was extremely public in his pro-Castro activities and went out of his way to be noticed by the media. One can almost imagine former CIA Director William

Colby saying, "We thought Army Intelligence or the FBI would take care of it."

Prior to the assassination, Carlos Bringuier put out a "press relief" and an "open letter" to the exile community. These items could well have been sent to intelligence agencies or officers as well. The missives sought to call attention to Oswald and his activities.[52] This markedly increased the likelihood of his coming to CIA attention as a red menace or potential mole. Yet he allegedly remained a domestic political unknown to the Agency.

The CIA never seemed to be able to gather data on Lee Harvey Oswald when he passed through their nets, whether in New Orleans or, as we will see, in Mexico. Yet Agency-linked persons and organizations were always around him, from Moscow to New Orleans to Dallas.

It is not as if the CIA had no apparatus in New Orleans. It is now known that the Agency's operational presence there in 1963 was extensive. In order to administer its array of Cuban-exile groups and activities, as well as to monitor international shipping in the port of New Orleans, the CIA established a very large domestic station—one of the key stations in the country.[53] A distinguished New Orleans attorney is believed to have served as a station chief in the early 1960s. His name has never been publicly revealed; neither (to the author's knowledge) has he ever been questioned by any official investigation.[54] A 1967 CIA memo obtained by the author under the Freedom of Information Act states that in that year the Agency had 26 employees in New Orleans.[55] In 1976 the Senate Intelligence Committee discovered that as far back as 1957 the Agency's New Orleans station was running its own mail-intercept program, Project SETTER, apparently with no approval from any executive or legislative oversight bodies.[56]

In conclusion, Oswald's ostensibly pro-Castro involvements were firmly enmeshed in the city's anti-Castro subculture. Moreover, as will soon be described, the nature and substance of his activities fit nicely, if not perfectly, with the role of agent-provocateur.

4

The Mohair Marauder

He oughta be shot!

David Ferrie, referring to President Kennedy
after the Bay of Pigs invasion

It is only fitting that Lee Harvey Oswald's clandestine tableau has in it
at least one character colorful enough to have sprung from a John LeCarré
spy novel. His name is David Ferrie, and his strange career rivals anything
in fiction.[1] Rejected by two seminaries because of behavioral problems,
Ferrie founded his own church, the Orthodox Old Catholic Church of
North America, and appointed himself bishop. A master hypnotist who
studied psychology and philosophy as well as religion, the library of his
apartment was stuffed with 3,000 volumes.[2] He became a senior pilot
with Eastern Airlines, but his on-the-job homosexual activities caused
him to be fired. Ferrie lost not only his airline pilot's job and his two
chances to become a Catholic priest, but all of his hair as well. He was
hairless from head to toe.

Ferrie dabbled in cancer research, an interest that led him to keep
hundreds of mice in his apartment. He reportedly built two miniature
submarines in hopes of attacking Havana Harbor. He developed ties to
organized crime and, at the time of the assassination, was employed by
an attorney who worked for New Orleans crime boss Carlos Marcello.
The day President Kennedy was killed, Ferrie was in a federal courtroom
in New Orleans watching as Marcello was cleared of charges that had

resulted in his temporary deportation.[3] Ferrie's precise relationship with Marcello is not known, but he may have piloted him on occasion.[4]

Physically, Ferrie was an unforgettable figure. He rejected a commercial hairpiece in favor of a homemade device: a reddish wig cut out of mohair, glued to his scalp with plastic cement. This was accompanied by outsized "eyebrows" drawn on with greasepaint.[5] These adornments looked eminently unnatural. Together with his slim, intense visage and small, beady eyes, they created an image that most people found difficult to forget—a cross between a sad clown and a heavy from a grade-C horror flick.

Ferrie did have friends. He worked sporadically as an investigator for Guy Banister, whose Camp Street "detective agency" was occasionally employed by crime boss Marcello.[6] Organized crime patronized a variety of anti-Castro endeavors and some of its bosses were in league with the CIA in plots to assassinate Castro.

Banister and Ferrie were close associates. In 1961, when the forty-three-year old Ferrie was in the process of being fired by Eastern Airlines, Banister flew to Miami to appear on Ferrie's behalf at his dismissal hearing.[7] Banister's secretary, Delphine Roberts, asserts that Ferrie was one of Banister's "agents." He worked out of a private office located behind Banister's. She was told that Ferrie did "private work."[8]

The two men were very compatible politically: Ferrie, like Banister, was a right-wing zealot. He was as intense about his superpatriotism as he was about his appearance, with results only slightly less grotesque. Ferrie once wrote to the United States Air Force: "There is nothing I would enjoy better than blowing the hell out of every damn Russian, Communist, Red, or what-have-you. . . . Between my friends and I we can cook up a crew that can really blow them to hell. . . . I want to train killers, however bad that sounds. It is what we need."[9]

Ordinarily such self-advertisements might lead to offers of psychoanalysis rather than job offers. But Guy Banister's was not the only agency to hire the weird-looking chap with the virulently anti-communist views. The organization that did not shrink from hiring men "of the worst moral character," as Allen Dulles admitted, found a place for Ferrie's high-flying militaristic fantasies.

Ferrie's work for the CIA involved, among other things, his considerable skills as a pilot. There are reports that in 1961, before the Bay of Pigs invasion, he flew missions to Cuba, sometimes conducting bombing raids, sometimes executing bravado landings in which he rescued anti-Castro commandoes.[10] In the summer of 1963, according to a number of witnesses, Ferrie also served as an instructor at the Cuban-exile training camp outside New Orleans where recruits were taught guerrilla warfare techniques to be used against Castro.[11] This camp was raided by federal agents seeking to enforce President Kennedy's order forbidding anti-Castro military activities on U.S. soil.[12]

Banister's secretary told journalist Anthony Summers that she believed Ferrie's work to be CIA-connected rather than FBI-connected.[13] Besides Banister, Ferrie's anti-Castro, CIA-linked associates included Sergio Arcacha Smith, the leader of the Cuban Revolutionary Council (CRC) who had an office at 544 Camp Street at the same time Oswald used this address on his pamphlets. Ferrie approached Arcacha Smith and offered to train exiles for the invasion of Cuba.[14] Smith helped Ferrie get out of jail after being arrested for homosexual assault.[15]

Former CIA man Victor Marchetti, who served as executive assistant to the deputy director, claims to have observed that then CIA Director Richard Helms and other senior Agency officers became disturbed when Ferrie's name was linked to the President's assassination by New Orleans District Attorney Jim Garrison in 1967. Marchetti asked a CIA colleague about Ferrie and was told that he had worked for the Agency as a contract agent in the early 1960s and was involved in some of the Cuban operations.[16] Marchetti now believes that Ferrie was "involved in some rather nefarious activities" as a contract agent.[17]

In 1967 the Justice Department posed a series of questions to the CIA regarding allegations stemming from Garrison's investigation. A deputy assistant attorney general in the Justice Department's Criminal Division asked the Agency in writing: "What was the exact relationship between CIA and David Ferrie? What was the extent of CIA's file on him before the assassination?" The Agency's terse reply was, "There was no relationship, and there was no file before the assassination."[18]

In 1963 Ferrie seems to have been a suspect in the President's murder because of his links to Oswald and his anti-Kennedyism (to be described shortly). He was taken in for questioning by the FBI but was released.[19] Even his telephone records provided a possibly coincidental but intriguing tidbit. Two months before the assassination he made a call to a Chicago apartment building. It has not been established to whom he talked, but the building was the residence of one Jean West. The night before the assassination West was staying at the Cabana Motel in Dallas with Lawrence Meyers, a friend of Jack Ruby. Ruby visited Meyers at the Cabana around midnight—twelve hours before the President's assassination.[20]

An FBI document indicates that Ferrie admitted to being publicly and privately critical of President Kennedy's withholding of U.S. air support during the Bay of Pigs invasion. In one instance, he gave a speech to a men's civics club in New Orleans after the Bay of Pigs debacle. He had to be removed from the podium by his hosts when he launched into an offensive verbal attack on President Kennedy.[21] Ferrie further admitted to using expressions such as, "He oughta be shot," in reference to the President.[22] The FBI decided that Ferrie did not mean this literally.[23]

Although he was in federal court in New Orleans at the time of the assassination, his strange and unexplained movements immediately afterward have aroused suspicion among many analysts. The night of November 22, 1963, Ferrie and two companions left New Orleans in the midst of a torrential rainstorm. They drove all night (a 400-mile drive) and arrived in Houston around 5:00 AM. Ferrie gave the FBI an interesting assortment of reasons concerning why he went to Texas. The visit was to "merely relax."[24] He and his friends wanted to do some "goose hunting," he said.[25] Downtown Houston, where Ferrie and friends checked into a hotel, is not renowned as a mecca for goose hunters; perhaps that's why Ferrie was smart enough not to bring along any guns.[26] The trip did not appear to be particularly relaxing. A gas station attendant who waited on the trio on November 24 said that they seemed to be "in somewhat of a hurry."[27] They did stop long enough to watch television at the gas station; the news was of Oswald's murder at the hands of Jack Ruby.[28]

The day after the assassination Ferrie et al. drove to a skating rink near Galveston. Naturally, they didn't skate. Ferrie told the FBI that he had been "considering for some time the feasibility and possibility of opening up an ice skating rink in New Orleans," and that this accounted for his visit to the rink.[29] Chuck Rolland, the proprietor of the Winterland Skating Rink, has a different memory of the visit. He told the Bureau that a man introducing himself as "Ferris" or "Ferry" asked for the skating schedule and indicated that he had come from out of town to do some skating.[30] Rolland said Ferrie mentioned nothing about equipping or opening a rink.

Skating and goose hunting aside, one of the main activities of the trip seems to have been telephoning. There were four calls placed from Ferrie's Houston hotel room to New Orleans, as well as one local call.[31] At another stop a call was made to Alexandria, Louisiana (number unknown).[32] At the skating rink, Ferrie spent the entire two hours hanging around the pay telephone. When it rang, he answered; after talking, he departed the rink with his two companions.[33]

By far the most significant of Ferrie's activities and associations are those involving Lee Harvey Oswald. In 1955 Ferrie was already a pilot of some renown. He led the New Orleans unit of the Civil Air Patrol

(CAP). The local CAP unit became a forum for his homosexual activities. There were reports of homosexual orgies involving the young cadets, nude gambling at Ferrie's residence, and free-flowing liquor.[34] Eventually he lost his CAP command.[35]

In 1955, while Ferrie led the New Orleans CAP, Lee Harvey Oswald joined. Oswald was living in the city with his mother.[36] House Assassinations Committee investigators found six witnesses whose statements confirmed that Oswald was in Ferrie's CAP unit.[37] One witness believed Oswald had attended at least one of Ferrie's parties.[38]

The House Committee noted that homosexuality and liquor aside, Ferrie seemed to exert "tremendous influence" on the cadets who were his pupils.[39] The Committee discovered that Ferrie "urged several boys to join the armed forces." At age sixteen, immediately following his experience in Ferrie's CAP unit, Oswald tried to enlist in the Marines.[40] He was so anxious to join that he lied about his age. When he was rejected by the Corps for being underage, he began studying his older brother's Marine Corps manual until he "knew it by heart."[41] He succeeded in joining the Marines shortly after his seventeenth birthday.

One might think this would be the end of any relationship between Ferrie and Oswald, since Ferrie went on to become an even more extreme right-wing militarist and Oswald ostensibly became a Russophile, a Marxist, a traitor to his country, and a supporter of Castro. But Oswald was again in Ferrie's company after returning from Russia, and immediately after he appeared to become a pro-Castro activist. Despite Ferrie's announced desire to "blow the hell out of every damn Russian, Communist, or Red," which might well have included Oswald and his wife Marina, the two men must have found a common ground. They were seen together by a variety of witnesses.

Guy Banister's secretary claims that Ferrie not only met Oswald at 544 Camp Street but, on at least one occasion, took him to the anti-Castro, guerrilla training camp on the outskirts of New Orleans where Ferrie was alleged to have been an instructor.[42] One friend of Ferrie's, Dante Marachini, worked at Reily Coffee while Oswald worked there. Marachini was hired on the same day as Oswald.[43]

Solid evidence of a post-defection association between Oswald and Ferrie stems from an incident that took place in Clinton, Louisiana in late August or early September of 1963—at the end of Oswald's FPCC summer in New Orleans and only three months before the President's murder. The incident was not known to the Warren Commission. It was discovered by the Garrison investigation in 1967 and confirmed by the House Assassinations Committee in 1978.

The Clinton event occurred in the summer of 1963, which was dominated by political activism and racial tension.[44] Dr. Martin Luther King, Jr. had proclaimed it "civil rights summer." Political mobilization and voter registration drives were underway all across the deep South. President Kennedy had invited black civil rights leaders to the White House and had committed his administration to the passage of a civil rights bill.

Clinton, Louisiana, then a small town of about 1,500 people located a hundred miles north of New Orleans, was caught up in the political swirl. There had been several arrests of blacks who were engaged in civil rights activities. The Congress of Racial Equality (CORE) was conducting a voter registration drive among local blacks. On the day of the incident there was a long line of blacks waiting to register to vote. Police watched anxiously for anything that might spark violence in racially tense Clinton. According to the composite accounts of the Clinton witnesses—chief among them being two CORE organizers, the mayor, the town marshal, and the registrar of voters—the incident began when a black Cadillac (a conspicuous car in poor, rural Clinton) arrived in town during the morning. The three men in the vehicle parked near the registrar of voters' office. One of them, a slim, young white man, got out of the car and stepped into the long, slow-moving line of blacks waiting to register. The young man, conspicuous by his color, stood in line for several hours. After the assassination the Clinton witnesses were positive that it was Lee Harvey Oswald.

Registrar of voters Henry Palmer dealt with Oswald personally. After spending hours in line, Oswald finally entered the registrar's office. Palmer asked the stranger for identification. The man produced a Navy ID card bearing the name Lee H. Oswald. According to Palmer, Oswald claimed that he was seeking work at a nearby state hospital in order to enhance his eligibility to become a registered voter in Clinton. Palmer thought it was odd that a white stranger was trying to register in the midst of a voter registration drive centering on indigent blacks. He told Oswald that he was not eligible because he had not lived in town long enough. Oswald thanked Palmer and left.

While Oswald was waiting in line to see the registrar, the black Cadillac remained parked on the street. The CORE activists were worried that the mysterious vehicle might harbor men who had come to disrupt the registration drive. A CORE worker asked the town marshal, John Manchester, to check out the car. He had already been eyeing the Cadillac, and he complied with the request. The marshal approached the vehicle and questioned the man behind the wheel long enough to conclude that the strangers presented no threat to local peace. The Cadillac stayed well

into the afternoon as its occupants continued to observe civil rights activities.

The marshal and other witnesses described the driver as a big man
with grey hair and a ruddy complexion. Several Clinton witnesses identified the man as Clay Shaw, the New Orleans businessman who was
unsuccessfully prosecuted for conspiracy to assassinate the President by
District Attorney Jim Garrison in 1969. The witnesses made this identification at the 1969 trial and to the House Assassinations Committee a
decade later. Still, the possibility that it was Guy Banister cannot be ruled
out. In their photographs, Banister and Shaw are not strikingly dissimilar
in general appearance. Neither Garrison nor the Committee has indicated
that the witnesses were shown photos of Banister. His presence in Clinton
would certainly be in keeping with the Camp Street interconnections
among Oswald, Ferrie, and himself and also with one of the interests
reflected in Banister's files. The reader will recall that among an array
of file categories dealing mostly with missiles, bombers, and national
security was the title "Civil Rights Program of JFK."

The third man in the Cadillac was more easily identifiable than the
driver. In fact, he was downright unforgettable. According to the CORE
chairman, his most salient features were his hair and eyebrows: "They
didn't seem real."[45] The CORE chairman had no trouble identifying the
bizarre stranger as David Ferrie.

It is a provocative incident—the mohair marauder and the pinko Marine together in rural Louisiana only months before the assassination.
The House Assassinations Committee (HSCA) found the Clinton witnesses very credible and believed that the incident did occur as they
described. Moreover, Oswald is remembered by other witnesses beyond
the scene of the registration drive.

The town barber in Jackson, Louisiana, another small town near Clinton, remembered Oswald. The appearance of strangers was a rare event
in these thinly populated, rural environs. The barber recalled that Oswald
asked for advice in getting a job as an electrician at the local hospital
(Oswald had told the registrar in Clinton that he was seeking work at the
hospital). The friendly barber sent Oswald to see a local politician who
might help in obtaining a job at the hospital. Louisiana State Representative Morgan Reeves confirmed that Oswald did visit him. Two people at the hospital also remembered Oswald; he appeared there and
actually applied for work. This chain of events occurred before he tried
to register to vote.

Like much in Oswald's life, these activities seem inexplicably strange,
perhaps even nonsensical. If we dispense with the explanation that he

had a sudden and compelling urge to be a hospital electrician in rural Louisiana and that his old CAP buddy David Ferrie, and some other man, drove upstate to help Lee settle in, then what was he doing? The House Assassinations Committee treated the Clinton incident as significant only in that it linked Oswald to Ferrie, but the Committee could not make any sense of the event itself. Implicitly, the HSCA leaves us hanging with the notion that Clinton was yet another serendipitous meander by a confused left-wing ideologue who had a curiosity about civil rights politics.

Professor James W. Clarke offers another explanation of Oswald's association with Ferrie, an explanation grounded on the flawed assumption that Oswald was genuinely pro-Castro. "Thus," says Clarke, "Oswald was probably in contact with Ferrie in an attempt to obtain information on anti-Castro activities that he hoped to relay to the Castro government."[46]

Some researchers who suspect that Clinton may have had a domestic intelligence dimension point to the FBI's infamous COINTELPRO program.[47] COINTELPRO was a massive counterintelligence effort conducted by the Bureau against radical and left-wing groups in the United States. Although the FBI was the organization with the broadest official mandate for domestic spying and while COINTELPRO is perhaps the most pervasive and best-known project of that era, there are problems in leaping to the conclusion that Oswald might have been working for the Bureau. Gay Banister—if he was the man in the car in Clinton—once was an FBI agent. But his Camp Street operation was firmly enmeshed in anti-Castro activities that were CIA, not Bureau, related. There has never been any suggestion that Ferrie worked for the FBI—only the CIA. Moreover, investigators have failed to notice how the Clinton incident relates to the lesser known CIA involvement in domestic spying in the early 1960s.

The Agency's 1947 charter forbade domestic spying; however, from its very inception, the CIA did spy inside the United States.[48] Sometimes it negotiated agreements with the FBI for strictly limited domestic activities; sometimes, as in the case of its Cuban exile networks, the Agency simply muscled into the Bureau's turf and expanded domestic spying without any specific authorization from Congress and in violation of its charter. The justification for a limited domestic role for the Agency was based on the argument that the CIA could not end its pursuit of foreign agents and of matters relating to foreign intelligence simply because the trail led back to the United States (except, of course, in Oswald's case). With this as an entrée the CIA developed an appetite for domestic spying that was voracious if not insatiable, expanding into surveillance and covert action activities that had little or no connection with international spying. This is precisely why the CIA and FBI were such bitter rivals. It is why the most ardent watchdog of the CIA's domestic role was not congressional oversight committees or the White House but J. Edgar Hoover, whose bulldog countenance was perfect for the role.[49]

The CIA's domestic activities of the early 1960s included organizing consumer boycotts against U.S. firms that traded with Castro and organizing demonstrations in Washington outside the foreign embassies of governments who supported Cuba.[50] But what of Clinton and CORE? No Cuban connection there.

The CIA steadily increased its domestic spying throughout the early 1960s. This activity peaked with operation CHAOS, which was formally constituted in 1967 and ended in 1975.[51] It was a massive effort to monitor and penetrate left-wing or radical organizations such as the Students for a Democratic Society (SDS). CHAOS also included a mail-opening program in which the Agency diverted 28 million pieces of mail belonging to U.S. citizens and organizations.[52] The watch list of targets for mail opening included organizations as tame as the American Friends Service Committee and individuals such as writers Edward Albee and John Steinbeck. The Agency opened CHAOS files on over 7,000 Americans.[53]

Long before CHAOS was formalized, the CIA was gradually increasing its domestic spying toward the massive levels reached in late 1960s and early 1970s. Networks of spies are built fairly slowly, whether in the domestic or foreign arena. Getting them in place ("building assets," as it is called in clandestine parlance) takes time, especially for an operation of the magnitude of CHAOS.

In 1967 the CIA formalized project MERRIMAC.[54] Its stated purpose was to provide advance warning of demonstrations by left-wing or anti-war groups that might "threaten" CIA personnel and facilities in Washington, DC. While there were protests that at times threatened to block traffic or shut down certain government agencies, the CIA had not been subjected to them (perhaps one of the advantages of being located on a 125-acre tract out in the Langley, Virginia woods). MERRIMAC's narrow mandate to gather intelligence about forthcoming disruptions to CIA headquarters was used as an excuse to infiltrate the left-wing and liberal political arena.

In all probability MERRIMAC was created as a formally approved project not to begin legitimate domestic surveillance activities, but rather to serve as a cover for illegitimate activities, some of which predated the project itself. The Agency used MERRIMAC as a pretext for spying activities that had nothing to do with possible demonstrations at Langley. One of the project's directors admitted, with considerable understatement, "I think it started out legitimately concerned with the physical security in . . . installations . . . it just kind of grew into areas and perhaps it shouldn't have."[55]

Under the guise of MERRIMAC the CIA justified its infiltration of no less than ten political organizations, most of which never even considered trying to demonstrate against the CIA or harass its employees. Agency operations shadowed the leaders of target groups, photographed the faces and license numbers of demonstrators, reported on the "attitudes" of group members, their relationships with the group, and even their sources of income.[56]

The ten groups targeted for surveillance and infiltration were not, by and large, coteries of bomb-throwing radicals. Four were targeted as soon as MERRIMAC opened up shop in February 1967.[57] The Agency claimed that these four were "bellwethers."[58] Bellwethers of what was not clear: ostensibly, of efforts to disrupt the Agency. The four were, the Women's Strike for Peace, the Washington Peace Center, the Student Nonviolent Coordinating Committee (SNCC), and CORE, whose civil rights activities never did include demonstrating against the CIA.

MERRIMAC's formal targeting of CORE occurred three and a half years after the Clinton incident, but it establishes the CIA's special interest in CORE. From the rest of what we know about the Agency's domestic operations, this interest surely did not start with MERRIMAC. In sum, MERRIMAC can be viewed as a device by which the Agency could justify and further expand its ongoing domestic spying under the caché of self-protection.

Former CIA administrator Victor Marchetti has described the many tactics "used by the CIA to cover its tracks" in domestic spying—deceptions designed to conceal its "numerous activities inside the United States."[59] Marchetti points to CIA training of local police in the late 1950s and early 1960s as a typical example of Agency duplicity in domestic operations. The Agency first tried to cover up its training of police, then chose to mislead the public, the press, and Congress about the scope and nature of its involvements. The Agency tried to use a provision of the Omnibus Crime Control and Safe Streets Act of 1968 to legitimize its domestic police-training program. But this provision, which encouraged federal law enforcement agencies to assist local police, was clearly inapplicable to the CIA because its charter forbade any "police" or "internal security" functions. Moreover, the CIA had been conducting police training long before the anti-crime bill was passed in June 1968.[60] In part, the Agency was forced to cover up this linkage in order to keep the FBI at bay: the Bureau maintained special facilities for police training and had a legal authorization for such activity.

From this perspective, the Clinton incident need not be viewed as FBI-related, as it has been by many analysts who have not understood the breadth of the CIA's domestic activities. A description of the Agency's modus operandi in MERRIMAC is provided by the Rockefeller Commission's investigation into CIA domestic spying:

> They were instructed to mingle with others at demonstrations and meetings open to the public, to listen for information and pick up literature . . . to attend meetings of the organization, to show interest in their purpose, and to make modest financial contributions. . . . They were directed to report on how many persons attended the meetings or demonstrations, what they said and what activities were conducted or planned.[61]

The mind reels at the vision of the premier U.S. foreign espionage agency dispatching its operatives to monitor poor blacks and a few white organizers involved in voter registration in rural Louisiana. It would sound like the paranoid speculations of those who see CIA agents behind every bush if it were not for the fact that CORE was targeted as a potential threat to the Agency.

The Agency itself seemed almost paranoid about the direction of black politics in the early 1960s. In 1978 the Center for National Security Studies in Washington, DC obtained, through the Freedom of Information Act, internal CIA memoranda revealing the extent of the Agency's domestic spying on blacks. The documents show that the CIA infiltrated black political groups in the Washington area, took photographs of a Malcolm X Day rally, infiltrated the Resurrection City encampment in 1968, and had informants inside the Washington school system to spy on black youths.[62] One informer, who was identified only as "a teacher and a department head," warned the Agency in 1969 that black students were becoming increasingly militant and that some carried weapons. The CIA also maintained a minute-by-minute log of the riots that took place following the April 1968 assassination of Dr. Martin Luther King, Jr. One Agency memo admits that at the time of these surveillance activities, black militant groups posed no threat to CIA property or personnel.[63]

A CIA memo obtained by the *Washington Post* in 1978 clearly manifests the Agency's fears concerning black power groups.[64] The CIA allegedly found that some of these groups had hostile attitudes toward it. It worried that this posed "a new threat" to its operations abroad—

although how this was so remains unclear—and a threat to its "image in the United States." Recognizing that threats to image did not exactly fall under project MERRIMAC's legal mandate of threats to property or personnel, the Agency memo cynically notes that it is the latter threats "which must be our official concern."

The Clinton incident is often dismissed as a harmless manifestation of Oswald's catholic curiosity about leftist causes, as further indication of the flightiness of his political involvements. The Clinton activities all occurred within 48 hours and seemed to be disconnected from Oswald's other involvements. Moreover, he was not an electrician; he did not move to Clinton, and so on. From the perspective of domestic spying *à la* MERRIMAC, some of what Oswald and his associates did does make sense as a one-shot intelligence-gathering foray—observing CORE's activities, and testing the registration process. The other activities—the job hunting, the intimations of staying around Clinton—could have been part of the 48-hour probe of CORE or perhaps something more. It has always been assumed that Oswald never intended to pursue anything further in Clinton or with CORE. Perhaps not, but it is a mistake to assume that the proof of this lies in the fact that he never followed up on anything.

There is another possibility. By the time of the Clinton incident in late August to early September 1963, Oswald's last public FPCC ritual had been performed; his role as a pro-Castro activist was over. He may have been in the process of getting into another role, another domestic spying assignment to be played out in Clinton and elsewhere. But his plans changed. Instead of going back to Clinton, or getting closer to CORE somewhere else, or continuing in his old role as FPCC activist, he departed for Mexico within weeks after Clinton. His assignment had apparently been changed.

Oswald went to Mexico City in late September. There, as will later be described, some of the most important espionage activity relating to his role in the President's assassination took place. What may have prevented further surveillance activities relating to Clinton or CORE was that Oswald was suddenly being moved back to Dallas via Mexico, along the trail that would lead to the Texas School Book Depository on November 22nd.

Ferrie's exact association with Oswald remains shadowy. Of course, he denied any association. When FBI agents showed him pictures of Oswald four days after the assassination, he said that the profile view of Oswald had "a very vague familiarity," but the full-face and full-length photos were not familiar.[65] In a personally typed statement submitted to the FBI two and a half weeks after the assassination, Ferrie tiptoed around his links to Oswald as if he were an apprentice lawyer who had not quite mastered the syntax of legalese.

In 1955, or thereabouts, I assisted, for a time, the Moisant Squadron of Civil Air Patrol, at Moisant Airport, New Orleans, Louisiana, though I cannot establish through personal records or recollection the exact dates of this connection. I have no records, or recollection, to my knowledge, to show that LEE HARVEY OSWALD was, or was not, a member of this particular unit of the Civil Air Patrol. To my best knowledge and belief I do not know LEE HARVEY OSWALD, and have no personal recollection of ever having met him. If I did ever meet him it was very casual and to my best recollection have definitely not seen him in recent years. [66]

Two witnesses asserted that Ferrie seemed to be in a state of panic immediately following the assassination, about—of all things—a library card. One of Oswald's former neighbors in New Orleans told the House Assassinations Committee that Ferrie visited her after the President's murder and inquired about Oswald's library card. [67] A second panicky inquiry about the card was reported by Oswald's former landlady in New Orleans, who stated that Ferrie visited her within hours of the assassination, just before he set off to Texas to hunt and ice skate. [68]

Why the concern? According to official records, no library card of any kind was found on Oswald when he was arrested in Dallas. But one of Ferrie's associates claimed that while Ferrie was on his Texas sojourn, Ferrie's lawyer, G. Wray Gill, showed up at his client's home and reportedly remarked, "When Lee Harvey Oswald was arrested by the Dallas police, Oswald was carrying a library card with Ferrie's name on it." [69]

Ferrie was taken into custody by the Secret Service shortly after his skating trip. He was questioned briefly and released. During this interview the Secret Service did ask Ferrie whether he had lent his library card to Oswald. [70] The reason for the question has never been explained. The Secret Service question might have been precipitated by Ferrie's own inquiries about the card, although there is no evidence of this. Alternatively, the question may have been sparked by something said or found in Dallas in connection with Oswald's arrest.

In late 1966 Ferrie was under intensive investigation by New Orleans District Attorney Jim Garrison as part of his reinvestigation of the assassination. Ferrie was under heavy surveillance: Garrison had targeted him as part of an alleged conspiracy in the President's assassination. On February 26, 1967, as Garrison was about to go to court, David Ferrie was found dead in his home. The cause of death was listed as "natural," due to a massive brain hemorrhage.[71] No trace of any toxic substance was found.

Ferrie's body was found nude amidst the singular artifacts of his bizarre life. The walls of his bathroom were dotted with hundreds of splotches of dried glue, marking the sites where his mohair wig was hung when out of service; hundreds of mice—fodder for Ferrie's experiments in cancer research—resided in unkempt cages. Books on medicine and pharmacology were strewn about. There were guns, a large bomb, military equipment, and three blank U.S. passports that needed only a picture and some basic data to appear valid.[72] There were also two suicide notes, presumably left by the mohair marauder to signal the onset of his naturally caused hemorrhage. One note was found on his piano; the other, on a table. Both were typed.[73] Each had a typed signature.

The night before Ferrie's body was discovered, he was in his apartment with *Washington Post* reporter George Lardner, Jr. from midnight to 4:00 AM. Lardner told Garrison's office that Ferrie seemed in good spirits when he last saw him. The reporter described the forty-nine-year-old adventurer as an "intelligent, well-versed guy [on] a broad range of subjects."[74]

Whatever the cause of Ferrie's demise, his friend and patron Eladio del Valle was murdered before Garrison's investigators could find him and question him about Ferrie and the assassination. Del Valle was a wealthy anti-Castro organizer who had reportedly financed some of Ferrie's activities against Castro. Garrison's investigators had been trying unsuccessfully to track him down in Miami. Twelve hours after Ferrie's body was found, del Valle's turned up in a Miami parking lot. He had been shot in the heart at pointblank range; his skull was split open with an ax. The case was never solved.[75]

The Clinton incident forced the House Assassinations Committee to wrestle with the implications of the Ferrie–Oswald association. In the end the Committee decided:

> Since Oswald consistently demonstrated a left-wing Marxist ideology, he would not have supported the anti-Castro movement. At the same time, the Committee noted that Oswald's possible association with Ferrie might be distinguishable, since it could not be simply termed an anti-Castro association. Ferrie and Oswald may have had a personal friendship unrelated to Cuban activities.[76]

The assumption that Oswald's left-wing involvements were real rather than a charade has forced all official inquiries into weak explanations like the one above. It would have us believe that Oswald and the volatile Ferrie trucked around together observing the political phenomenon of the civil rights summer as a part of their "personal friendship," spiced, one is led to imagine, by point-counterpoint discussions concerning communism and Castroism. It is far more logical to view the two men as pursuing the same goals in the service of the same organization.

5

Smearing the Left Kremlin-Red

According to Director Helms, to "monitor" a group is merely to attend its public meetings and hear what any citizen present would hear; to "infiltrate" a group is to join it as a member and appear to support its purposes in general; to "penetrate" a group is to gain a position of leadership and influence or direct its policies and actions.
Rockefeller Commission Report on CIA domestic spying[1]

Clinton, Louisiana was the beginning and the end of Oswald's brief foray into civil rights politics. Like his flurry of pro-Castro activities in New Orleans, the CORE incident was a never-to-be-repeated phenomenon. Oswald never spoke publicly on behalf of Castro or conducted FPCC leafletting after he closed up shop in New Orleans the summer before the assassination; neither did he have anything to do with the political struggles of blacks. There was, however, one last domestic political involvement before the assassination. Like the Clinton incident, this one was brief. It is seemingly inexplicable or insignificant in the view of most researchers.

This incident occurred in Dallas the month before the assassination, after Oswald had left New Orleans, gone to Mexico, and then returned to Dallas. It involved the American Civil Liberties Union (ACLU), a group of liberal activists staunchly committed to the defense of political freedoms. As with CORE, Oswald's brief contact with the ACLU has been dismissed by most investigators as significant only as a manifestation of his leftism or political curiosity. Again, as with CORE, there is another perspective concerning the ACLU episode: it may have been the final domestic spying assignment for agent Oswald before he was moved into whatever role he played in the President's assassination.

Oswald's contact with the ACLU began when he accompanied his acquaintance Michael Paine to a meeting of the organization's Dallas chapter on October 25, 1963.[2] (Ruth Paine befriended Marina Oswald. Marina and Oswald's two daughters lived in the Paine home in Irving, Texas while Oswald took apartments in Dallas and visited his family on weekends.) His strange behavior at the meeting is often viewed as evidence of the mental turmoil that would induce him to commit murder the very next month. Like so much of his ostensibly unstable behavior (wrist slashing, street brawls), it may have been very rational, from a covert activity frame of reference.

Oswald spoke briefly at the meeting. In a short, coherent speech he took issue with a previous speaker who had asserted that members of the John Birch Society were not, ipso facto, anti-Semites as well. Oswald's friend Paine (who was never called to testify before the House Assassinations Committee)[3] described to the Warren Commission Oswald's rather contentious and intolerant remarks as "out of keeping with the mood of the meeting."[4] The ACLU was founded, in major part, out of an abiding commitment to the principle of tolerance. Oswald seemed determined to test that commitment.

After the meeting broke up, people stayed and had discussions in small groups. Oswald joined Paine's friend Frank Krystinik and a third man.[5] The third man's identity was not known to Paine, but he thought the man was a member of the local chapter. During the discussion, Oswald took a strident leftist position. He railed against free enterprise and began a heated argument with Krystinik, who was defending certain facets of the free enterprise system. Krystinik employed a few workers in a small-scale business and was irritated by Oswald's criticisms.[6] The two men nearly came to blows.[7]

To the Warren Commission this incident was further evidence that Oswald was a left-wing hothead. If, in fact, he was this aggressive about his Marxist beliefs, it is surprising that he and the volatile David Ferrie made it to Clinton intact.

After the meeting Oswald and Paine rode home together in Paine's car. Pain remembers that Oswald seemed singularly unimpressed by the ACLU. Paine described the organization's goals and purposes. Oswald responded that he could not join such a group. He expressed surprise that Paine would join an organization whose purpose was to defend free speech per se.[8] Paine's impression was that Oswald seemed not to be aware of "the more general principle of freedom of speech for everyone which has value in itself."[9] In contrast, unknown to Paine, Oswald had stated during his New Orleans radio appearance that the FPCC represented a minority viewpoint which, in a democracy, deserved a full and free exposition—an assertion very much attuned to the principles of the ACLU.

Paine certainly did not encourage Oswald to join, or even suggest that he do so, in light of Oswald's behavior and his comments, which seemed to question the organization's raison d'être.[10]

Unknown to Michael Paine, Oswald did join the ACLU. Within a few days of attending the local meeting, he joined via the national headquarters. Almost as surprising as his joining was the question posed in his letter: he asked the national headquarters how he might get in touch with "ACLU groups in the area."[11] Both his request and his joining seem inconsistent, if not patently phony. Michael Paine and his wife Ruth were ACLU members, and Oswald had already made contact with the local branch.

Then, on November 1, 1963 (ten days after attending the meeting) he did two things that may indicate the real purpose of his apparently fickle relationship with the ACLU. First, he wrote to the American Communist Party. In his letter he described the meeting that he had attended, including its location (indicating that he had not forgotten where the local chapter could be found, despite his query to the national ACLU). The letter described the political "friction" between the left and the right in Dallas. But the last two paragraphs are the most revealing:

> Could you advise me as to the general view we had on the American Civil Liberties Union? and to what degree, if any, I should attempt to heighten its progressive tendencies?
> This Dallas branch of the ACLU is firmly in the hands of "liberal" professional people (a minister and two law professors conducted the Oct. 25th meeting). However, some of those present showed marked class-awareness and insight.[12]

Suddenly Oswald seems to have a purpose for his ACLU activities: he wants advice on how to "heighten" the organization's "progressive tendencies." As for those who manifested "marked class-awareness," was Oswald referring to the ACLU speaker with whom he had disagreed, to Krystinik, who had defended free enterprise? Was Oswald so starved for the company of fellow leftists that he invented them, like a child inventing imaginary playmates, or did he invent persons with "marked class-awareness and insight" for another purpose?

Arnold Johnson, who was then the national secretary for the American Communist Party, recalled that his only response to Oswald's letter was to send out some literature.[13] Yet Oswald's letter had, in essence, invited the national Communist Party to commit to paper its advice for making the Dallas ACLU more attuned to communist ideology. This letter, by itself, established a linkage between the two organizations. However artificial or limited this linkage may have been, it now existed on paper.

On the very same day that the letter to the Communist Party was postmarked (November 1), Oswald established another pro-communist link for the ACLU. He opened up a new post office box in Dallas. On the rental form he authorized the receipt of mail for two organizations—the ACLU and the Fair Play for Cuba Committee.

Oswald surely did not anticipate much mail relating to either of these organizations. His FPCC activities were finished; there were no FPCC members remaining in New Orleans (they had all moved to Dallas in the person of Oswald). Neither did he set up a chapter or pursue any public FPCC activities in Dallas. As for the ACLU, his correspondence consisted of writing to the national chapter to join, then writing to the Communist Party about tactics. He did not make any further ACLU contacts that might produce mail for his new box.

Most likely, the primary purpose of the box was not to receive mail but, rather, to establish a link between the ACLU and the FPCC. There, in the paper trail of the U.S. Postal Service, was the second communist link for the ACLU, forged by Oswald on the same day as the first.

Whatever happened with Lee's leftist cubbyhole in Dallas, the federal intelligence bureaucracy may well have known about it. As author Sylvia Meagher pointed out, the FBI admitted to the Warren Commission that informant "T–2" had furnished the Bureau with a copy of a letter Oswald had written to the FPCC from Dallas. The FBI provided a copy to the Commission. T–2 "did not know Oswald personally and could furnish no further information," said the FBI.[14]

Did T–2 intercept only one Oswald letter, or was the government privy to all the leftist missives sent by Oswald? Was it also monitoring his new FPCC/ACLU box? If the box was under surveillance, wasn't someone worried when the Mannlicher-Carcano Italian carbine rifle was mailed there, to be received by "A. J. Hidell"? This rifle was the alleged murder weapon in President Kennedy's assassination. It was supposedly mail-ordered by Oswald to his box using the Hidell alias, as was the .38 revolver alleged to have been used by Oswald to kill Dallas police officer J. D. Tippit in the aftermath of the President's assassination.

In January 1963 Senator Thomas J. Dodd (Dem., CT) began hearings in Washington conducted by his Senate subcommittee (known as the Dodd Committee). Dodd was gathering evidence to bolster his push for gun-control legislation. He was particularly concerned with mail-order guns which could be obtained by any criminal or psychopath without restriction. Could Oswald have been proving the point that pro-Cuban subversives could do the same? Dodd himself was specifically concerned about the subversive threat posed by the FPCC.[15] The two companies from which Oswald allegedly mail-ordered the guns (Klein's Sporting Goods in Chicago and Seaport Traders of California) were specific targets of the Dodd Committee's investigation.[16] Perhaps Oswald or his handlers wanted to create some data on the threat of subversive firepower. If he merely wanted a rifle with which to assassinate the President, he could have bought it over the counter anywhere in Texas with no questions asked and only the salesclerk's recollection to tie him to the weapon.

The possibility that Oswald's Dallas mail was being diverted is strengthened by the strange history of the November letter he wrote to the Communist Party seeking advice about rendering the Dallas ACLU more progressive. It arrived in New York City four weeks after its postmark. As Sylvia Meagher has noted, for three of the four weeks (until November 22) Oswald was not an infamous, accused assassin, so this cannot account for the delay.[17]

If, as the House Assassinations Committee believed, Oswald was a leftist ideologue, then forging links among these various groups would make some sense in terms of his political worldview. After all, the ACLU was an ultra-liberal defender of political freedoms, including those of far-left political action groups like the FPCC. But there is also the other pattern, which recognizes that Oswald had about as much need for information from the ACLU national headquarters as he did to register to vote in Clinton—the pattern of domestic spying.

The CIA's domestic spying activities escalated dramatically in the 1960s. As previously described, they did not suddenly emerge full-blown with the inception of CHAOS in 1967, or begin with CHAOS's inception. The surveillance of 1,000 organizations, which surely included the ACLU, may have been formally constituted into a program under the code name CHAOS in 1967, but a good number of those organizations—certainly the FPCC and quite possibly the ACLU—must have been targeted in the early 1960s. The fact that a thousand groups were targeted indicates that the ACLU must have been included, given its size, prestige, and activities in defense of the political rights of radical groups.[18]

The CIA has been extremely sensitive and ultra secretive about its domestic spying activities.[19] Because of the limitations imposed by its charter, the almost certain flak from liberal elements of Congress and the press, and the FBI's defense of turf, the Agency has tended to minimize and obscure its domestic operations, even to the point of lying to Congress and the press about their scope and existence.[20] Thus the Agency's grudging admission to the Rockefeller Commission that it had an interest in certain domestic organizations (names withheld) dating to 1964 increases the likelihood that Oswald's 1963 activities with the FPCC, CORE, and the ACLU were part of the Agency's ongoing spying.[21]

There are other indications of a potential Agency interest in the ACLU. The CIA was concerned about the legal aspects of radical/leftist politics in the United States—the ACLU's turf. The Agency monitored the legal proceedings of all 28 persons indicted following the riots that occurred during the 1968 Democratic National Convention in Chicago.[22]

In addition, the major premises underlying project CHAOS reveal much about the CIA's domestic clandestine mentality and much about the nature of Oswald's domestic spying activities. The premises of CHAOS were that the American Communist Party was a surrogate of the Kremlin and that, in general, foreign regimes were influencing and nurturing left-wing political organizations in the United States for subversive purposes.[23] CIA field offices were instructed to search out links between U.S. political groups and "communist, communist-front, or other anti-American foreign elements abroad."[24] There was never any doubt that such connections existed; CHAOS was designed to expose them, not to discover whether they were real. These assumptions were not born suddenly in 1967 but, rather, reflected the Cold-War, clandestine mentality that has dominated the CIA's organizational culture since its inception.[25]

Oswald's activities regarding the FPCC and the ACLU manifest a striking similarity to each other and to the CIA's worldview and modus operandi concerning domestic spying. If we reexamine his FPCC involvement from this perspective, we find an artificially created paper trail leading to the American Communist Party, similar to the one he would create for the ACLU. The contrived quality of his FPCC actions was

manifested in Dallas, even before he went to New Orleans. In a letter
to the national FPCC (April 19, 1963) he described an incident in which
he claimed to have been distributing leaflets in Dallas.

> Since I am unemployed, I stood yesterday for the first time in my life with
> a placare [sic] around my neck, passing out Fair play for Cuba pamplets
> [sic], etc. I only had 15 or so.
>
> In 40 minutes they were all gone. I was cursed as well as praised by
> some. My home made placare [sic] said *Hands off Cuba!* and *Viva Fidel!*
> Now I ask for 40 to 50 more of the fine, basic pamplets [sic].[26]

Oswald was unemployed, but there is no evidence that this incident
ever occurred. In May 1964, during the Warren Commission investigation, a Dallas policeman recalled that he had seen an unidentified
white male passing out pro-Castro literature the previous year, but the
policeman never got a close look at the subject and could not identify
him.[27] Some researchers think that it might have been Oswald.[28] The
policeman remembered this incident as taking place "on a day in the
late spring or early summer 1963."[29] Oswald had departed Dallas for
New Orleans by April 25.

His letter describing the alleged incident did not mention anything
about moving to New Orleans or pursuing FPCC activities there, although he moved within a week after writing it. He again wrote the
FPCC's national headquarters after arriving in New Orleans and declared his intention to set up a New Orleans chapter. He also mentioned the possibility of renting a small office.[30] This letter was written
in late May after he had settled into his new job at Reily Coffee near
the Camp Street offices of Guy Banister. Banister's modus operandi was
in keeping with the style of CIA domestic spying that would later be
manifested in CHAOS and MERRIMAC. He hired young men to infiltrate college campuses in New Orleans and search out pro-Castro
sympathizers and activists.[31]

As described previously, the FPCC national director was not thrilled
by Oswald's announced intention of starting a New Orleans chapter.
The director cautioned that the city's right-wing political culture would
not be hospitable; he admonished Oswald not to get involved in "un-
necessary incidents that frighten away prospective supporters."[32] As the
director was probably well aware, the FPCC was a prime target of U.S.
intelligence and thus had reason to be worried about being disrupted or
discredited.

One of the most active agencies, by virtue of both its Cuban fixation and its expanding domestic spying, was the CIA. The Agency was not only interested in collecting documents, mailing lists, and photographs relating to FPCC but announced its intention to conduct covert activities as well.[33] According to an FBI document, the Bureau was advised on September 16, 1963, that the CIA was "giving some thought to planting deceptive information which might embarrass the Committee [FPCC] in areas where it does have support."[34] The Agency went on to assure the Bureau that it would make certain that "the CIA activity will not jeopardize any Bureau investigation."[35] Given the CIA's panoply of anti-Castro groups and the scope of its Cuban operations (which, as of the date of the above memo, had outstripped the Bureau's Miami operation in personnel), it is likely that the CIA was really thinking that it was time to protect itself on paper vis-à-vis the Bureau or Congress concerning its expanding surveillance.

We now return to Oswald's FPCC agenda. After passing out his pamphlets to the sailors from the *U.S.S. Wasp* on June 16, he discontinued his public activities until early August. After being in such a rush—presumably motivated by ideological zeal—that he had to print his own literature (3,000 copies), his own membership applications (500 forms), and his own membership cards (300), he handed out a few pamphlets to some sailors one afternoon and then called it quits for nearly two months.[36] There is no evidence that the founder, president, and sole member of the New Orleans FPCC ever attempted to broaden the chapter's membership base—no recruiting, no real proselytizing of any kind. After working feverishly to create a small mountain of paper, Oswald simply dropped out of action. This is the consistent pattern that runs through Lee Harvey Oswald's domestic political involvements, which were primarily concerned with paper, not people.

Perhaps this pattern arose because Oswald was a loner; however, he was able to associate with people on the extreme political right like Ferrie and, as we shall see, George de Mohrenschildt. Perhaps Oswald found right-wing New Orleans too tough a place to make a go of a chapter, as the FPCC national director had warned. If this was the problem Oswald certainly exacerbated it: during the two-month hiatus between passing out leaflets on the docks and his next FPCC event in August he worked at Reily Coffee, in the heart of the anti-Castro bastion at Camp Street. Given William Reily's anti-Castro politics, his coffee company was probably an unlikely place for seeking out pro-Castro supporters.

Not much is known about what Oswald did during his break from public displays on behalf of the FPCC, but he apparently did a lot of reading. A post-assassination inventory of the books he checked out of the New Orleans library that summer is itself interesting reading. The six-page analysis of Oswald's reading habits was compiled by the Warren Commission's staff, based on Secret Service and FBI documents.[37] Of 34 books listed, not one has anything to do with Oswald's ostensible preoccupation that summer—Cuba. There are four books on communism: one is on China, two on Russia, and one is a general work. Five titles had to do with another topic in which Oswald may have been more conversant than communism. There was Ian Fleming's *Thunderball, Goldfinger, Moonraker, From Russia with Love,* and an edited collection entitled *Five Spy Novels.* Katherine Ford, an associate of Marina and Lee Oswald in Dallas, told the Bureau that "Oswald read some books about how to be a spy."[38]

Maybe it's an occupational spin-off or a busman's holiday sort of thing—that spies like to read or write spy tales. One recalls clandestine warrior E. Howard Hunt writing numerous cloak-and-dagger paperbacks under a pseudonym. Oswald also read two books dealing with his alleged victim—*Profiles in Courage* and *Portrait of a President,* the former written by John F. Kennedy.

Just before Oswald's June 16 leafletting near the *Wasp,* and before he went underground for two months, he did something significant. Again it was on paper. He wrote to *The Worker,* the official organ of the American Communist Party. The letter requested yet more paper, in the form of Communist Party pamphlets. The importance of this incident lay in the letter itself, not in the pamphlets it requested. The letter established a link between the FPCC and the Communist Party. Moreover, it indicated that the New Orleans FPCC was, in the view of its president, a vehicle for a broad "popular struggle" of the kind promoted in communist ideology. To strengthen the linkage, Oswald sent along some honorary FPCC membership cards to American Communist Party luminaries Gus Hall and B. Davis (hardly a sacrifice on Oswald's part since he had 299 unused cards lying around).[39]

> L. H. Oswald
> P.O. Box 30061
> New Orleans, La.

The Worker
23 W. 26th St.

Dear Sirs:

As a long time subscriber to the Worker I know I can ask a favor of you with full confidence of its fulfillment.

I have formed a "Fair Play for Cuba Committee" here in New Orleans,

I think it is the best way to attract the broad mass of people to a popular struggle.

I ask that you give me as much literature as you judge possible since I think it would be very nice to have your literature among the "Fair Play" leaflets (like the one enclosed) and *pamphlets* in my office.

Also please be so kind as to convey the enclosed "*honorary* membership" cards to those fighters for peace Mr. Gus Hall and Mr. B. Davis.

Arnold Johnson, the Communist Party secretary, responded that literature would be sent but cautiously pointed out that the Party did not have any organizational ties with the FPCC.[40] Johnson's guarded response may have resulted from the recognition that the political right in the United States, as well as the intelligence community, was striving to demonstrate that the American Communist Party was linked to nearly everything left of center, and that the Party was trying to use such ties to broaden its subversive activities. Johnson was wrong in a very important sense: if the Party had no organizational ties with the FPCC in the past, it did now. Oswald was creating them on paper.

After the two-month respite Oswald's activity became feverish. In August he thrust the FPCC into the media spotlight, on both radio and television; he also posed as an anti-Castro militant at Carlos Bringuier's store, and he got into the street scuffle with Bringuier and friends. The reader will recall that latter incident allegedly resulted when Bringuier received a "tip" from a friend that Oswald was passing out pro-Castro literature. The scuffle that led to Oswald's arrest seemed to one policeman to have been "set up."[41] At the scene of the leafletting Bringuier approached Oswald menacingly. Undaunted, Oswald taunted Bringuier: "OK, Carlos," he said, smiling, "if you want to hit me, hit me."[42]

The suspicious nature of this incident is augmented by the fact that Oswald reported it to the national FPCC *before* it occurred. In a letter dated August 4, 1963, he erroneously reported that he had distributed "thousands" of pamphlets before being attacked by Cuban exiles in the street and then approached by police. He further asserted, "The incident robbed me of what support I had, leaving me alone."[43] Of course, Oswald never was anything but alone, except for anti-Castroites. His letter was as contrived as the incident it claimed to report. This was, most likely, his second false report to the FPCC, the first being his claim to have been "cursed as well as praised" while distributing pamphlets in Dallas before moving to New Orleans.

He eventually reported the street scuffle four days after it occurred, not to the FPCC but to the American Communist Party. He wrote Party secretary Arnold Johnson and forwarded a newspaper clipping describing the incident. Oswald asked for still more pamphlets and dispensed yet another chapter membership card.[44]

Arnold Johnson
23 W. 26th St.
New York, 10, NY

Dear Mr. Johnson:

I wish to thank you for the literature which you sent me for our local branch of the "Fair Play for Cuba Committee," of which I am the secretary-president.

As you can see from the enclosed clipping I am doing my best to help the cause of new Cuba, a cause which I know you approve of also.

Would you from time to time send us literature? Any at all will be greatly appreciated.

Please accept an *honorary* New Orleans branch membership card as a token of esteem.

> Thank you
> [signed] Lee H. Oswald
> P.O. Box 30061
> New Orleans, La.

Oswald also wanted to be sure that the FBI knew all about the Bringuier confrontation and about the New Orleans FPCC. As mentioned previously, after his arrest by police (on August 9, 1963) he requested that a representative of the Bureau come to his cell. Agent John Quigley obliged, and Oswald provided a wealth of information. Quigley's summary report runs for five single-spaced pages.[45] Oswald had much information to dispense, but most of it was false. It seems that he wanted to salt the Bureau's files and set the stage for his subsequent unmasking as a Soviet defector, all as part of his job of discrediting the FPCC by tying it to communist subversion. He also saw to it that Quigley received a sampling of FPCC literature and membership cards.

One of the first points that Oswald made was to tell Quigley that the FPCC was not a communist or communist-controlled group, a claim which Oswald's letters to the Communist Party and his radio appearance (to be described shortly) were designed to belie. Oswald described the New Orleans chapter in ways that made it appear clandestine. He told Quigley that he did not know where the groups' offices were located or the home addresses of members. He showed the agent his chapter membership card, which bore the membership number 33, implying that there were at least 32 other members. The card was signed "A. J. Hidell," a man Oswald portrayed as the shadowy leader of the New Orleans FPCC. Oswald claimed that he had never seen Hidell in person but contacted him by letter or by phone to inform him when and where meetings would be held and what the agenda for political activities would be. While the national FPCC emphasized public lobbying and outreach, Oswald described the New Orleans operation as more akin to an underground cell: its meetings were not advertised but were communicated to members by phone and held at shifting locations. At these meetings no last names were used, only first names. Oswald had similarly told New Orleans Police Lieutenant Francis Martello, who participated in his arrest, that the local FPCC had 35 members, but that members' names and the location of meeting places were not to be revealed.[46]

Oswald set about the work of using the street scuffle as a springboard for a media blitz. The day after the incident he was in the office of the city editor of the *New Orleans States-Item* trying to persuade him to give more coverage to the FPCC.[47] Three days later he reportedly phoned New York radio personality Long John Nebel and offered to travel north at his own expense to appear on Nebel's show.[48] Then, on August 16, he performed his last activist ritual—handing out pamphlets in front of the New Orleans Trade Mart with the help of his paid recruit from the unemployment line. This leafletting lasted only a few minutes, but it was just long enough for a mobile unit from TV station WDSU to capture it on film.[49] It would be interesting to know what brought WDSU to the scene so promptly. Perhaps there was another lucky tip like the one that brought Bringuier to confront Oswald, or perhaps the tip came from Oswald himself. If it was a tip, it wasn't the last: there was another within a few days.

The day after the TV camera recorded Oswald and his recruit outside the Trade Mart, he was interviewed by a local radio station.[50] The interviewer found Oswald's performance to be "oddly deliberate."[51] A few days later the climactic event of his FPCC summer occurred—a radio debate conducted before a large metropolitan audience. Oswald took on two anti-communists. One was Ed Butler, the head of a stridently anti-communist organization called the Information Council of the Americas.[52] It functioned as a private propaganda mill whose principal activity was to taperecord interviews with Cuban and iron-curtain refugees and distribute the tapes to the hundred or so radio stations that aired them.[53] The second of Oswald's debate opponents was none other than Carlos Bringuier.

Oswald held his own in the early part of the program, conducting himself with poise. Ed Butler remembered that Oswald seemed "very articulate," especially for a young man twenty-four years old. Butler said that the public image of Oswald as being inarticulate was inaccurate.[54] After listening to an audio tape of the program, the author too was impressed with Oswald's performance.

Even so, the radio debate was a no-win situation for Oswald-the-leftist and especially for the FPCC. His opponents had a secret weapon, a bombshell to drop. They had discovered that the president of the New Orleans chapter of the FPCC was, in reality, a Soviet defector. His Russian Communist ties were dramatically revealed to the listening audience. From that point on, the program focused almost exclusively on this sensational revelation. The FPCC's links to the Kremlin, in the person of Lee Harvey Oswald, were exposed for all to hear.

Both of Oswald's debate opponents had ties to the CIA's anti-Castro network. Bringuier's *Directorio Revolucionario Estudiantil* (DRE) was the outgrowth of a militant, CIA-funded anti-Castro student group that was heavily involved with the CIA at the time of the Bay of Pigs invasion.[55] There was also a DRE chapter in Dallas. An FBI document indicated that Oswald attended a DRE fundraising meeting the month before the assassination.[56] A witness said that Oswald did not speak to anyone but listened for a while and then left.[57] Bringuier's DRE published a newsletter that was also backed by the CIA-funded Crusade to Free Cuba Committee, the organization patronized by William Reily of Reily Coffee. This group served as a fundraising arm of the Cuban Revolutionary Council (CRC) headquartered at Camp Street above Guy Banister and led by Ronnie Caire, whose address appeared (in scrambled form) in Oswald's notebook.[58]

Oswald's second opponent, Ed Butler, headed the Information Council of the Americas (INCA), whose manager was a member of the Cuban Revolutionary Council.[59] This interface helped INCA obtain taped interviews with Cuban exiles.

There was no chance that Oswald's Soviet defection would not be aired. All three participants (his two opponents and the radio host) found out about it before the program. Bringuier claimed to have sent a spy to Oswald's New Orleans home. Bringuier's friend allegedly posed as a pro-Castro sympathizer and talked with Oswald (as Oswald had done in posing as an anti-Castro supporter when visiting Bringuier's store).[60] Bringuier's man supposedly heard Oswald speak Russian to his family and thereby became suspicious of a Soviet connection. According to Bringuier, he and his friend visited Ed Butler two days before the debate and informed

him of the Russian dimension, whereupon Butler allegedly called "someone at the House Un-American Activities Committee" in Washington,
DC and obtained confirmation of Oswald's Soviet ties.[61] By whatever
method, the two anti-Castro supporters arrived at the radio station primed
to expose Oswald.

The program's host, William Stuckey, would certainly not dispute
their charge that Oswald was a Soviet defector. He too had found out,
and by the usual method—a tip. One of Stuckey's "news sources" in
Washington—a source which to this day remains unidentified—called
him and told of Oswald's stay in the Soviet Union.[62] It is unclear as to
how the Washington source divined that Oswald was about to appear on
a New Orleans radio show. The caller gave Stuckey a list of dates by
which to find Washington newspaper clippings that reported the defection.[63] We know of at least one Washington-based organization that kept
a clipping file on this event. When the CIA sent the Warren Commission
the Agency's Oswald dossier, it included "four newspaper clippings" from
the *Washington Post* and the *Washington Evening Star* dealing with
Oswald's defection.[64]

The full transcript of the radio "debate" reveals that it was less a debate
than an Oswald monologue. After initially exposing Oswald as a former
Soviet defector, his two opponents didn't have much to say.[65] Oswald
said all that needed to be said—not about Castro or Cuba, of which
Oswald said little of substance, but about the nature of the FPCC and
its relationships with the American Communist Party. Speaking in a
poised, articulate, and deliberate manner, he exaggerated the size of his
one-man chapter, claiming it had several officers and a number of members. He refused to reveal its exact size, causing Butler to chide him
about it being a "secret society." Oswald's description of the local FPCC
was hardly reassuring on that score. He portrayed the membership as
publicity-shy if not clandestine: "Yes, as secretary I am responsible for
the keeping of the records and the protection of the members' names so
that undue publicity or attention will not be drawn to them, as they do
not desire it."

Oswald used the show to set up the FPCC for a political and public
relations disaster. It was he, and not any of the other three participants,
who announced that "the Fair Play for Cuba Committee is now on the
Attorney General's subversive list." But his main message, repeated again
and again so that there would be a lasting impression on the listeners,
was that the FPCC had absolutely no ties with the Communist Party.
Oswald himself posed the issue of whether the FPCC was communist-
controlled, before his opponents did. Oswald's "reassurance" to the right-

leaning political culture of New Orleans must have sounded to most listeners like the non sequitur that it was (which is doubtless how he intended it to sound): "That is correct, and I think it is the fact that I did live for a time in the Soviet Union that gives me excellent qualifications to repudiate charges that the Fair Play for Cuba Committee is communist-controlled."

Again and again, Oswald eschewed discussions of Castro, Cuba, or ideology in favor of harping away at denials of FPCC–communist links.

> The Senate Subcommittee, who have occupied themselves with investigating the Fair Play for Cuba Committee, have found that there is nothing to connect the two committees [communist and FPCC]. We have been investigated from several points of view. That is, points of view of taxes, allegiance, aversion and so forth. The findings have been, as I say, absolutely zero.

The frequency of his denials must have made the audience suspicious that the young former defector "doth protest too much". Moreover, the denials highlighted the case against him better than his opponents might have.

> We are not all communist-controlled regardless of the fact that we have been investigated, regardless of any of those facts, the Fair Play for Cuba Committee is an independent organization not affiliated with any organization.

Asked whether his New Orleans FPCC would "benefit the Communist Party or the goals of international communism," Oswald replied:

> It is inconsistent with my ideals to support communism, my personal ideals. It is inconsistent with the ideals of the Fair Play for Cuba Committee to support international communism. . . . In other words, we do not feel that we are supporting international communism or communism in supporting Fidel Castro.

Within a week of the radio show Oswald would write to the American Communist Party, establishing on paper the very links he was denying on the air. He would claim to have used the FPCC "to foster communist ideals."

Oswald made one other notable comment during his radio appearance. It was about a topic he never publicly mentioned at any other time before or after—the CIA.

Although I feel that it is a jest [sic] and a right development in Cuba, still we could be on much friendlier relations with them and had [sic] the Government of the United States, its Government Agencies, particularly certain covert, undercover agencies like the now defunct CIA.

Oswald's comment about the Agency was intriguing. The show's moderator was taken aback by his reference to the "now defunct" CIA, and questioned Oswald about it. "Well," Oswald replied, "its leadership is now defunct. Allen Dulles is now defunct." This is an odd comment for a leftist ideologue, but not for an Agency spook. No self-respecting leftist would consider the CIA defunct simply because it changed directors. The organization would still be seen as a very powerful, malevolent tool of U.S. capitalism, whose reputation as a brutal counter-leftist force around the world remained undiminished by Dulles's departure. Within the CIA's clandestine culture, however, the sudden departure of the founding father, who was fired by President Kennedy, was viewed as a severe blow that seriously weakened the Agency. Oswald was in the Soviet Union when Dulles was fired and did not return to the United States until nine months later. Yet the pinko Marine seemed to be aware that Dulles's loss was significant for the CIA.

After exposing Oswald as a Soviet Communist, Carlos Bringuier urged his supporters, via a missive he called a "press relief," to ask their Congressmen for a full-scale investigation of Oswald and his communist background.[66] There is no evidence that the plea was successful in getting the House Un-American Activities Committee, or anyone else, to investigate Oswald. But if it had been successful, there was certainly a clear paper trail to communist links for investigators to follow.

The events of Oswald's New Orleans summer were a disaster for the FPCC, whose announced goal was to cultivate sympathy for the Castro regime. Conversely, it was a major public relations and propaganda coup for Bringuier and the anti-Castroites.

There was to be one last addition to Oswald's FPCC paper trail. He never wrote to the national FPCC to inform it of his unmasking as a Soviet defector, but he did write to the Central Committee of the American Communist Party to ask for its advice in dealing with the problem it created—that his Soviet background could be used by his opponents to the detriment of the FPCC. The letter (dated August 28, 1963, and replete with spelling errors) contributes to the very problem it is ostensibly trying to solve: Oswald confesses that he was using the FPCC "to foster communist ideals."[67]

Central Committee
CP, U.S.A.

Lee H. Oswald
P.O. Box 30061
New Orleans, La.

August 28, 1963

Comrades:

Please advise me upon a problem of personal tactics.

I have lived in the Soviet Union from Oct. 1958 to July 1962.

I had, in 1959, in Moscow, tried to legally dissolve my United States citizenship in favor of Soviet citizenship, however, I did not complete the legal formalities for this.

Having come back to the U.S. in 1962 and thrown myself into the struggle for progress and freedom in the United States, I would like to know weather, in your opinion, I can continue to fight, handicapped as it were, by my past record, can I still, under these circumstances, compete with anti-progressive forces, above ground or weather in your opion I should always remain in the background, i.e. underground.

Our opponents could use my background of residence in the U.S.S.R. against any cause which I join, by association, they could say the organization of which I am a member, is Russian controled ect. I am sure you see my point.

I could of course openly proclaim, (if pressed on the subject) that I wanted to dissolve my American citizenship as a personal protest against the policy of the U.S. government in supporting dictatorship, ect. But what do you think I should do? Which is the best tactic in general?

Should I dissociate myself from all progressive activities?

Here in New Orleans, I am secretary of the local brach of the "Fair Play for Cuba Committee," a position which, frankly, I have used to foster communist ideals. On a local radio show, I was attacked by Cuban exile organization representatives for my residence ect., in the Soviet Union.

I feel I may have compromised the FPCC, so you see that I need the advice of trusted. long time fighters for progress. Please advise.

With Ferternal Greeting
Sincerely

[signed] Lee H. Oswald

It is an incredible letter, offering up a scenario that would confirm the worst paranoias of zealous anti-communists: a former Soviet defector using a pro-Castro group as a front for advancing communist ideals is unmasked, then writes his comrades in the American Communist Party to ask whether or not he should go underground. Here is proof that the

insidious tentacles of Kremlin subversion reached into domestic politics
in the United States, proof that the Kremlin, Castro, and the American
Communist Party were linked in political action as well as ideological
affinity.

The national FPCC would surely have been touched by Oswald's
sensitivity to the adverse effects that his background might have on the
organization's efforts. After disregarding its warning and creating a plethora of negative publicity, he never did inform the group that he had
placed it in a situation in which its opponents could give new force to
charges that it was communist-controlled.

There is also evidence, neglected by most researchers, that Oswald's
efforts to lump leftist groups together and link them to domestic and
foreign communism extended to the Socialist Workers Party (SWP) as
well. As we would expect from Oswald's now-familiar modus operandi,
his SWP interactions were confined to paper. In November 1962, while
living in Dallas, he wrote the SWP and applied for membership. The
Party's national secretary replied that the organization's constitution required five members before a chapter could be formed and that without
a chapter no individual memberships could be granted.[68] A month later,
while working at the Dallas photo-optics firm of Jaggars-Chiles-Stovall,
Oswald sent samples of his photographic work to the SWP and offered
to do photo chores.[69]

He may have intended to establish—or been in the process of establishing—a Dallas chapter of the Socialist Workers Party. Perhaps it was
to be another one-man paper-chapter. In any case, among his possessions
in Dallas was an item described in the FBI evidence log as:

Negative Bearing:

Join

The Socialist Workers Party

fight for a better world!

Write

Box 2915

Dallas, Texas

Short of forming a chapter, Oswald may have been content with mixing
the socialists into the left-wing melting pot that was his Dallas post office
box, thus establishing linkages with the FPCC and the ACLU.

According to a secret memorandum written in 1963, an FBI source
advised the Bureau:

[D]uring the first two years of the FPCC's existence there was a struggle between the Communist Party (CP) and Socialist Workers Party (SWP) elements to exert their power within the FPCC and thereby influence FPCC policy. However, during the past year this source observed there has been a successful effort by FPCC leadership to minimize the role of these other organizations in the FPCC so that today their influence is negligible.[70]

It seems Oswald was out to prove the Bureau's informant wrong single-handedly. Through his maze of letters, memberships, and ostensible sympathies, he was linking up the three organizations and—in the case of the Communist Party, at least—was claiming on paper that external influence over the FPCC did indeed exist.

A truly committed communist would certainly be disposed to using other organizations to foster Party ideology, as Oswald's letter to the Communist Party claimed he was doing with the FPCC. But his pursuit of communist ideals was, like the rest of his leftist involvements, a paper-thin veneer. His ties to the American Communist Party consisted of his subscription to its newspaper (*The Worker*) and his letters, the primary thrust of which was to link the party to the FPCC and the ACLU. In fact, Oswald was not a member of the American Communist Party. There is no evidence of his ever having sought out communists in Dallas or New Orleans. He never attended any communist meetings or attempted to socialize with his alleged ideological "comrades." His associate Michael Paine told the Warren Commission that Oswald had apparently not made contact with any communist elements in Dallas; neither had Oswald ever mentioned having any communist affiliation.[71]

There was a Communist Party in Dallas. The FBI was worried that the former Soviet defector might pose some security threat upon his return to the United States, so the Bureau checked Oswald out with two of its informants within the Dallas communist organization. It found that Oswald "was not a communist, was not a member of the Communist Party."[72] The FBI's informers had never heard of him. When queried by the Warren Commission as to the reliability of its sources, the Bureau described them as "excellent."[73] The FBI also checked with its informants in New Orleans and found that Oswald was unknown in Communist Party circles there.[74]

If the "loner" image fits Oswald at all, it fits his leftist domestic politics. It seems he was incapable of seeking out and contacting his supposed ideological brethren. He made not one convert to his FPCC chapter and, beyond handing out a few leaflets, never tried to do so. He had no known contact with leftists of any description in New Orleans. In Dallas he made brief contact with the ACLU, but no communist or leftist associations. In contrast, he was able to make contacts on the right. He also had no trouble being outgoing with the media—visiting a newspaper editor to ask for more FPCC coverage, seeking out radio interviews. And he was not afraid to confront the supposed opposition, whether on the radio, at Bringuier's store, or in the street. He could strike up a friendly conversation with Captain Davison at the U.S. Embassy in Moscow or ride to Clinton with David Ferrie (and perhaps Banister). Regarding the political left, however, it was all solo performances surrounded by piles of pamphlets and cards, set in a red tableau sketched by Oswald's numerous letters.

In the 1960s the CIA's expanded domestic spying went beyond monitoring to what a Senate investigation would later describe as "actual penetration [of] the dissident organization."[75] Oswald's activities seemed aimed not so much at spying on the FPCC or the ACLU as painting them as part of a communist monolith whose subversive intentions could be traced back to Moscow. This fit the CIA's assumptions concerning the Kremlin's domestic incursion.[76] It also fit the Agency's expressed intention of "planting deceptive information which might embarrass the Committee [FPCC]."[77]

Tying leftist groups in the United States to the American Communist Party and to Moscow would also serve another goal in addition to discrediting them: it would help to legitimize domestic spying by the CIA. The more foreign links there were, the broader a domestic spying role the Agency could claim under its charter, and the better it could fend off its critics in Congress and its rivals in the intelligence community.

Oswald's New Orleans summer was indeed productive. It generated negative publicity for the FPCC and was a propaganda coup for the anti-Castroites; it produced a paper trail supporting the Agency's professed theory of communist subversion while simultaneously legitimizing domestic spying. Beyond these payoffs, there was another one which—whether or not it was specifically intended at the time—would be crucial within three months. Oswald's pro-Castro involvement would be a central element in the purposely crafted image of Oswald-the-assassin.

6

Dallas: The Long Arm of Langley

The point of this is that the CIA is not simply an agency that gathers foreign intelligence for the United States in far-off corners of the globe. It is deeply involved in many diverse, clandestine activities right here in the United States in at least twenty metropolitan areas.

David Wise and Thomas B. Ross
The Invisible Government, 1964

The pattern manifested in Moscow, in New Orleans, and throughout much of Oswald's life continued in Dallas. The unseen hand was there, moving events toward the climax of the President's assassination. As usual, the CIA is there too, officially and unofficially, overtly and covertly. The events of Oswald's life in Dallas are often obscured by the mistaken assumptions that Oswald was not an intelligence agent, and that the CIA had no domestic clandestine involvements.

It was assumed by the Warren Commission that the Agency had no presence in Dallas beyond overt intelligence gathering, and thus no leverage by which to influence events surrounding Oswald. The House Assassinations Committee reached much the same conclusion, which was less understandable given the post-Warren Commission revelations about the CIA's broad role in domestic spying and domestic clandestine activities. From the ignorance of the Warren Commission's perspective and from the myopia of the House Committee's perspective, searching for a CIA role in the events of Dallas (events occurring before, during, and after the assassination) would be an exercise in paranoiac fantasy to be pursued only by those who mistakenly view the CIA as omnipotent and omnipresent.

Both the Commission and the Committee interpreted the events of Dallas through the prism of Oswald-the-leftist-ideologue. Having followed him on the long and mysterious trail from his days as the pinko Marine to his role as a provocateur, we can approach these events with a much different perspective.

CIA linkages to Oswald, so clearly manifested in New Orleans, begin to emerge in Dallas immediately upon his June 1962 arrival when he returned from the Soviet Union. Then, George de Mohrenschildt became his closest friend and became a, if not the, primary influence in the young man's life. De Mohrenschildt would also provide some of the most damning testimony about Oswald to the Warren Commission. His accounts were a key element in the Commission's image of Oswald as an ill-tempered malcontent and a violence-prone crackpot who, according to de Mohrenschildt, assassinated the President because "it made him a hero in his own mind." De Mohrenschildt asserted that Oswald was extremely jealous of Kennedy, "who was young, attractive, had a beautiful wife, and had all the money in the world and was a world figure. And poor Oswald. He had nothing. He had a bitchy wife, had no money, and was a miserable failure in everything he did."[1]

Who was this man who helped cast his young friend into historical infamy? George de Mohrenschildt, the baron, was a descendant of Russian nobility. Along with his friends in the White Russian community in Dallas, he despised the Soviet Communist regime. The baron's close relationship with Oswald, 30 years his junior, was very strange if one assumes that Oswald's Marxist-communist credentials were bona fide.

Like David Ferrie, de Mohrenschildt's political philosophy and background were hardly leftist: George too was a zealous anti-communist. He liked to brag that he was a staunch Republican. He belonged to such conservative establishment organizations as the Dallas Petroleum Club and the local country club.[2] He once stated to friends that he favored Nazi Germany and thought that Heinrich Himmler was "all right."[3] An FBI memo written in 1942 described him as "very pro-Nazi," so much so that the FBI suspected him of being a German spy during World War II. He was detained by authorities, searched, and interrogated after allegedly sketching cargo facilities in Port Arthur, Texas.[4] At the end of the war it was not uncommon for U.S. intelligence to take over former German agents and use them in the Cold War against the communists.[5]

A Dallas associate of de Mohrenschildt remembered warning an acquaintance not to hang around George, partly because he had no visible means of support and yet appeared to live comfortably. According to the associate, de Mohrenschildt heard about the conversation and called up to say, "A good friend of mine told me that you said I was a communist. If I hear any more statements of this nature I will come over and beat the hell out of you."[6] George's sensitivity about communism was understandable given his background.

According to one associate, de Mohrenschildt claimed to have had a troubled childhood, suffering under the Soviet Communist regime.[7] His father was a member of the artistocracy who was arrested by the communists shortly after the revolution. The senior de Mohrenschildt had been an official in the czarist government and had helped mobilize the czar's army against insurgents.[8] The Bolshevik revolution deprived George of his future barony. Then eight years old, young George was forced to wander the streets in search of food.

He finally escaped to Poland, where he trained for a career as an army officer. But he had lost the wealth needed to sustain this position: Polish officers were expected to personally finance their careers. Eventually George found his way to the United States.[9] His wife Jeanne had suffered at the hands of Chinese Communists, who had allegedly executed her father.[10]

Whether George de Mohrenschildt worked for the French underground during World War II, as he claimed, for the Germans, or for both, his involvement in intelligence work is a certainty. In 1942, only a year after he was detained for possibly spying in the United States, he showed up in Mexico. He stayed for nine months, doing what he later described as "painting" and "investing."[11] The Mexican authorities seemed to suspect that there was more to his visit than straightforward pictures and portfolios. He was declared persona non grata and deported. The reason, as George described it, was that, "they [the Mexican authorities] said 'that is the best way, for you to leave, because you cannot fight the constitutional forces of Mexico.' "[12]

There are some clues as to de Mohrenschildt's activities in Mexico. A letter sent to him by one of his relatives shortly before the Mexican trip instructed George to "get the necessary letters of credit from Nelson Rockefeller."[13] When he was booted out of Mexico, he was indeed carrying letters of credit worth thousands of dollars, issued by the Rockefellers' Chase Manhattan Bank.[14] During World War II, Nelson Rockefeller was active on behalf of U.S. intelligence through an organization called British Security Co-Ordination. One of Rockefeller's aims was to prevent Latin American oil from reaching Nazi Germany.[15]

Whatever George's role in Mexico, he and his trusty sketchpad were to become tools of U.S. intelligence after the war. A House Assassinations Committee staffer whose work centered on de Mohrenschildt commented in 1978 that George "had contacts with intelligence again and again."[16]

He traveled widely in Ghana, Yugoslavia, Guatemala, Haiti, and Costa Rica. The Warren Commission described him as a "petroleum engineer," but his activities went far beyond the collection of rock and silt samples. In 1957 he went to Yugoslavia, ostensibly on a geological field survey. He was accused by the Yugoslavian government of sketching military facilities.[17] This is not surprising since he was then working for the American CoOperation Administration, which was subsequently exposed as a CIA-funded subsidiary of what would become the Agency for International Development (AID).[18] AID became infamous as an umbrella for the CIA's clandestine activities abroad.

On his return from Yugoslavia, de Mohrenschildt was debriefed by the CIA both in Washington, DC and Dallas. The debriefing took place over the course of "several meetings" which generated no fewer than "ten separate intelligence reports."[19]

George and his wife Jeanne took an eight-month hike through Central America in 1960, traveling from the United States to Panama over primitive jungle trails. One photograph shows George in the company of the U.S. ambassador to Costa Rica.[20] The couple kept a log of their unusual trip and took extensive film footage.[21] The trip happened to put them in Guatemala City during the Bay of Pigs invasion. Guatemala was a major staging area for CIA-backed Cuban exiles.[22]

While in Haiti, de Mohrenschildt became friendly with a man named Clemard Charles, a banker and close associate of the president of Haiti. Charles was involved in the U.S.–Haitian arms deals.[23] House Assassinations Committee sources described him as having "many connections" with the CIA. One source believed that the CIA had "planted" a secretary on Charles's staff.[24] Committee sources who knew de Mohrenschildt in Haiti described his activities there as "strange." One said that George "followed people in his car."[25] Another source, who was introduced to de Mohrenschildt by Charles, observed that George claimed to be in Haiti to scout for oil but that it was difficult to figure out what he actually did. The source believed that George had "intelligence connections." He asserted that de Mohrenschildt and Charles hung out in an establishment "frequented by many American intelligence personnel from the American embassy."[26] It is also rumored by sources with CIA connections that de Mohrenschildt was involved in the abortive coup that tried to topple Haitian president-for-life "Papa Doc" Duvalier. Subsequently the CIA would attempt to have Duvalier assassinated.[27]

George was apparently very well connected to a variety of important persons. Peggy Adler Robohm, who has conducted in-depth research on de Mohrenschildt, has told the author that he had extensive, elite ties to U.S. military and intelligence officers, State Department officials, prominent oil men, socialites, and politicians, many of whom were, or would become, national figures. In numerous instances, he possessed the home address and phone numbers of these notables. Such information would be difficult, if not impossible, for an outsider to obtain.

Some of George's associates in Dallas were puzzled by his finances. One noted that at certain times he seemed to have very little money; at others, "plenty."[28] Gary E. Taylor, a former son-in-law, wondered to the FBI how George was able to finance his extensive travel when he seemed to be in financial need.[29] Taylor could not understand how the de Mohrenschildts outfitted themselves so well for their hike through Central America.[30] Another associate observed that George "did not work steady" but "got along well financially" and traveled extensively.[31]

The House Assassinations Committee obtained information that de Mohrenschildt had received a "substantial sum" of money shortly after the assassination (paid to his account in Haiti). Jacqueline Lancelot, who owned a Haitian restaurant frequented by intelligence types, reported that she learned from a source in a Haitian bank that $200,000 to $250,000 had been deposited in de Mohrenschildt's account and had been paid out shortly before he left Haiti and returned to the United States after the assassination. Lancelot did not claim to know to whom the funds were dispensed.[32] The Committee also discovered that in May 1963 George went to Washington, DC and met with the CIA. The purpose of the meeting is not known.[33]

De Mohrenschildt was frequently seen in the company of a man reported to be a CIA operative in Cuba.[34] In fact, the White Russian community in Dallas, into which George introduced his ostensibly Marxist friend Oswald, received financial assistance from the CIA. Most of the White Russians had fled Communist persecution and had been brought to the United States by the Tolstoy Foundation, an anticommunist lobby that received yearly subsidies from the Agency.[35] The Russian Orthodox Church, a centerpiece of the very conservative and religious White Russian community, also received Agency philanthropy.[36]

The pattern of de Mohrenschildt's CIA links caused his friend and lawyer Patrick Russell to state in 1978, "I personally have always felt that George was a CIA agent."[37] As we will see later in this chapter, George's CIA connections in Dallas included J. Walton Moore, the Agency's Domestic Contact Service officer in Dallas. The connection specifically involved Oswald.

As previously mentioned, de Mohrenschildt had worked for AID (the Agency for International Development), an organization with extensive CIA ties. Part of the time that Oswald was in New Orleans and while he lived in Dallas and worked at the Texas School Book Depository, his family lived with Ruth and Michael Paine in Irving, Texas. Ruth Paine's father, William Avery Hyde, was a retired AID employee.[38] Michael Paine's brother was employed in the Washington, DC area, also by AID.[39] During the House Assassinations Committee investigation, a Haitian associate of de Mohrenschildt recognized the name William Avery Hyde as one mentioned by George.[40]

William Avery Hyde was not unknown to the CIA. An FBI memo reporting on the Bureau's post-assassination check of the Paine family gave Hyde a clean bill of health so far as "subversive" activity was concerned. One source for this conclusion was the Agency, which vouched for Hyde. The CIA reported to the Bureau that it had such confidence in him that it considered using him to head a "cooperative educational center" in Vietnam in 1957, although it did not actually use him in that capacity.[41] The House Committee found the possible link between AID alumni Hyde and de Mohrenschildt to be "intriguing."

Oswald's ability to associate with people who had government connections was uncanny. Michael Paine moved out of his home when Oswald's family moved in. He then moved back with his wife Ruth after the assassination, when Marina and her two children found other quarters. He was employed as a security-cleared engineer at Bell Helicopter, a defense department contractor.[42]

Intriguing too is a Warren Commission document only declassified in 1976.[43] It refers to a telephone conversation recorded by the FBI the day following the assassination. As the Bureau described it, "a male voice was heard to say that he felt sure Lee Harvey Oswald had killed the President but did not feel Oswald was responsible, and further stated, 'we both know who is responsible.' " The male voice was that of Michael Paine, who was talking to Ruth Paine when recorded by the Bureau's telephone tap.

George de Mohrenschildt, the displaced aristocrat, the spook with pro-Nazi sympathies, became Lee Harvey Oswald's patron and guiding force. He was most likely his CIA babysitter as well. In the words of George's lawyer, Patrick Russell, the relationship with Oswald "went a little deeper than friendship."[44] When Oswald was arrested in Dallas following the assassination, he had in his possession what the FBI evidence log described as "#208-Note bearing the telephone number EM3-1365." The log does not indicate whose number it was. In one place, the Warren Commission volumes erroneously list the number as EN3-1365. Dallas assassinologist Mary Ferrell, whose research has included the identification and cataloguing of several thousand telephone numbers relevant to the case, told the author that the number found on Oswald was that of de Mohrenschildt's unlisted phone.[45]

George's influence over Lee seems to have been quite extraordinary. As de Mohrenschildt's former son-in-law Gary E. Taylor described it, "Whatever his [George's] suggestions were, Lee grabbed them and took them, whether it was what time to go to bed or where to stay."[46] Taylor told the FBI he thought Oswald would do anything George told him to do.[47] Yet George would describe Oswald to the Warren Commission as an unstable, insufferable lout whom he could barely endure. Why did de Mohrenschildt bother to befriend Oswald and become his patron?

He befriended the Oswalds and introduced them socially to members of the White Russian community, many of whom were suspicious of Oswald's pro-communist background. George telephoned friends to set up appointments to help Lee find a job.[48] He seems to have been the guiding force behind most, if not all, of Oswald's movements.

One thing George evidently told Lee to do was to move into Dallas from Fort Worth. On October 7, 1962, a group of White Russians, including George and Jeanne de Mohrenschildt, visited Lee and Marina at their dumpy apartment in Fort Worth.[49] Oswald announced to the group that he had lost his job at a nearby metal factory. It was a lie, like so many that Oswald told about losing and seeking jobs.[50] His announcement of his putative firing precipitated a group discussion about what he might do next. Not surprisingly, George had a ready-made plan.

Lee and Marina would move to Dallas, 30 miles from Fort Worth. She would stay with one of the White Russian families there while Lee looked for work. Those present remember that George seemed surprisingly certain regarding Lee's job prospects in Dallas.[51] De Mohrenschildt also gave the impression that he was subsidizing the Oswalds.[52] In fact, Oswald did pay off a $200 debt to his brother around this time, in spite of his apparent poverty.

The day after George had announced the plan, Oswald moved to Dallas. Only four days after arriving there he secured a new job. Although the job was ostensibly found through the services of the Texas Unem-

ployment Commission, de Mohrenschildt's wife and daughter claim that
it was George who found Oswald the position.[53] Contrary to what Oswald
told the White Russian group back in Fort Worth, he had quit his factory
job there. His new job in Dallas paid him, within a few pennies, the
same wage he had been making in Fort Worth. His new employer,
however, was markedly different from his old one.

In Dallas he worked for the firm of Jaggars-Chiles-Stovall, a graphic
arts company that did newspaper advertising layouts and catalogues. It
also did sophisticated photographic work. Jaggars processed and analyzed
photos taken by the U–2 spy plane.[54] The U–2 material was theoretically
available only to security-cleared workers, which Oswald was not. In
reality, however, the firm's employees worked in cramped quarters that
made strict security and limitation of access nearly impossible.[55]

It seems that Lee Harvey Oswald could not avoid crossing paths with
the black lady of espionage. He was near the U–2 in Atsugi, Japan; he
was in the Soviet Union when it was shot down; now, back in Texas, he
was working at a firm that did U–2 photo analysis. It is not as if the
U–2s were like McDonalds restaurants—so ubiquitous one expects to run
into them everywhere. It is more likely that Oswald and the spy plane
kept crossing paths because they were programmed by the same source.

One of Oswald's fellow employees at Jaggars-Chiles-Stovall recalled
him as being quiet and reserved. Occasionally, however, he would discuss
the Soviet Union in a most peculiar manner. As previously mentioned,
co-worker Dennis Ofstein said that Oswald would describe the disperse-
ment patterns of Soviet military units—infantry, armor, and planes.[56]
These are strange remembrances for a Marxist ideologue whose defection
was allegedly motivated by a simplistic political idealism. Perhaps Oswald's keen eye for the deployment of military hardware gave him something in common with his patron George de Mohrenschildt, who made
a habit of observing military facilities during his frequent travels abroad.

As we would wearily expect, Oswald's Jaggars-Chiles-Stovall tenure is
an enigma. Sometimes he would literally disappear at the end of each
workday until he showed up at work the next morning. No official investigation has discovered what he was up to, or even where he was living,
for most of the period between October 8 and November 3.[57]

While at Jaggars he became acquainted with sophisticated camera
techniques and equipment.[58] He asked the firm if he could use their
facilities to do his own photo developing.[59] Oswald probably used Jaggars
equipment to forge the "Hidell" draft card found in his wallet when he
was arrested on the afternoon of the assassination. An FBI expert stated

that the forgery involved a very accurate camera "such as are found in photographic labs and printing plants."[60]

Perhaps Oswald knew what he was talking about when he told Dallas police that the infamous photo of him posing with guns in his backyard was a fake. He calmly asserted that the picture had been fabricated by persons unknown, that the face was his but the body was not.[61] He told police that he "knew about photography." There is no doubt about that; however, the question is how he was using this knowledge.

In Dallas Oswald had a cache of strange and expensive equipment, especially for a lowly stock boy living on a menial income. Among the items found by police after the assassination was a Minox camera, generally referred to as a "spy camera." There was also a 15-power Wollensak telescope, a pair of Nippon Kogaku binoculars, several camera filters, a slide viewer, an Ansco flash assembly, a 35-mm camera, another pair of binoculars, a lens hood, a 7×18 telescope, yet another camera, and a variety of film. In addition, there was a pedometer and a compass.[62]

Police found several rolls of pictures taken with a Minox camera.[63] It was not until 1978 that a Freedom of Information Act suit against the FBI forced the release of some of the photos. Strangely, the majority of the 25 released photos show scenes shot in Europe; five are of military facilities thought to be in Asia or Latin America.[64]

In Oswald's address book, found by police after the assassination, there is one page containing the following notations:[65]

Jaggars-Chiles-Stovall
TYPOGRAPHY
522 BROWDER
RI11550
micro dots

These references have been only partially deciphered by previous research. The Dallas address of 522 Browder Street belonged to the Jaggars firm; RI1 1550 was its telephone number. "Typography" can refer to almost any aspect of the advertising or printing trade, from typesetting to photographic composition. In May 1981 the author talked with Mr. Steven Baker, who then worked in Jaggars' advertising department.[66] He indicated that at Jaggars, typography had a more specialized meaning: it described the sophisticated techniques of photographic reduction and modification performed by the firm in its advertising work. In 1962–63,

Baker asserted Jaggars used "modification cameras" and other complex equipment that were more sophisticated than the photographic equipment available in most photo labs.[67]

"Microdot" is a system employed in espionage to store and transmit intelligence data. Using sophisticated techniques of photographic reduction, the system affords the storage of large volumes of strategic information within a tiny spot the size of a semicolon or an exclamation point. Such a spot is then concealed within the text of a letter or document for storage or transmittal.

From the perspective that Oswald was not a foreign intelligence agent, there would seem to be no reason for him to be microdotting information at Jaggars to ship abroad, and no logical reason to employ such a cumbersome process for the transmission of domestic data to U.S. intelligence. However, his knowledge of this unique process could relate to the espionage context of his Soviet sojourn: perhaps he knew of the technique being used there to transmit data to U.S. intelligence.

Jaggars' work involved reducing photographs in size, photosetting typescript, photographing words and sentences, and using sophisticated lenses and equipment to arrange advertising displays and charts.[68] One Jaggars employee told the Warren Commission that the firm did many things with letters in ways that differed from ordinary photography.[69] The employees and management of Jaggars who testified before the Commission claimed to be unfamiliar with microdotting.[70] Most thought that it had to do with microfilm; none knew of any microdot work being done at Jaggars. Indications are that Jaggars had equipment sophisticated enough to do microdotting. Oswald did hands-on work in the photographic department.[71] His job was described as that of "camera man."[72] He was taught how to operate the specialized equipment: distortion cameras, phototypesetters, and Robertson vertical cameras.[73]

Although no one else at Jaggars knew what microdotting was, Oswald did. There was one employee who became friendly with him. Dennis Ofstein was twenty-four, the same age as Oswald.[74] He too had served in the military (Army) and had an interest in the Russian language. He had studied Russian while working for the Army Security Agency and was still trying to improve his skills. Although Lee generally kept to himself, he and Ofstein conversed quite a bit. In one discussion which Ofstein described to the Warren Commission, Oswald explained microdotting:[75]

> *Warren Commission Counsel Albert Jenner:* Do you know what a microdot is?

Dennis Ofstein: That was explained to me by Lee Oswald.

Jenner: Tell us about that.

Ofstein: He asked me one day if I knew the term "microdot" and I told him no, I wasn't familiar with it and he told me that that was the method of taking a large area of type or a picture and reducing it down to an extremely small size for condensing and for purposes, such as where you had a lot of type to photograph to confine them into a small area, and he said that that is the way spies sometimes sent messages and pictures of diagrams and so on, was to take a microdot photograph of it and place it under a stamp or send it. I presumed that he had either read this in a book or had some knowledge of it from somewhere, but where, I didn't know.

Ofstein was friendly enough with Oswald to invite him and Marina to his house for "social activities." Ofstein asked Oswald to introduce him to some of Lee's Russian-speaking friends. Oswald promised to do so "in time," but never did. The two men didn't talk politics much, but Ofstein recalled that Lee simply shrugged when Ofstein cursed Fidel Castro.

Oswald showed Ofstein a photograph of a building situated on the bank of a river. Ofstein asked if it was taken in Japan, knowing that Oswald had served there. Oswald said that it wasn't Japan but would say no more, except to discuss with Ofstein the possibilities of enlarging the photo. Ofstein later learned from subsequent conversations that the picture was taken in Minsk and was of a Soviet military headquarters of some sort.[76] The building was guarded by troops whom Lee described as having orders to shoot anyone trying to enter without permission.

It is no wonder Ofstein assumed that Oswald was "with the [U.S.] government" while he was in the Soviet Union (Ofstein did not know about Oswald's supposed defection). Oswald's eye for details of Soviet military disbursement smacked of professionalism. As Ofstein described:

He also mentioned about the disbursement [dispersal] of the military units, saying that they didn't intermingle their armored divisions and their infantry divisions and various units the way we do in the United States, that they would have all of their aircraft in one geographical location and their tanks in another geographical location, and their infantry in another, and he mentioned that in Minsk he never saw a vapor trail, indicating the lack of aircraft in the area.[77]

Oswald also said the Soviets kept tanks north of Minsk.

Oswald criticized Soviet military logistics, telling Ofstein that their disbursement patterns were ineffective because they neglected the mutual support needs of various kinds of units and because of the time it took to move units from one section of the country to another. And, said Oswald, the Soviet units were quite far apart: he never saw jet trails where he saw tank treads and vice versa, and infantry units were not meshed with air or ground support.[78] Ofstein had the impression that Oswald's analyses of military logistics was not confined exclusively to Minsk but extended to Moscow as well.[79] Lee also seemed to be familiar with the Soviet MVD, which he told Ofstein was like our FBI. He described MVD headquarters in Minsk.[80]

After six months Oswald was fired from Jaggars, allegedly because his photographic work manifested excessive errors resulting in too many do-overs.[81] If he did not deliberately precipitate his firing for some reason related to his covert activities, and if his dismissal was genuine, then it may well have resulted because Oswald was rushing through the firm's work to do his own—developing his own pictures, forging a Hidell ID card.

During his tenure at Jaggars he also seems to have been busy using the equipment of the national-security-connected firm to do leftist photographic work. He sent samples of his left-wing photography to the Gus Hall-Benjamin Davis Defense Committee (closely linked to the American Communist Party); he sent blow-ups to the American Communist Party newspaper *The Worker*; he mailed still more blow-ups to the Socialist Workers' Party national headquarters. To all three he intimated that he was available and expert regarding photographic work for "the cause." All three letters, with accompanying samples, were mailed within ten days of each other.[82] It is a familiar scene: Oswald ensconced in a governmental, national security, or anti-communist context while emitting left-wing paper trails. And it is surely not coincidentally a vision that would drive the House Un-American Activities Committee to distraction: a former Soviet defector infiltrates a firm that does sensitive government work and uses the facilities for his subversive activities.

Oswald's alleged inability to hold a job is one of the traits central to his profile as a malcontent and a loser, the profile accepted by all official investigations and many researchers. We know, however, that in at least one of these employment terminations he actually quit while pretending to be fired. By whatever circumstances, his two jobs in Dallas brought him in proximity to the U–2 and the President's assassination.

Oswald was supposedly fired from Reily Coffee in New Orleans for having poor working habits, after working there from May 9 to July 19, 1963. Adrian Alba, the manager of a garage located near Reily Coffee, remembered that Oswald was pleased about leaving Reily, saying that he had "found his pot of gold at the end of the rainbow"; he expected to work at the New Orleans facility of NASA (National Aeronautics and Space Administration).[83] At first, this seems to be just another of Oswald's fairy tales about jobs. One might imagine that with Oswald's background and employment history, he had about as much chance of working at NASA as he did of landing a job as an electrician in Clinton. He never did work at NASA, but there may have been more to his comment than idle chatter or fantasy.

Whatever went on inside Reily Coffee, the firm seems to have been a primary recruiting ground for the aerospace industry. It is not clear how a coffee company would train its personnel in such a way that several of them could make an easy transition to aerospace work. But a clue to the Reily–aerospace connection may lie in the fact that it was not a random sample of employees who made this transition: it was those who worked with Oswald.

In July, the same month Oswald was allegedly fired, Alfred Claude, the man who hired Oswald at Reily, went to work for the Chrysler Aerospace Division of the NASA facility in New Orleans.[84] Within days of Oswald's separation, Emmett Barbee, Oswald's immediate superior, left the coffee works for a new job at NASA in New Orleans.[85] Several weeks later John D. Branyon, a co-worker of Oswald's, also went to NASA.[86] Dante Marachini, who also went from Reily to Chrysler Aerospace, was a friend of David Ferrie's. He had been hired at the coffee company on the same day as Oswald.[87] One of Ferrie's associates who did not work at Reily also found his way into aerospace work. Melvin Coffee, who accompanied Ferrie on his ice-skating foray to Texas on the night following the assassination, found work at Cape Kennedy.[88] Another Ferrie associate, James Lewallen, who lived in the same apartment building as Marachini, went to work for Boeing at the NASA facility.[89]

Melvin Coffee and James Lewallen also had some connection with the Civil Air Patrol.[90] Coffee denied knowing or recognizing Oswald but told the FBI that Ferrie had coordinated weekend bivouacs for the New Orleans-area CAP while Coffee was a member. He joined the group in 1954 and left in 1957; Oswald joined in 1955. Lewallen had no formal connection with the New Orleans CAP but stated that he had assisted David Ferrie as a volunteer during Ferrie's tenure with the squadron. Lewallen too claimed he had never met Oswald.

The aerospace connection did not touch Oswald as he had allegedly boasted to Adrian Alba, but it did touch everyone around him at the coffee company. One wonders what was happening here. Did the firm have some established pipeline to the defense–aerospace industry? Was everyone who worked with Oswald being placed in some national security context for some reason relating to him? It is impossible to discern. But the occupational connection between working on coffee beans and rockets is intriguing.

George de Mohrenschildt, who clearly seems to have played a major role in shaping at least some of Oswald's employment history, used this as part of the highly negative portrait of his deceased associate that he presented to the Warren Commission. When Oswald and de Mohrenschildt falsely announced to the White Russian social group that Lee had been fired, he had actually performed satisfactorily for three months before he quit the Leslie Welding Company in Fort Worth, according to his supervisor.[91]

De Mohrenschildt told the Commission that "hating" jobs was but another facet of Lee's "unstable" personality.[92] When asked by Commission lawyer Albert Jenner whether Oswald would be capable of doing government work requiring a high degree of intelligence and equilibrium, de Mohrenschildt volunteered that Oswald was unsuitable for "confidential work." The Commission was unaware just how much expertise George had on this subject.

> *Commission Counsel Jenner*: Did you form any impression in the area, let us say, of reliability—that is, whether our Government would entrust him with something that required a high degree of intelligence, a high degree of imagination, a high degree of ability to retain his equilibrium under pressure, a management of a situation, to be flexible enough?
>
> *de Mohrenschildt*: I never would believe that any government would be stupid enough to trust Lee with anything important.
>
> *Jenner*: Give me the basis of your opinion.
>
> *de Mohrenschildt*: Well, again, as I said, an unstable individual, mixed-up individual, uneducated individual, without background. What government would give him any confidential work? No government would. Even the government of Ghana would not give him any job of any type.
>
> *Jenner*: You used the expression "unstable." Would you elaborate on that?
>
> *de Mohrenschildt*: . . . unstability—his life is an example of his instability. He switched allegiance from one country to another, and then back again, disappointed in this, disappointed in that, tried various jobs. But he did it, you see, without the enjoyment of adventure—like some people would do in the United States, a new job is a new adventure, new opportunities. For him it was a gruesome deal. He hated his jobs. He switched all the time.

While de Mohrenschildt may have been one of the CIA's unofficial operatives in Dallas, J. Walton Moore was the official one. He was with the Agency's Domestic Contact Service (DCS). He had known de Mohrenschildt since at least 1957 when he debriefed him upon his return from Yugoslavia (where he was accused of sketching military facilities).[93] It is not surprising that de Mohrenschildt should have much to talk to the CIA about. Like Oswald, he had a habit of showing up where the Agency action was heavy—Guatemala, during preparations for the Bay of Pigs invasions; and in Haiti, where the Agency had been involved in a coup plot.

In a 1977 CIA memorandum written to refute a claim by a Dallas television station that Oswald had been employed by the CIA, Moore denied knowing Oswald before the assassination. He also "recalled" that he had met de Mohrenschildt only twice.[94] But the House Assassinations Committee found other documents in de Mohrenschildt's CIA file that revealed "more contact with Moore than was stated in the 1977 memorandum."[95] In 1961 de Mohrenschildt showed Moore the extensive film footage of his eight-month backpacking tour through Central America.[96]

Jeanne de Mohrenschildt claimed that Moore was such a close associate of her husband's that the local Agency man dined once a fortnight at their home.[97] She also remembered hearing at least one conversation between Moore and her husband, occurring before the assassination, in which "Moore seemed to be aware of Oswald."[98] She asserted that Moore was instantly familiar with Oswald when his name was brought up during dinner.[99] Still, Moore claimed that "to the best of my recollection I hadn't seen de Mohrenschildt for a couple of years before the assassination."[100]

It was de Mohrenschildt himself who first implied the existence of a special relationship between Oswald and the CIA. George was questioned by the FBI while he was living in Haiti after the assassination. He told Agent James Wood that after he first met Oswald, Moore had indicated that it was "safe"—whatever that meant—for him to associate with Lee, that the returning defector was "okay."[101]

It has always been a mystery as to how the spooky baron and the leftist ideologue became close friends. De Mohrenschildt claimed that he met Oswald by chance in the fall of 1962 when they were casually introduced by other members of the White Russian community. An early version of this explanation had George being introduced by a Dallas businessman of Russian extraction, Colonel Lawrence Orlov, who took Oswald to meet the baron. But Orlov stated during an interview with author Edward

Epstein that at that meeting, it was clear to him that Lee and George had already met.[102]

After the assassination de Mohrenschildt told the FBI that it was George Bouhe, a leading figure in the White Russian community, who first introduced them. Bouhe did not confirm that version.[103] Another de Mohrenschildt associate, Samuel B. Ballen, then chairman of the board of Highplains Natural Gas Company, thought that the acquaintance had somehow materialized via "members of the White Russian community," but he did not know how.[104] He told the FBI that the de Mohrenschildts "went out of their way to befriend the Oswalds."[105]

George de Mohrenschildt may finally have revealed the truth as to how this friendship really got started during his last interview on the subject. In 1977 he told the *Dallas Morning Star* that it was, in fact, CIA officer J. Walton Moore who encouraged him to see Oswald, and that he never would have done so without Moore's encouragement.[106]

In 1977 the House Assassinations Committee tried to locate de Mohrenschildt as a key witness.[107] Students of the Kennedy assassination looked forward to his being questioned about his mysterious background and his association with Oswald, questions that had arisen since the erstwhile "petroleum engineer" had testified before the Warren Commission. In March 1977 Committee investigators finally located him in Florida. They called and arranged for an interview. He seemed to take the call calmly.[108] Several hours later he was dead—shot through the mouth with a 20-gauge shotgun. The coroner ruled it a suicide.

Two of the best sources on Oswald's relationship to U.S. intelligence were never thoroughly questioned by investigators. Both Ferrie and de Mohrenschildt allegedly took their own lives within days of their impending interrogations about Oswald.

Lee Harvey Oswald, Minsk, USSR, radio factory, circa 1960
Credit: National Archives

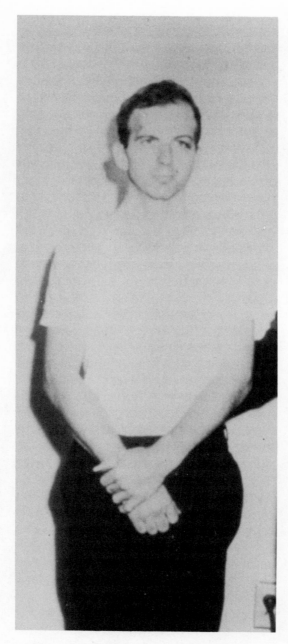

Lee Harvey Oswald under arrest in Dallas, November 23, 1963
Credit: Newcomb Collection, Southeastern Massachusetts University Library

David Ferrie
Credit: Assassination Archives and Research
Center, Washington, D.C.

Guy Banister
Credit: Assassination Archives and Research
Center, Washington, D.C.

George de Mohrenschildt
Credit: Assassination Archives and Research
Center, Washington, D.C.

Snapshot of "Oswald" with rifle, 1963
Credit: National Archives

7

Mexican Mystery Tour

The Central Intelligence Agency advised that on October 1, 1963, an extremely sensitive source reported that an individual identified himself as Lee Oswald, who contacted the Soviet Embassy in Mexico City inquiring as to any messages. Special Agents of this Bureau who have conversed with Oswald in Dallas, Texas have observed photographs of the individual referred to above and have listened to a recording of his voice. These Special Agents are of the opinion that the above-referenced-to individual was not Lee Harvey Oswald.

Memo by J. Edgar Hoover, Nov. 23, 1963[1]

In the last week of September 1963, after finishing his FPCC activities in New Orleans and his brief but active stint in Clinton, Louisiana with David Ferrie, Lee Harvey Oswald went to Mexico.

His trip is a mystery within a mystery. It is complex and has posed many unanswered questions. Before we examine in detail the events and puzzles of the Mexican sojourn, it is useful to begin with what is known or seems manifest. Again, Oswald is shadowed by persons with demonstrable or probable CIA connections. Again he is snared in an Agency surveillance system but allegedly goes unmonitored and unrecorded. The ostensible purpose of the trip was that he was desperate to return to the Soviet Union via Cuba. He supposedly visited the Soviet and Cuban consulates in Mexico City desperately seeking assistance for his return to the Soviet Union to give communism another try—pinko Marine II? He allegedly failed and returned to Dallas in psychological turmoil.

Oswald announced to the Passport Office that the Soviet Union was his destination. In reality, since his leftism was a thin veneer, this must be assumed to be yet another layer of Oswald's cover. His trip was rather sudden, and he must have believed that he had some mission or task to perform. Whatever he did in Mexico City, whatever he thought his mission was, he was being impersonated while he was there: someone flitted between the Cuban and Soviet consulates posing as a desperate Oswald. If Oswald was directed to Mexico by his handlers so that he could be set up (which is the most logical option), then someone was working to create for him an image of motive and madness for the impending assassination of the President. This image was created by having Oswald do certain things that would enhance his established leftist cover and, simultaneously, by using Oswald impostors both in Mexico City and back in Dallas to create an aura of political and mental insta- bility, and of a potential for violence, that would ultimately point to his guilt as an assassin. While someone played the role of Oswald becoming psychologically unhinged in Mexico City, yet another impostor(s) was back in Dallas impersonating him in more provocative incidents designed to cement his future guilt. (These incidents are discussed in the next chapter. In one, an Oswald impostor talks of assassinating President Ken- nedy.) Finally, there is overwhelming circumstantial evidence that the CIA covered up proof of an Oswald impostor at work. Thus the Agency may have had a lead to whomever was working to implicate Oswald in the President's murder.

Oswald's Mexican trip seems to have been shadowed closely by various intelligence operatives. Travel is often a seasonal activity: in summer the French head for European resorts; in winter Americans flock to Florida. Evidently, the last week in September is the season in which anti-Castro intelligence agents rush to Mexico like lemmings. There was Lee Harvey Oswald himself. There was Manual Porras Rivera, an anti-Castro op- erative on a covert mission. And there was a CIA agent who knew Oswald. All three went to Mexico at the same time and left at approximately the same time.

During its post-assassination investigation, the FBI sought out the iden- tity of those who had applied for entry into Mexico at the same time as Oswald. The Mexican authorities cooperated fully and a list of names was obtained by the Bureau and given to the Warren Commission. Re- garding persons who had gotten a Mexican visa on the same day as Oswald, the name of visa-holder FM 824084 did not appear. An FBI document indicated "no record of FM 824084 located."[2] The traveler who had received his visa immediately before Oswald (and who stood in the visa queue in New Orleans ahead of Oswald) was William Gaudet, a CIA agent.[3]

Gaudet was officially listed as the editor of *Latin American Traveler*, a small Costa Rican-based newsletter. In fact, by his own admission, he worked undercover for the Agency for two decades.[4] Gaudet claimed he did not travel to Mexico by bus with Oswald but went by air. He insisted that the timing of his trip was purely coincidental. He asserted that he could not remember the nature of his business in Mexico or recall whether it involved intelligence work. The "coincidence" of Gaudet's proximity to Oswald is not confined to the Mexican trip. He admitted to having observed Oswald handing out FPCC leaflets in front of the New Orleans Trade Mart.[5] He told one interviewer that he had known Oswald in New Orleans and went on to describe Lee's physical characteristics and personality traits in rich detail that seemed to stem from close contact.[6]

Gaudet, now deceased, was an elderly man living out his retirement in Mississippi when his proximity to Oswald was discovered. He was angered that his name had surfaced. His most striking revelation came in a 1977 interview with journalist Anthony Summers, when he stated, "I did see Oswald discussing various things with Banister at the time and I think Banister knew a whole lot of what was going on. . . . I suppose you are looking into Ferrie. He was with Oswald."[7] Although Gaudet would not discuss his work for the Agency and flatly denied any links to the assassination, he opined that Oswald "was a patsy."[8]

Gaudet too may have known "a whole lot of what was going on" for he worked out of an office in the anti-Castro bastion of Camp Street, only a few doors from Guy Banister.[9] It seems that Gaudet had some knowledge concerning another key figure in the assassination. In 1959 Jack Ruby traveled to New Orleans on his way to Havana. The extent of Gaudet's interest in or knowledge of Ruby is not clear, but in 1963 he volunteered to authorities information on Ruby's 1959 visit to New Orleans.[10]

In 1978 the House Assassinations Committee asked the Agency for Gaudet's file. It revealed only that he provided "foreign intelligence information" during the 1950s. There was no record of any contact with him after 1961, yet he claims to have worked for the Agency for 20 years, including 1963.[11]

Gaudet ran a Costa Rican newsletter. Another man who visited Mexico at the same time as Oswald was a Costa Rican anti-Castroite named Manual Porras Rivera. As journalist Anthony Summers has pointed out, his Mexican travel parallels Oswald's very closely.[12] Four days before Lee obtained his Mexican visa in New Orleans, Porras entered the United

States and went to Miami, the hub of U.S. anti-Castro activity. He admitted to authorities that he met with anti-Castro activists there. Then he traveled to Mexico City and departed by bus on the same day as Oswald, October 3.

It is what Porras did while in Mexico City that places him centerstage in the mysterious events that occurred there. Porras visited the Cuban consulate at least once, Saturday, September 28, one of the days that Oswald allegedly was there. Like the Oswald impostor, Porras tried to obtain a Cuban entry visa. He told U.S. authorities after the assassination that he traveled to Mexico to try to gain entrance to Cuba but was refused, so he gave up and left Mexico. Costa Rican intelligence claimed that he was on a mission to infiltrate Cuba.

Perhaps he was, but he may well have had another mission as well. It seems that Porras was only about five-foot-seven. Could he be the shorter "Oswald" who made such a fuss about getting to Cuba? As we will see, three Mexico City witnesses who had dealings with "Oswald" during his visit there remember him as being around five-foot-six. The real Oswald was five-foot-nine or five-foot-nine and a half. When Porras departed Mexico, he did not return to his native Costa Rica or to Miami but went directly to Dallas. His activities and affiliations deserved intense investigation, which neither the Warren Commission or the House Assassinations Committee provided.

The parade of shadowy characters on the Mexican trip is not over. In addition to Oswald and the two other intelligence agents, there is yet another figure whose activities appear clandestine enough to suggest the possibility of an intelligence connection. This man not only rode the same bus as Oswald but, according to other passengers, sat with him during the trip.

Passengers recalled that Oswald sat next to a man with an English accent. The two conversed. In its efforts to interview the passengers, the FBI sought out this English-speaking man, whose name was listed as "John Bowen" on the bus's baggage manifest. The Bureau could not find Mr. Bowen. It finally located a man allegedly named Albert Osborne, who claimed to be an acquaintance of Bowen (although his recollection of Bowen was hazy).[13] The FBI interviewed Albert Osborne three times. Finally, agents discovered that Osborne was indeed well acquainted with Bowen; they were one and the same. Osborne admitted to using the alias "John Howard Bowen."[14] The FBI was perplexed and angered by the deception. Bowen-Osborne denied sitting next to Oswald on the bus. But even the Warren Commission was troubled by this strange character with the false identity. The Commission concluded:

Osborne's responses to Federal investigators on matters unrelated to Oswald have proved inconsistent and unreliable, and, therefore, based on the contrary evidence and Osborne's lack of reliability, the Commission has attached no credence to his denial that Oswald was beside him on the bus.[15]

There was more to the spooky Osborne than just an alias. He appeared to be in his fifties but claimed to be in his seventies. He told the Bureau that he had used an alias in his work for 50 years, but never explained why. He claimed to be a "missionary" who traveled around the world bringing the word of God to Latin America, Spain, France, and Italy. He traveled almost continuously, conducting what he described as one-man "missionary tours."[16] But he told fellow passengers that he was a retired teacher writing a book on earthquakes.

Osborne's missionary work seems to have had a lot in common with the international wanderings of another shadowy figure—George de Mohrenschildt, who claimed to be a geologist. Like de Mohrenschildt, Osborne traveled extensively, almost continuously, with no explanation as to how he financed these sojourns.[17] Like de Mohrenschildt, his itineraries are puzzling. Extensive checks of the border-crossing points for entry into France and Spain failed to turn up any record of the prevaricating preacher's entrances to do missionary work there.[18] Also like de Mohrenschildt, Osborne had been pro-Nazi during World War II.[19] In Osborne's case, fanatically so.

Osborne returned to New Orleans after the Mexican trip. Nine days before the assassination he departed the United States for Spain and Italy. It is not surprising, in light of all this, that unconfirmed reports surfaced in the early to mid–1970s that he was a CIA operative of some sort.[20]

Whether it is purely coincidence or whether Oswald knew Osborne before the Mexican City bus trip, Oswald used the alias "Osborne" on two occasions when he ordered the printing of his FPCC literature. This occurred in New Orleans before the Mexican bus trip.

In attempting to track down the passengers on the bus, the FBI was forced to work from the baggage manifest rather than from the more complete and official passenger manifest. According to the bus terminal manager in Mexico City, the passenger manifest was "borrowed by investigators of the Mexican government soon after the assassination."[21] The terminal manager had kept a copy. But five days later some "unidentified investigators" claiming to be from the Mexican government showed up and "borrowed" the copy. The passenger manifest has never been found. Mexican officials disputed the claim that their investigators had taken the lists.[22]

Some of the passengers who were located by the FBI presented a rather odd picture of Oswald's behavior on the bus ride. His fellow workers at his various jobs described him as reserved, if not reclusive. He was never known to be gregarious or outgoing. On this occasion he acted as if he were the social director for the tour. He left his seat to introduce himself to two Australian women, then told them a series of stories about his experiences in the Marine Corps and the Soviet Union. He showed them his 1959 passport as proof that he had been there.[23] Lee initiated another conversation with a British couple, the McFarlands. In addition to informing them that he was the secretary of the FPCC in New Orleans, he asserted that he was headed for Havana, Cuba in hopes of meeting Fidel.[24] Since it was illegal for U.S. citizens to travel to Cuba, which Oswald surely knew, he was announcing his intention to break the law. But then he had already announced his illegal travel plan to the U.S. government by indicating on his passport application that he was headed for the Soviet Union via Cuba. The usually secretive Oswald seemed compelled to leave an indelible impression among passengers concerning his pro-communist background and his alleged plans. It worked.

In obtaining his passport, Oswald continued his run of inexplicably favorable treatment, or tremendous luck, when dealing with the federal bureaucracy. The lookout card—flagging him as a defector, or as a person whom it would be undesirable to permit travel abroad—was not there. As Sylvia Meagher pointed out, this was an era in which U.S. citizens alleged to have pro-communist sympathies were the subject of particular attention by the Passport Office. This happened, for example, to a Harvard professor who had advocated disarmament—but not to the U-2 defector.[25] Oswald obtained his passport in 24 hours, faster than most citizens who are not an object of suspicion regarding their loyalty to the United States. It is not as if Oswald had been deceptive: he indicated on his application that his previous passport had been cancelled. This alone should have served to red-flag his passport even in the absence of a lookout card. True to form, it had no effect.[26]

Oswald allegedly continued to leave vivid impressions at the Soviet and Cuban consulates in Mexico City, in terms of both emotions and exhibits. He made a conspicuous display of leftism; he frenetically talked of returning to the Soviet Union. He also exhibited an array of leftist materials: correspondence he had had with the American Communist Party, a membership card for the FPCC, a photo of himself being arrested by New Orleans police during his street scuffle, a membership card for the American Communist Party. He flew into a rage when informed that it would take several months to process his application to enter the Soviet Union.[27] But was this the real Oswald?

The evidence seems solid that the real Oswald went to Mexico. Passport documents, signatures, and other evidence convinced both the Warren Commission and the House Assassinations Committee.[28] But there is also very strong evidence that he was not the man who visited the consulates claiming to be "Oswald" and proffering credentials.

Cuban consul Eusebio Azcue, who dealt with "Oswald," testified before the House Assassinations Committee. Azcue described "Oswald" as thirty-five years old, of medium height, with dark blond hair. The real Oswald was then twenty-four and had brown hair. Azcue claimed that when he saw television coverage of Ruby shooting Oswald, he noted that the Oswald killed in Dallas did not even resemble the man who visited his consulate.[29]

The other person at the Cuban consulate who had the most contact with "Oswald" was Sylvia Duran, Azcue's assistant. Her recall was less certain than that of her boss. She had no reason to suspect that the man she dealt with was not the real Oswald. She knew that the names matched, and the brief film of Oswald's murder had not created any doubts.[30]

In 1979 journalist Anthony Summers made it possible for Sylvia Duran to study more extensive film footage of Oswald than she had seen previously. The House Committee had not bothered to afford her a fresher, longer look at the man who was the subject of her testimony. The film was of a television interview he had given in New Orleans only a few weeks before his Mexican trip. Mrs. Duran could thus hear as well as see the subject. Her conclusion was that "the man on the film is not like the man I saw here in Mexico City." She observed that the real Oswald had a strong voice and seemed confident. The man she dealt with was small, had a trembling voice and seemed "weak."[31]

This impression was partly reiterated by the Soviet consul in Mexico City, Pavel Antonovich Yatskov. Eight months after the assassination he described his encounter with "Oswald" as follows:

I met Oswald here. He stormed into my office and wanted me to introduce and recommend him to the Cubans. He told me that he lived in the USSR. I told him that I would have to check before I could recommend him. He was nervous and his hands trembled, and he stormed out of my office. I don't believe that a person as nervous as Oswald, whose hands trembled, could have accurately fired a rifle.[32]

Duran told the House Assassinations Committee that the man she dealt with was "gaunt and short," about her size (five-foot-three).[33] In her contemporaneous notes about the 1963 Mexican episode, she wrote that "Oswald" was short, about five-foot-six. The real Oswald was five-foot-nine.[34] Both Duran and Azcue remembered the Mexican "Oswald" as having blond hair; Duran recalled that he had blue eyes.[35] The real Oswald had neither.

Anthony Summers, whose energetic investigation of the Mexican trip has provided important new data, also interviewed a man named Oscar Contreras, whom the House Committee investigators were unable to find.[36] At the time of Oswald's visit to Mexico, Contreras was a member of a leftist, pro-Castro student group. He asserted that a man calling himself "Lee Harvey Oswald" approached him and three of his friends and began to express discontent with life in the United States and a desire to go to Cuba. "Lee Harvey Oswald" said the Cuban consulate was refusing to give him a visa, and he asked Contreras and friends for help in dealing with the officials. They did have contacts there. "Oswald" saw the group a second time and repeated his request for assistance. Contreras and his associates provided none: they were distrustful of the American, fearing that he might be trying to infiltrate their group.

Contreras described "Oswald" as being over thirty years old and short. Contreras, himself five-foot-nine, remembered looking down at him. Moreover, he was understandably suspicious as to how this man knew that he and his friends had left-wing political ties. When the American first approached them they were sitting drinking coffee, discussing a movie; there was no talk of politics. How, Contreras wondered, out of the thousands of students in Mexico City, was "Oswald" lucky enough or savvy enough to find four who had contacts with the Cuban consulate? This aroused Contreras's suspicion that the man might be some sort of spy.

There are two pieces of physical evidence that point to the real Oswald instead of an impostor, but they are not definitive. First, Sylvia Duran's name and phone number were found in Oswald's notebook when he was arrested in Dallas. However, the Duran listing hardly ensures that it was Oswald who made the visits. Second, House Assassinations Committee's handwriting experts concluded that the signature on the visa application filed with the Cuban consulate was that of the real Oswald, although they could not rule out a skillful forgery.[37] There is a gap in this chain of evidence, however.

When "Oswald" entered the Cuban consulate to apply for a visa, he claimed not to have any photographs of himself. He left, supposedly to get his picture taken at a nearby photographic studio. A post-assassination investigation could find no record in any local photographic establishment showing that "Oswald" had his picture taken. Yet "Oswald" returned with a photo of the real Oswald. When he returned with the photo, Sylvia Duran evidently did not notice the discrepancy between the man's face and the photo of the real Oswald.

The man was gone from the consulate for four hours. In 1986 former HSCA investigator Edwin Lopez appeared in the television production "On Trial: Lee Harvey Oswald." Lopez, the author of HSCA's report on its Mexico City investigation, asserted that Duran "could never tell us that he signed it in her presence." The possibility exists that the signature could have been carefully forged, or perhaps it was somehow obtained from the real Oswald.

It seems that other artifacts proffered by "Oswald" were of suspicious origin. One was an American Communist Party membership card. It appeared to Consul Azcue to be suspiciously pristine, as if newly minted. [38] The question arises as to whether the Party dispensed membership cards at all, a question that the author was unable to answer. The real Oswald had never become a member of the American Communist Party. [39] Then there was the proffered photo of him supposedly being taken into custody, with a policeman on each arm. The real Oswald had been arrested by New Orleans police after the scuffle with anti-Castroites. Sylvia Duran later reflected that the photo exhibited by "Oswald" looked "phony." [40] Indeed it might have been, for there is no known photograph of the arrest.

The Mexican episode has been obscured by a CIA cover-up that has gone on since 1963. In September of that year, two months before the assassination, the Agency reported in a teletype sent to other government agencies that a man named "Lee Oswald" had contacted the Soviet embassy in Mexico. [41] At the time of this alleged visit, the CIA had both the Soviet and Cuban consulates under photographic surveillance. The night of the President's assassination the Agency forwarded to the Dallas FBI office a picture of "Oswald" entering the Soviet consulate. But the man in the picture was not Oswald; he was taller, older, heavier, had a crewcut, and bore no resemblance to Oswald. This incongruity spawned a host of questions, some of which remain unresolved. The Agency's conflicting explanations have led many investigators to the conclusion that this complex matter of CIA photos represents much more than an innocent bureaucratic error, and that the Agency was covering up vital information about an Oswald impostor. To this day, the man in the picture remains unknown to researchers and official investigators. Then CIA Director William Colby alleged in 1975, "We don't know who he is."[42]

One explanation as to how this man was mistaken for Oswald was that the Agency had simply guessed wrongly about his identity.[43] Part of the problem, it was claimed, was that the CIA had no picture of the real Oswald anywhere in its files, and thus it could not determine that the heavyset, crewcut man was not Oswald.[44] Not so. There was a picture of Oswald in CIA files allegedly taken by a tourist in the Soviet Union. The CIA's Oswald file that was sent to the Warren Commission in 1963 contained two newspaper photos of him from articles dealing with his defection. A December 9, 1960 CIA document from Oswald's "201 file," obtained by the author from the Agency's Kennedy assassination file, has a check mark in the "yes" column under the heading "photo."

The Warren Commission tried to resolve the matter of the "mistaken" photo but was frustrated by the Agency. The CIA dragged its feet in replying to the Commission's inquiries. Internal memoranda reveal that the Agency considered waiting out the Commission, stalling until it went out of business.[45] It was Richard Helms, then deputy director, who wrote a memo to Commission chief counsel Rankin explaining Oswald's visit to Mexico.[46] Helms asserted that full disclosure of the Mexican incident might compromise the Agency's sources and methods.[47]

In a memo sent to the Commission in July 1964, the CIA claimed the mystery man had been photographed at the Soviet consulate on October 4, 1963, the day after the real Oswald allegedly departed Mexico to return to Dallas.[48] This must have made the mystery man seem to the Commission to be less important, less potentially relevant to Oswald. The memo was silent about the fact that the man had also appeared at the Soviet consulate on October 1, the date Oswald allegedly appeared there.[49] The Agency went on to assure the Commission that the unidentified man had no connection either to Oswald or the assassination; therefore, the Agency urged, there was no reason to publish his photo.[50] The CIA wanted it both ways: it had no idea who the man was, but it was certain he had no connection to anything important.

The question arose as to whether the real Oswald was photographed by Agency surveillance cameras, since he entered on the same day as the unidentified man. This surveillance operation was not set up to capture Oswald: it was a continuous monitoring system.[51] Was the real Oswald missed? If so, how? Were there pictures of someone impersonating Oswald that were withheld or destroyed by the Agency? The reasons given by the CIA for the absence of the real Oswald's picture have been far from satisfactory.

A former CIA officer who served in Mexico during the period of Oswald's visit claimed in 1977 that photographic surveillance was not operational 24 hours a day.[52] But "Oswald" made no less than five visits to the two communist consulates. This provided a series of ten entrances and exits spread over a three-day period; CIA cameras had more than their share of chances to catch him.[53] It was asserted that hundreds of photos produced by the surveillance systems during this same period were scrutinized, but there was not one of "Oswald."[54]

In 1976 a Freedom of Information Act suit filed against the Agency succeeded in liberating a dozen additional pictures of the mystery man who was "mistaken" for Oswald. In these, the man is wearing several different outfits, indicating several episodes of photographic surveillance.[55]

In 1975 the Agency claimed that the Soviet consulate cameras did not operate on weekends, and that this explained how Oswald's Saturday-night visit was missed. Meanwhile, the story went, CIA photographic surveillance of the Cuban consulate had simply broken down while "Oswald" was there.[56] Not only is it hard to imagine why a surveillance system would be given weekends off—perhaps the Agency had determined that espionage was a five-day-a-week activity—but we have a photo of the unidentified man taken on one of the very days "Oswald" visited the Soviet consulate.

If the CIA did have pictures of the real Lee Harvey Oswald visiting communist consulates in Mexico City, it would surely have provided them to the Warren Commission. Doing so would have saved considerable trouble and embarrassment. If the Agency had captured on film not Oswald but his impostor, it could hardly have turned such pictures over to the Warren Commission without raising the specter of conspiracy in a form impossible to ignore.

In 1989 Anthony Summers presented additional information, derived in part from interviews with former HSCA staffers.[57] He asserted that two former CIA employees had lied under oath to the HSCA when claiming that the surveillance cameras missed "Oswald" because of malfunctioning or part-time usage. Summers says that Committee staffers felt certain that photographic surveillance was operational during "Oswald's" various visits.

Summers offers a provocative quote from former HSCA investigator Edwin Lopez, stating that the CIA was definitely covering up but that he and his colleagues weren't sure whether it had to do with some element of the CIA being involved in the assassination. During the Mexico City investigation, the Agency allegedly tried to refuse the Committee access to interviewees and dragged its feet in responding, knowing the Committee had a limited, two-year lifespan.

Summers seems persuaded that a surveillance photo of the real Oswald in Mexico City did exist but was suppressed by the Agency. He reports that HSCA was told of the photo by a retired senior CIA officer who served in Mexico City and that three other CIA employees told Committee investigators they too had seen the photo at the CIA office in Mexico City; two others claimed to have known about its existence. The photo was allegedly kept for years in the private safe of retired Mexico City station chief Winston Scott, until it was removed by a senior CIA officer after Scott's death. If true, why would only one photo exist or be preserved? There should have been numerous Oswald photos, if HSCA investigators are correct in their belief that blanket surveillance was operational during his visits.

Summers speculates that perhaps the photo was suppressed because it showed someone with the real Oswald—perhaps someone with CIA links or even a communist affiliation (Cuban or Soviet). However, given the strong evidence of an Oswald impostor and given the Agency's record of deception and disinformation in this matter, there are other possibilities. Perhaps there really was no photo at all and the story was concocted; perhaps the putative photo was not of the real Oswald and this accounted for its spooky history; or perhaps it was a photo of Oswald but not an authentic surveillance photo of his visiting a consulate in Mexico City. The alleged existence—or even the actual existence—of a single Oswald surveillance photo does not refute the evidence that he was being impersonated.

At the time of the Mexican episode the CIA had more than photographic surveillance to work with. It is now known that both consulates were extensively bugged, with phone taps and covert electronic surveillance devices.[58] Were Oswald's conversations captured on audio tape?

In a 1975 television interview with CBS reporter Dan Rather, then CIA Director William Colby was queried about the possibility.[59]

> *Rather*: Did you make voice recordings of him?
> *Colby*: [pause of several seconds] I'd say . . . I think there were, yes.

In 1976 CIA officer David Phillips, who was in the Agency's Mexican station during the relevant period, said that tapes once existed but had been routinely destroyed.[60] If this occurred after the assassination, the Agency had trashed vital evidence, even if the tapes were of the real Oswald.

There is some indication from another source that the tapes may have captured an impostor. The day after the assassination FBI Director J. Edgar Hoover wrote a memorandum to President Johnson summarizing the state of the evidence, as part of the Bureau's role as the primary investigative agency in the case. Hoover mentioned the Oswald tapes. He stated that two FBI agents who had conversed with Oswald prior to the assassination listened to the tapes, and they did not think it was Oswald's voice.[61]

It was noted by consulate personnel that "Oswald" spoke "broken" Russian that was "hardly recognizable."[62] The real Oswald spoke fluent Russian.

The Hoover memo was the only mention of the tapes in FBI files. The two FBI agents named as listeners were called to testify before the House Assassinations Committee. They claimed to have no recollection of hearing any tape of Oswald.[63]

It seems certain that tapes existed. The Warren Commission's own documents clearly establish that the CIA bugged, at the very least: a phone call made by "Oswald" from the Cuban consulate to the Soviet consulate, a conversation with a guard at the entrance to the Soviet consulate (in which "Oswald" specifically identified himself), and a third conversation in which "Oswald" indicated that he wanted to go to the city of Odessa if granted a Soviet visa.[64] This alone was sufficient data to determine if it was the real Oswald or an impostor. As with the pictures, if the speaker was really Oswald the Agency should have been delighted to circulate the tapes widely rather than suppressing or destroying them. Such recordings could validate the CIA's account of Oswald's Mexican visit and could largely dispose of the impostor question.

In 1976 *Washington Post* reporter Ron Kessler was able to track down a typist and a translator who worked in the CIA's Mexican station during the Oswald affair.[65] They recalled translating and typing up the "Oswald" tapes. They also recalled that their bosses were in a rush for the data. As the translator described, "Usually they pick up the transcripts the next day. This, they wanted right away."[66]

In his appearance on the 1986 television production "On Trial: Lee Harvey Oswald," former HSCA investigator Edwin Lopez expressed his conclusion about the Mexico City affair.[67] HSCA's 265-page investigative report remains sealed until the year 2028. As the report's author and one of the chief investigators, his observations carry considerable weight.

Lopez asserted his belief that there was definitely an Oswald impostor and that "the only plausible explanation was that they were trying to set him up [as a patsy in the president's assassination]." Lopez also stated that the evidence suggested the real Oswald was not really trying to go to Cuba. When asked if Oswald was involved with the CIA, Lopez responded: "Oh, I have no doubt that he was in some way." The former investigator could not provide details because he had signed a legally binding secrecy pledge when working for HSCA.

The Mexican episode is not the only CIA cover-up regarding crucial data about Oswald. It is not the only instance in which someone clearly seemed to be impersonating him. Back in the United States, incidents and artifacts designed to implicate him in the President's assassination appeared with striking frequency.

8

Legend I: Incidents

I'm just a patsy.

Lee Harvey Oswald to reporters in the
Dallas police station, Nov. 22, 1963

It is indeed a facet of certain criminal mentalities that they seek, subconsciously, to get caught. Therefore they implicate themselves or make
mistakes that lead to arrest in a compulsive manifestation of self-loathing
or a desire for notoriety. It is certainly logical that if Oswald wanted to
enter the history books as the world's most famous Marxist assassin, he
would consciously or subconsciously delight in leaving a trail that any
correspondence-school gumshoe could follow. Regardless of whether Oswald did or did not shoot at the president, regardless of whether he
knowingly participated in the assassination (either alone or in concert
with others), and regardless of whether he left a trail of self-implicating
evidence for reasons of stupidity or to ensure his place in history, there
remains a basic problem: he was not entirely responsible for the orgy of
incriminating activity that surrounded him before, during, and after the
assassination. He had help, whether he wanted it or not. To some degree

Note: In clandestine terminology a "legend" is a cover story created to mask the real
activities of a spy or operative, or the real purpose of a project. Depending on the scenario
being run, the operative(s) for whom the legend is crafted may or may not be aware of
all or part of it.

at least, depending on his actual role, Oswald *was* set up. A legend was built for him.

When an alleged assassin's face is flashed across the TV screen, whether it is Oswald, James Earl Ray, or Sirhan Sirhan, dozens of persons come forward with stories of sightings. Law enforcement files in all three cases are glutted with such reports. Sometimes the sources are seeking media attention; sometimes they are mistaken, having seen someone who bore a resemblance to the alleged assassin. Sometimes they are correct but their report has no significance to the case, as in witnessing Sirhan buying lunch. But Oswald's case is different.

We begin with the strange machinations in Mexico City that lend credence to the basic notion that someone was impersonating him. In most of the incidents that followed, witnesses rendered very positive identifications, but it could not have been Oswald; he was known to be at his job, with Marina and his two children, or in Mexico. These instances are all provocative, because they form a consistent pattern in which each contributes to the false portrait of a violence-prone, left-wing hothead who is increasingly frustrated and out of control. Most significantly, the impostor(s) not only verbally identifies himself as Oswald in half of the incidents, but proffers some information or artifact that relates to the real Oswald—experience in the Marine Corps, in Russia, or Mexico, use of a rifle (an uncommon Italian carbine) like the one with which Oswald allegedly shot the president. Several of the sightings are far more than fleeting and involve multiple witnesses.

On September 25, 1963, while the real Oswald was on a bus somewhere between New Orleans and Mexico City regaling passengers with tales of his leftism, a young man calling himself "Harvey Oswald" appeared at the Selective Service Office in Austin, Texas.[1] He requested help in upgrading his Marine Corps discharge.[2] He talked for over a half hour to the assistant director of the office's administrative section and explained his problem in detail. "Harvey Oswald" had been in the Marines, he said, and had gotten into some trouble resulting in an undesirable discharge. This prevented him from obtaining a good job. He said that he had a family living in Fort Worth and needed the upgraded discharge in order to support them. He was given a sympathetic ear but was informed that he should try the Veterans Administration, since Selective Service had no jurisdiction over discharges.

The real Oswald did receive a downgraded discharge from the Marine Corps and had lived in Fort Worth in 1962. The Selective Service administrator never saw "Harvey Oswald" again until she saw his name and picture flashed across her TV screen the evening of the assassination.

It was, she believed, the same man who had visited her office. Two other people in Austin claimed to have seen Oswald there on or near September 25.[3]

There were additional incidents of "Oswald's" discontent with his treatment and his status. On November 9, 1963, a customer calling himself "Lee Oswald" walked into a Lincoln-Mercury showroom in Dallas and expressed interest in buying a car.[4] The prospective customer would not easily be forgotten by the salesman, for "Lee Oswald" took him for a nerve-wracking test drive that reached speeds of 85 miles an hour on the crowded Stemmons Freeway. When they returned to the showroom to discuss financing, "Lee Oswald" announced that he did not presently have enough money for a downpayment, but that he would be coming into "a lot of money in the next two or three weeks."[5] This event occurred two weeks before the assassination. "Lee Oswald" delivered an ideologically charged statement about money to the credit manager: if financing could not be arranged, he just might return to the Soviet Union, "where they treat workers like men."[6]

Three witnesses at the car dealership vouched for this encounter. The Warren Commission concluded that they were mistaken. According to the Commission's evidence, the real Oswald was at home in Irving, Texas the day of the incident.[7] Even if he had been in Dallas that day, he was an unlikely candidate for a high-speed test spin; the real Oswald did not know how to drive.[8]

An Irving, Texas grocer claimed that "Harvey Oswald" appeared in his store on November 9 and tried unsuccessfully to cash a check for $189.[9] The Warren Commission rejected the sighting because Oswald was accounted for elsewhere and there did not appear to be any corroboration for the story. However, there was some corroboration.

Clifton Shasteen is not mentioned in the *Warren Report*, although the grocer does appear. Shasteen owned a barber shop a few doors away from the grocery store. He asserted that Oswald had come to his shop on several occasions to get a haircut. He had seen him enter the grocery store but could not recall the date.[10]

Shasteen vividly remembered one encounter with "Oswald," who was accompanied by a fourteen-year-old boy.[11] (The real Oswald had two young daughters.) In the presence of Shasteen and several customers, "Oswald" and the boy made leftist remarks about the unfairness of there being "one leader over everyone else," about Shasteen keeping part of the money earned by the barbers who worked for him, about the inequity of allowing one man " to hog up the whole country and let another man starve," about world "greed" ending when "you don't have a leader in every little old country." Shasteen admired "Oswald's" shoes. They were purchased in Mexico, said "Oswald."

On November 1, a young man entered Morgan's Gun Shop in Fort Worth and purchased ammunition for a rifle.[12] His rudeness and abrasiveness managed to draw the attention of three witnesses. He boasted that he had served in the Marine Corps. After the assassination all three witnesses identified the man as Lee Harvey Oswald. The real Oswald was accounted for in Dallas that day.[13]

On November 9 (the same day as the test-drive incident, while Oswald was at home in Irving) a man appeared at the Sports Dome Rifle Range in Dallas and drew the attention of a number of people by his obnoxious behavior.[14] Witnesses said the man was a good shot but was shooting at the targets of neighboring riflemen as well as his own, a violation of one of the cardinal rules of range conduct. The man fired rapidly—another violation of the rules. One witness who talked with the man and saw his weapon said that he was using a 6.5mm Italian carbine, similar to the one allegedly used to kill the president. After the assassination witnesses recognized the undisciplined marksman as Lee Harvey Oswald.[15]

Journalist Henry Hurt reported another incident involving "Oswald" and a 6.5mm Italian carbine.[16] Mrs. Lovell Penn, a Dallas high school teacher, lived on a farm 15 miles outside the city. About six weeks prior to the assassination she was startled to hear blasts of gunfire coming from her cow pasture. She confronted three trespassers, one of whom held a rifle, and told them to stop shooting because they might hit her livestock. The man she thought might have been Oswald became angry. When Mrs. Penn threatened to call the police the trio departed.

Following the assassination she thought she recognized Oswald. She presented authorities with an empty cartridge case she had picked up in her field. (Mrs. Penn thought one of the other man might have been of Latin extraction.) The FBI determined that it was a cartridge case from a 6.5mm Mannlicher-Carcano rifle but that it was not fired from the rifle that had allegedly killed the president.

By far the most significant impersonation occurred in late September, when three strangers visited the home of Annie and Silvia Odio in Dallas.[17] The women were active in the anti-Castro efforts of the Cuban exile community. The three men, two Latins and an American, claimed to be members of JURE, a mildly anti-Castro exile group but one that was very far to the left on the spectrum of exile politics. The American was introduced as "Leon." He said only a few words during the brief discussion of exile politics at the Odio home.

Forty-eight hours after the trio of visitors departed, one of the Latins

phoned Silvia Odio. He again requested that she help the JURE movement, as he had done at her home, but he also seemed keen to discuss
his American companion "Leon Oswald." According to Odio, the Latin
asked her opinion of the American. Then the caller went on to char-
acterize "Oswald" in a manner that she found chilling even at the time:

> Well, you know, he's a Marine, an ex-Marine, and an expert marksman.
> . . . He's kind of loco, kinda nuts. . . . The American says we Cubans don't
> have any guts. He says we should have shot President Kennedy after the
> Bay of Pigs. He says we should do something like that.[18]

After the assassination, with a profound sense of shock and fear, both
sisters recognized the Oswald they saw on TV as the man who had visited
them. The Warren Commission found the Odio story very credible, as
did the House Assassinations Committee. Silvia Odio seemed an intelligent, articulate woman. Moreover, she had told portions of her story
to others *before* the assassination. This was substantiated by her father's
reply to a letter she had written.[19] She placed the incident as occurring
sometime between September 24 and September 29, probably in the
middle of that span.[20]

During that time, the real Oswald was ending his stay in New Orleans
and heading for Mexico; he was not in Dallas.[21] It is interesting to note
that while this incident seems to contrast with the others in that it has
an anti-Castro thrust instead of a leftist one, it can be seen as fostering
a leftist image from the perspective of Cuban exile politics. JURE, the
organization with which the visitors identified themselves, espoused a
program of Castroism without Castro. It was considered to be dangerously
left-wing by many elements within the exile community.[22] To the most
militant anti-Castro groups, JURE was viewed as little better than the
Communist Party.[23]

The Warren Commission was troubled by the implications of what it
regarded as Mrs. Odio's very credible story. Since the Commission's own
evidence placed Oswald in New Orleans or Mexico at the time of the
incident, someone might well have been trying to frame him. Commission Chief Counsel J. Lee Rankin wrote to J. Edgar Hoover insisting that
the Odio story must be either "proved or disproved."[24] In a sense this
was one of the most crucial problems to face the Commission: Proof of
the Odio story would constitute circumstantial proof of conspiracy.

The Warren Commission breathed a collective sigh of relief when the
matter was allegedly settled. J. Edgar Hoover took the Commission off
the hook of conspiracy, or so it appeared. The FBI turned up a witness,

Loran Eugene Hall, who claimed to be one of the men who had visited Mrs. Odio. Hall identified the other members of the trio as Lawrence J. Howard and William Houston Seymour. Seymour, claimed Hall, bore a striking resemblance to Lee Harvey Oswald.[25] The FBI showed photos of Howard and Seymour to Silvia Odio. She could not identify either of them, or Hall, as the men who visited her. And there was another problem: Seymour did not look anything like Lee Harvey Oswald. He denied to the FBI being in Dallas at the relevant time or even meeting the Odios. Despite all this opposing evidence, the Commission chose to consider the matter settled. As Chief Counsel Rankin told a colleague who remained troubled by the incident, "We are supposed to be closing doors, not opening them."[26]

Ten days after the Commission presented its final report to President Johnson, Loran Eugene Hall retracted his version of the Odio story.[27] In fact, Hall now admitted, he had never so much as met Mrs. Odio. The retraction came too late for the Commission, whose conclusions were now carved in granite.

Loran Hall's career as a witness in the Kennedy assassination was only half over. He surfaced again in 1967, this time in New Orleans. Again Hall managed to confuse an assassination probe—that of New Orleans District Attorney Jim Garrison. Hall gave Garrison information that led to the ill-conceived investigation of a California man in connection with an alleged New Orleans conspiracy to assassinate the president, an investigation based largely on Hall's stories.[28]

Who was this mysterious witness whose fraudulent testimony had dead-ended the Odio affair? For one thing, he was an operative with impressive anti-Castro credentials. He was linked to the CIA as well as to the anti-Castro activities of organized crime (which, in turn, were linked to each other).[29] In 1963 he worked with the CIA-backed Free Cuba group.[30] He was reportedly detained twice for violating President Kennedy's ban on exile military activities in the United States.[31] He reportedly visited Dallas twice in the fall of 1963—once to raise funds for a Cuban-exile group, a second time with a trailer full of weapons bound for exiles in Miami.[32] Hall was also a leader of Interpen, a militant anti-Castro group composed of Cuban exiles and CIA contract agents.[33]

After the assassination, Dallas Deputy Sheriff Roger Craig reported what apparently turned out to be an Oswald look-alike fleeing the crime scene. Craig was a meritorious twenty-seven-year-old law officer. He was across the street from the Texas School Book Depository 15 to 20 minutes after the shooting when he saw a white male running away from the building.[34] A light-colored Rambler with a luggage rack, driven by a dark-complected individual, pulled up and the running man got in. Several witnesses from different vantage points independently corroborated the presence of such a vehicle. Craig ran afoul of his superiors and his career went into a tailspin because of his unwavering insistence that the fleeing man was Oswald, or someone who looked very much like him. (Craig saw Oswald being interrogated at police headquarters.) The real Oswald had departed the crime scene earlier and was heading back to his apartment.

Apparently unknown to the Warren Commission, there were two men in Dallas at the time of the assassination who were involved in supplying or obtaining firearms for anti-Castro efforts. Both men apparently bore a resemblance to Oswald. Although there is no evidence linking either individual to the president's murder, the existence of two persons in the anti-Castro arena who resembled Oswald should have sparked a more energetic investigation of the alleged Oswald sightings.

There was a glaring lapse in the advance protective work done for President Kennedy. Alpha–66, an anti-Castro group, was in Dallas. The Secret Service didn't know of its presence, even though the Service had previously foiled one Cuban-exile assassination plot in which a small plane was going to ram *Air Force One*.[35]

While the question of why the FBI did not report Oswald to the Secret Service would receive great attention after the assassination, the question of why the CIA did not report Alpha–66 or its "violently anti-Kennedy" leader was never asked. The CIA was conspicuously silent about Dallas Alpha–66 head Roberto Ruiz (a pseudonym provided by the author), both before and after the assassination. Local police had the major responsibility for discovering local threats to a visiting president, but federal agencies also had an important role.[36] There were no precise guidelines as to the types of individuals that the FBI or CIA should report to the Service as constituting potential threats, but the violently anti-Kennedy leader of a commando group noted for openly challenging the president's ban on military activities against Castro clearly should have been reported.

That the CIA had no knowledge of Ruiz or his group is unlikely. Alpha–66 was in many ways a creature of the Company, receiving resources and encouragement in the CIA's covert war against Castro. CIA case officers were with the exiles at their Dallas meetings.[37] Alpha–66 and its leader came to the belated attention of the Secret Service after the assassination. The CIA responded to a Secret Service inquiry by stating that it had no data on Ruiz.[38] This is highly unlikely given the Agency's operational interest in the group and its direct contact with Ruiz and his group in Dallas.

After the assassination an FBI informant in Dallas reported that Ruiz was "known to be violently anti-President Kennedy."[39] The Bureau interviewed him twice in 1964.[40] On both occasions he claimed that he was an admirer of the president, both as a person and as a politician. Neither could he remember ever hearing any derogatory comments about Kennedy uttered at Alpha–66 meetings, although he had "heard rumors" that many Cubans were critical of Kennedy's policies. One Warren Commission memorandum describes Ruiz as "apparently a survivor of the Bay of Pigs episode," a debacle for which many anti-Castro Cubans blamed Kennedy personally.

Ruiz also seems to have born a resemblance to Oswald. At 8:00 AM the day after the assassination, the Dallas County sheriff's office passed along a report to the Secret Service: "Oswald" had been meeting with a Cuban political group before the assassination, "possibly the Freedom for Cuba Party [sic] of which Oswald was a member."[41] The address at which "Oswald" was seen had nothing to do with the pro-Castro Fair Play for Cuba Committee (FPCC)—it was the Dallas headquarters of Alpha–66.

The man attending Alpha–66 meetings who was mistaken for Oswald was very likely Roberto Ruiz. The FBI discovered an instance in which several witnesses had made this mistake.[42] While investigating a report that Oswald had been in Oklahoma on November 17 with several other men who might possibly have been confederates, the Bureau established that the witnesses had seen Ruiz.[43] Thus we appear to have two independent instances of this confusion of identity. Both men were five feet nine inches tall, had brown hair, and weighed approximately the same.

Around the time of the assassination, an agent of the Alcohol, Tobacco and Firearms Bureau (ATFB) of the Treasury Department was working undercover in Dallas gathering evidence against a local gun shop owner for violating the National Firearms Act.[44] The undercover ATFB agent learned that Roberto Ruiz and another Cuban had contacted the gun shop owner about the purchase of machine guns, bazookas, and "other heavy equipment." The gun shop owner confided that Ruiz had made purchases from him and that Alpha–66 had a large cache of arms somewhere in Dallas.

The undercover agent was interviewed by the Secret Service on December 16, 1964 (in order for the Service to learn more about Ruiz). In the Secret Service interview, the ATFB agent stated that he had "recently" worked undercover gathering evidence, thus indicating that the cache of arms referred to was probably in existence on November 22 when the president was shot.

But there is more to this gun shop than simply helping to establish that the commandoes of Alpha–66 were well armed at the time of the assassination. It seems that an exhaustive search by federal authorities revealed that this was one of the only two gun shops in Dallas in which bullets for a Mannlicher-Carcano rifle could be obtained.[45] The gun shop owner told the FBI that he had sold ten boxes of Mannlicher-Carcano ammunition in 1963, but it is not known to whom.

The ammunition that would fit "Oswald's" gun was uncommon in the United States in 1963. The shells found on the sixth floor of the Texas School Book Depository (from which the shots that killed the president were allegedly fired) were quickly traced to the manufacturer: the Western Cartridge Company of East Alton, Illinois. "Oswald's" ammunition came from a batch of four million rounds manufactured by Western Cartridge in 1954. An FBI document reveals that shortly after the assassination, an FBI agent made an interesting allegation about the manufacture—one that the Bureau would proceed to ignore. The depository shells were allegedly manufactured under government contract (DA–23–296–ORD–27) for the United States Marine Corps. But a high-ranking FBI criminalist, R. H. Jevons, claimed that this type of ammunition "does not fit and cannot be fired in any of the USMC weapons." Jevons' memo concludes: "This gives rise to the obvious speculation that it is a contract for ammunition placed by CIA with Western under a USMC cover for concealment purposes."[46] Jevons's "speculation" has neither been confirmed nor disproved.

It was not only Ruiz who resembled Oswald. It seems that, according to a federal agent, the gun shop owner looked like Oswald's "twin." In 1976 investigative journalist Dick Russell discovered some additional information.[47] He interviewed ATFB agent Frank Ellsworth, the man who had worked undercover in investigating the gun shop and its dealings with Ruiz and Alpha–66. Ellsworth broke his silence and told Russell an intriguing story. Immediately after the assassination Ellsworth was summoned to Dallas Police headquarters where, as the local federal firearms man, he was brought in to question Oswald concerning the alleged assassination weapon. Ellsworth was shocked when he entered the interrogation room and confronted the prisoner, for he thought Oswald was the man he had been investigating in the months prior to the assassination.

"Oswald was sitting in a chair about ten feet from the door," Ellsworth recalled, "and all I could see was headlines that I'd just turned loose the man who killed the president." Ellsworth later discovered that he was wrong, much to his relief. It was not Oswald that he had been investigating, but another man in Dallas who was Oswald's "twin." That man turned out to be the gun shop owner.

Ellsworth revealed that the owner had been interrogated by federal authorities after the assassination and was found to have been "nowhere near downtown Dallas" at the time of the shooting. Ellsworth claimed that a number of federal, state, and local officials were aware of the look-alike situation: "we talked about it. We laid it to rest and satisfied ourselves that it was merely coincidence."

The notion of an Oswald impostor apparently cropped up long before the assassination. It was referenced in a January 3, 1960 FBI memo, which none of the Warren Commission's lawyers could recall having seen (neither could relevant FBI or State Department officials).[48] The document was initialed by Hoover and went out under his name. Among other things, it states that "since there is a possibility that an impostor is using Oswald's birth certificate, any current information the Department of State may have concerning the subject will be appreciated."[49] Former Commission Counsel David Slawson, who had not seen the memo even though his investigative responsibilities related to it, opined when the memo surfaced that, "It conceivably could have been something related to CIA. I can only speculate now, but a general CIA effort to take out anything that reflected on them may have covered this up."[50]

Since Oswald was in the Soviet Union during this period, one might presume there would be concern that an Oswald impostor was lurking about in Russia.[51] If so, this should have caused great concern among the sleuths in U.S. counterintelligence. But it apparently did not. Even though Oswald was unaccounted for during part of his stay in the Soviet Union, and Hoover and the State Department referred to the possibility of an impostor, he was given his U.S. passport to return to the United States weeks before he had completed his travel plans. This occurred despite a specific State Department request that the passport be issued only at the last minute so as to reduce the potential for Soviet mischief in misappropriating the valid passport for espionage purposes.

Whether or not there was any domestic impostor data or warnings in U.S. files, we do know of one instance in which Oswald's name was usurped. Recall the January 20, 1961 incident at a truck dealership in New Orleans, while Oswald was in the Soviet Union. A Cuban and an American sought a bid for ten pickup trucks, implying that the vehicles were to be used for a special purpose and should be sold at cost (this was six months before the Bay of Pigs invasion and an active buildup was underway). The men claimed to be with the anti-Castro group Friends of Democratic Cuba. The American, in his early twenties, allegedly identified himself as "Lee Oswald" and printed the name on the bid form.

Legend-building for Oswald extended beyond the provocative, sometimes overlapping impersonations of him in Mexico and Texas prior to the assassination. It also included some artifacts and events concocted after the crime.

$$\underline{\underline{9}}$$

Legend II: Artifacts and Evidence

Don't believe the so-called evidence against me.
                    Lee Harvey Oswald to his brother Robert,
                    Dallas County Jail, Nov. 23, 1963

After the assassination, Dallas police claimed to have found two incriminating photos in the garage of the Paine home in Irving where the Oswalds were staying. In the infamous photos Lee is standing in the yard of his Neely Street apartment in Dallas dressed in black, holding leftist political literature in one hand and a Mannlicher-Carcano rifle in the other, while wearing a holster containing a revolver. One of the photos was published on the cover of *Life* magazine, captioned "Armed for Murder."[1] The picture did much to establish Oswald's guilt, leftism, and derangement in the minds of millions of Americans.

When police confronted him with a blow-up of the picture, he calmly asserted that the face was his but it had been superimposed on the body. He claimed never to have seen the photo before. Stating that he knew about photography (which was true), he contended that persons unknown to him had forged the item. He further asserted that, in time, he would be able to demonstrate this.[2]

Indeed, the pictures seemed replete with anomalies. Critics alleged, for example, that in one photo Oswald's nose casts a V-shaped shadow; in the other, his nose is in a different position because his head is slightly cocked. But the V-shaped shadows appear identical in both pictures. The shadows should have shifted at least slightly from one picture to the other when the position of the nose changed.[3] The chin in both pictures manifests a fine horizontal line—possibly betraying the grafting of Oswald's face onto the body of another man. The chin in the pictures is broad and rather square, with no cleft. Oswald's is narrow, pointed, and has a cleft.[4] One picture is taken at closer range than the other. Logically, the figure in that picture should be somewhat larger than in the other picture, which it is. The problem is that the heads, measured just above the chin, are of identical size.[5] Using Oswald's height as a baseline, calculations show that the rifle held in the pictures is 2.4 inches longer than the weapon found in the depository: either the rifle in the picture is not the alleged murder weapon or the body holding the rifle is shorter than Oswald's.[6]

The "Oswald" in these photos is holding two different kinds of left-wing newspapers: *The Worker*, the newspaper of the American Communist Party, and *The Militant*, the paper of the Trotskyite Socialist Workers Party.[7] The two publications, like the organizations that produced them, represent sharply conflicting ideological viewpoints. For someone conscious about ideological distinctions, as Oswald was supposed to have been, holding both *The Worker* and *The Militant* is somewhat odd—not unlike posing with copies of *National Review* and *The Nation* to portray an ideological orientation toward U.S. politics.

The incriminating photos smacked of forgery. In 1977 the Canadian Broadcasting Corporation retained an expert to study them. Major John Pickard, from the Canadian Department of Defense, concluded that the photos manifested "the earmarkings of being faked."[8] Journalist Anthony Summers retained another consultant, with the backing of the British Broadcasting Corporation (BBC). Detective Superintendent Malcolm Thompson, a past president of the Institute of Incorporated Photographers and of the Evidence Photographers International Counsel, had spent a lifetime in police identification work and was recommended to the BBC by both Kodak and Scotland Yard. Thompson found that the photos had been retouched in at least three places (Oswald's head, the rifle butt, and a pillar in the background of the scene). He also noted the anomalous shadows. Because of the disparity in the chins, Thompson asserted that the rest of Oswald's face had been grafted onto someone else's body and chin. Thompson concluded the photos had been faked.[9]

Experts often disagree. Despite all the problems manifested in the photos, the House Assassinations Committee retained a panel of distinguished experts who concluded that the pictures were authentic. The experts admitted, "It is possible to make a fake photograph that we would not be able to detect."[10] Nevertheless, the panel addressed the anomalies and Thompson's allegations point by point and concluded that they were the natural results of various facets of film processing and/or picture taking. Thompson ultimately deferred to the HSCA experts on many points but remained troubled by the striking differences in the chins when the rifle pictures are compared to pictures of the real Oswald.

In 1967 George de Mohrenschildt brought forward another copy of the infamous picture. He claimed to have discovered it among some of his possessions that had languished in storage since he went to Haiti in 1963. The photo was allegedly wrapped in paper and nestled in a stack of old phonograph records gathering dust in a Dallas warehouse.[11] Unlike the two photos found by police in 1963, George's had an inscription on the back. It read, "To my friend George, from Lee Oswald 5/IV/63." There was an additional inscription as well—one most damning to Oswald. It was written in Russian Cyrillic script. Translated, it read, "Hunter of fascists ha ha ha!!!"[12]

How self-incriminating! Except that the "Hunter of fascists" inscription was not written by Oswald. According to the House Committee's handwriting experts, it was not Oswald's handwriting; neither was it that of Marina Oswald, George de Mohrenschildt, or his wife Jeanne.[13]

The experts ruled out Marina and the de Mohrenschildts because the inscription had been written by someone not versed in the Cyrillic alphabet, while these three were. This deduction does not preclude the possibility that George de Mohrenschildt wrote it himself, in deliberately defective Cyrillic. The experts did not exclude his participation based on scientific analysis of handwriting samples. In this sense their work was inconclusive.

In 1967, when de Mohrenschildt brought forward the new photo, the Warren Commission Report and the authenticity of the original photos were under sharp attack by critics. If the photos were not a forgery, the autograph certainly was not authentic.

In the mid to late 1970s new and troublesome information surfaced which further clouded the murky record regarding the number, origin, and chain of possession of the infamous photos. In 1976 the Senate Intelligence Committee was examining the roles played by intelligence agencies in investigating the president's assassination. The Committee discovered yet another picture showing a different pose of Oswald with the rifle—a photo that seemed to be in the same series as those previously made part of the official record.[14] It was possessed by the widow of a Dallas police officer who said her late husband obtained it while performing his official duties after the assassination. He had told her that one day it would be very valuable. The most serious question spawned by this revelation is not the efficacy of historical souvenir-hunting by a police officer but why an item of such obvious importance to the case never found its way into the official record. Just how many of these controversial photos were there? Who had them, when, and how?

The matter is further complicated by the 1978 assertions of Dallas commercial photographer Robert Hester.[15] He had done photo work for the Dallas police and FBI following the assassination. Hester contended that he saw a rifle picture, or some version of it, on the very day of the president's murder, one day before the police allegedly found the photos among Oswald's possessions. Moreover, Hester remembered the rifle photo he saw as being a color transparency. All the known photos are black and white.

Another key evidentiary item was the "sniper's nest" discovered on the sixth floor of the Texas School Book Depository. According to the official conclusions of the Warren Commission and House Committee, depository employee Oswald, acting entirely alone, stacked two dozen boxes full of books in a semi-circle shield to hide himself from fellow workers. He also placed several boxes near the window so that he could shoot from behind them. In 1978 the House Committee's panel of photographic experts made a rather startling discovery which the Committee all but ignored.

There were two photographs of the sniper's nest window taken shortly after the shooting ended. They were snapped by two different photographers: bystander James Powell and professional photographer Tom Dillard, who was riding in the press vehicle in the presidential motorcade. Using sophisticated, high-tech methods of analysis that compared these photos to others, the experts verified the testimony of the photographers that both pictures were taken after the last shot had been fired at the president. The Dillard photo was taken first; Powell's was taken sometime between 30 seconds and two minutes after Dillard's.[16]

In the Dillard photo only two book cartons are visible in the window. The panel discovered that the Powell photo manifests "several additional boxes."[17] To the naked eye it appears to be either two or three new boxes. The experts conducted extensive trigonometric calculations and shadow analyses to see if the change was real—if the objects were really additional boxes rather than images created by shadows or a different viewpoint. The conclusion was that they were real: "The additional boxes visible in the Powell photograph were moved during the interval between the Dillard and Powell photographs."[18]

The Committee's final report blandly states that "there is apparent rearranging of boxes within two minutes after the last shot was fired at President Kennedy."[19] This single sentence is the only mention of what is actually an evidentiary bombshell whose logical implications the Committee refused to confront. Describing this as "rearrangement" gave the reader the false impression that a box could have fallen or been nudged. What the experts actually discovered is that someone was constructing what would become known as the sniper's nest *after* all of the shots were fired.

Inside the book depository there were no employees on the sixth floor during or immediately after the shooting (except, allegedly, Oswald). No one saw Oswald leaving the sniper's nest or departing the sixth floor. Law enforcement personnel were not yet on the upper floors and would not discover the nest until nearly a half hour later. Who was up there feathering the nest? Was someone planting the rifle and shells and creating the nest to incriminate Oswald?

Why would Oswald move extra 50-pound boxes into place after shooting the president? Just after the shooting, he was encountered by a Dallas policeman and the depository manager as he stood calmly drinking a soda on the second floor. Reconstructions by investigating authorities place this encounter at between one minute and 30 seconds to two minutes after the gunfire. There has been controversy about whether Oswald could escape the sixth-floor nest, hide the rifle, and descend four flights of stairs—the elevator was not available to him—in time for the encounter. Secret Service reenactments had Oswald down in time, but some corners were cut (throwing the rifle down instead of concealing it among the boxes). Even then there was little time to spare. It simply would not have been possible for Oswald to be up on the sixth floor moving boxes (possibly up to one half minute after the last shot) and arrive on the second floor in time to be seen by the officer. Oswald was neither breathing hard nor acting suspiciously. The policeman, who pointed his gun at Oswald, let him go when the Depository manager said he worked there. The officer then went upstairs in search of the gunman.

There are also oddities about the evidence linking Oswald to the alleged murder weapon. For example, all official reports and most historians and journalists assert that his fingerprint was found on the alleged murder weapon. But this evidence would never have been allowed in court because it was not properly validated. After Dallas authorities had twice told the press that no Oswald prints were found on the rifle, and after the FBI laboratory in Washington examined the weapon and found no prints, it was flown back to Dallas. Shortly thereafter, local authorities announced they had found Oswald's palm print on a portion of the rifle that can only be accessed when it is disassembled. Because the requisite procedure of photographing the alleged print before it was lifted from the rifle was not followed, there is no way to certify that the print came from the weapon instead of from Oswald's cell.[20]

Another suspect item of evidence relates to the mail-ordering of the rifle. Adrian Alba operated the Crescent City Garage in New Orleans, located next to Reily Coffee where Oswald worked. In addition to serving the general public, the garage housed and maintained U.S. government cars. The local Secret Service and FBI offices were nearby. Oswald frequented the garage's waiting room on his breaks; there was a coffee pot and a soda machine. There were also numerous gun magazines because Alba was a hobbyist. According to Alba, Oswald manifested a keen interest in how to order guns by mail and asked questions about it.[21] Oswald would leaf through the gun magazines and occasionally borrow one.

After the assassination authorities found among Oswald's effects two coupons for mail-ordering guns. One was an advertisement offering the Mannlicher-Carcano rifle from Klein's Sporting Goods in Chicago. Moreover, researcher Paul Hoch discovered that the jagged edges of the clipping perfectly meshed with those found in one of the magazines obtained by the FBI from Alba's waiting room. Oswald's fingerprint was allegedly found on the magazine itself.

There are problems with this evidence. Before the FBI and Secret Service descended on the garage, a stranger showed up at 9:00 AM the day after the assassination. The man told an employee that he was one of Alba's "very best friends" and had come to borrow some magazines. He was allowed into the waiting room. Then, he simply disappeared.[22] Alba does not know who the stranger was. But someone had unsupervised access to the magazines before the FBI seized them. Destroying evidence could not have been the stranger's mission since an Oswald print and a space matching the ripped-out coupon were found in one of the magazines: planting evidence seems a more likely possibility.

The alleged Oswald magazine found in Alba's garage was a June 1963 issue of *American Rifleman*. However, records produced by Klein's Sporting Goods showed that "Oswald" had ordered his rifle from the February issue.[23]

Following the crime, information targeting Oswald as the suspect surfaced very quickly—under mysterious circumstances. He was focused on as the exclusive suspect at a time when numerous Depository employees had not been accounted for or cleared. There was no logical reason to single out Oswald. He had been confronted on the second floor by a policeman and the depository manager within minutes after the shooting and had, in a sense, passed the test by not appearing out of breath or suspicious. Moreover, police would pursue him with information that could not have come from the available, overt sources.

Shortly after Oswald encountered the policeman inside the building, he departed and took a bus to his Dallas apartment. Why did the police pursue him? Roy Truly, the Depository manager, claimed to have brought Oswald's name to the attention of authorities after he and the policeman had encountered Oswald on the second floor. According to an FBI report of November 23, Truly "tried to account for the employees under his supervision about fifteen minutes after this [encounter] and OSWALD was missing. He advised Chief Lumpkin and shortly thereafter Captain FRITZ, both of the Dallas Police Department, of this."[24] As Truly described it to the Warren Commission:

> When I noticed this boy was missing, I told Chief Lumpkin, "We have a man missing here." I first called down to the other warehouse and had Mr. Akin pull the application of this boy so I could get—quickly get his address in Irving and his general description, so I could be more accurate than I would be.[25]

One would think that even though Oswald had left the Depository, he would not be at the very top of Truly's suspect list. Truly and the policeman had, in a sense, already checked out Oswald. He was by no means the only employee unaccounted for. Fifty people worked there at various times. Truly had no punch-card system to determine precisely when each employee entered and left. It would have been virtually impossible for him to glance around quickly and accurately determine who was or was not there and who had come and gone.

At least a dozen employees besides Oswald were unaccounted for. There is no indication that these men were accounted for, and were therefore beyond suspicion, until after Truly allegedly told the police about Oswald.[26] Only Oswald was pursued, almost instantly.

Most likely, the Dallas police did not target Oswald because of the information provided by Truly. The chain of this alleged information has too many missing links. Even if the chain were complete, Truly did not have the information that police came up with.

Captain Will Fritz told the Warren Commission, "Mr. Truly then came with another officer and told me that a *Lee Harvey Oswald* [italics added] had left the building."[27] Not quite. Truly actually told Fritz that "Lee Oswald" was missing.[28] By the time Fritz testified before the Warren

Commission, the whole world knew the alleged assassin as "Lee Harvey Oswald." But at the time of the assassination, Truly knew his employee only as "Lee Oswald." Oswald had never listed his middle name on any of his employment forms—the very forms Truly allegedly consulted so he could give the police Oswald's address.[29] Neither did Oswald ever call himself by his full name when interacting with fellow employees on various jobs.

The only address listed in Oswald's Depository employment records was that of 2515 West 5th Street, Irving, Texas, where he and Marina and his two young daughters stayed at the Paine home. But the Dallas police were operating several steps ahead of Truly's information, even though he was supposedly their source. Magically, officers did not rush out to Irving but instead showed up at Oswald's current Dallas apartment at 1026 N. Beckley Street. The Depository had no knowledge of the N. Beckley address, and neither did Marina Oswald or the Paines. Oswald had kept it secret. Author Robert Sam Anson also asserts that when police arrived at N. Beckley they asked the landlady the whereabouts of a "Harvey Lee Oswald."[30]

On the list of Depository employees compiled by the Criminal Intelligence Section of the Dallas police, twelve employees were unaccounted for. At the very top of the list was their first and only suspect, "Harvey Lee Oswald."[31]

Neither the Dallas address nor the name "Harvey Lee" could have come from Truly or depository records. Where did this information come from? It is clear from post-assassination investigations of the Secret Service's procedures that the Service's Protective Research Section had no file on Oswald. He did not manifest any of the characteristics that would cause the Service to open a file on him, given their 1963 data system.[32] The FBI was not in contact with the Dallas police about Oswald until after his arrest.[33] FBI agent James Hosty, who oversaw Oswald's FBI files, referred to the former Soviet defector as "Lee Oswald" when discussing Lee's case with the police after the arrest.[34] FBI files on Oswald prior to the assassination never—to the author's knowledge, based on examination—referred to him as "Harvey Lee." The Dallas police claimed to have no files on Oswald whatsoever, and none were ever found. Army intelligence in San Antonio checked their files following Oswald's arrest. They found a file on a "Lee Harvey Oswald."[35]

There is no known instance in which Oswald ever used the name "Harvey Lee" Oswald—not for any of his myriad cards, letters, post office boxes, and so on. He did use the alias "A. J. Hidell." He used the name "O. H. Lee" to rent the Dallas apartment that he moved into the day before he took a job at the Depository. He used the name "Osborne" when ordering FPCC application forms from a New Orleans printer. He generally referred to himself as "Lee Oswald." He never used "Harvey Lee," yet it appeared on the top of the list of Depository employees.[36]

There exists an intelligence practice of having two files on a person— John Baker Doe and Baker John Doe. The regular name is used for overt material; the transposed one, for covert material. With technical veracity, an intelligence organization can say that it has little or no material on John Baker Doe.

The name "Harvey Oswald" did appear two times, without the "Lee," in two of the legend-building incidents. "Harvey Oswald" appeared at the Selective Service Office in Austin to complain about his Marine Corps discharge (while the real Oswald was making his trip to Mexico). Then in November, "Harvey Oswald" allegedly tried to cash a check in a supermarket in Irving, Texas. The real Oswald was not in Irving at the time.

There is an intriguing but unexplained reference to "Harvey" in Oswald's CIA file. In 1978 former CIA director Richard Helms was testifying before the House Assassinations Committee when he was asked about a CIA memo dated November 25, 1963. The document mentioned consideration of "the laying on of interviews with Lee Harvey Oswald" in 1960, which caused Committee counsel Goldsmith to ask if the CIA had ever contacted Oswald. Helms responded negatively (this testimony is excerpted from Committee hearings and appears in Appendix B). Goldsmith also asked about the "Harvey" reference:[37]

Michael Goldsmith: I would like to draw your attention to the last line on this memorandum. It makes reference to the Harvey story.

Richard Helms: Yes.

Goldsmith: Do you know what Harvey story that is referring to?

Helms: No, I do not.

In the absence of an Agency explanation one can only speculate as to the reference's meaning. Did it relate to the CIA's own data on Oswald? Was the "story" one of the incidents in which an Oswald impostor used the name "Harvey Lee"? Or did it refer to William Harvey, the blustering, gun-toting CIA officer who headed the Agency's Executive Action Unit, formed to assassinate foreign leaders. We will probably never know.

The Criminal Intelligence Section of the Dallas police sent out a cable the night of the assassination. It was a secret one and was not declassified until May 1973. It originated with police intelligence, and then went from the 4th Army Command in Texas to the U.S. Strike Command at MacDill Air Force Base in Florida (a rapid deployment force.)[38] The urgent message contained two false statements: "Don Stringfellow, Intelligence Section, Dallas Police Department, notified 112th Intelligence Group, this headquarters, that information obtained from Oswald reveals that he had defected to Cuba in 1959 and is a card carrying member of the Communist Party."[39]

In Mexico only two months earlier, "Oswald" had tried to go to Cuba for the first time and had proffered a Communist Party ID card, although the FBI knew that the real Oswald had never joined. There was no indication from Oswald's interrogators that he asserted the false data. Was the police intelligence unit just sloppy or was it being fed information from federal intelligence sources trying to blame Castro for the president's assassination? At least one intelligence agency had direct ties to local police. Elsewhere, the author has documented the extensive, clandestine relationship between the CIA and the intelligence units of major metropolitan police departments during the 1960s and 1970s.[40] The CIA also seems to have been involved in one post-assassination attempt to portray Oswald as a hired gun working for Castro: the story of "D."

The day after Jack Ruby murdered Oswald in the basement of the Dallas police station, a Castro-conspiracy story cropped up. The source, a man identified only as "D," came to the U.S. Embassy in Mexico City and asserted that he had directly witnessed Oswald plotting to assassinate the president.[41] D alleged that he had observed Oswald at the Cuban consulate in Mexico receiving $6,500 from two men. According to D, one man said to Oswald that he wanted someone killed. Oswald replied, "You're not man enough. I can do it."[42]

D's revelation was flashed throughout Washington to the FBI, the State Department, and the Johnson White House by the CIA's Mexican station.[43] But why should this story be believed? The answer came 24 hours later. The Agency set the wires humming again with a follow-up message: information from a "sensitive and reliable" CIA source had confirmed D's story (electronic surveillance of the Cuban consulate perhaps?).[44]

Richard Helms brought D's story to the Warren Commission.[45] In his memo describing the evidence he did not reveal D's identity to the Commission. It remained for the FBI to discover that D was Gilberto Alvarado, a Nicaraguan intelligence agent who claimed that his mission was to spy on the Cuban consulate in Mexico.[46]

Despite the CIA's supposedly "reliable" corroboration of D's story, it did not hold up under scrutiny. First, as with so many other incriminating incidents, Oswald was elsewhere when D had him plotting in the Cuban consulate: he was visiting the New Orleans office of the Louisiana State Unemployment Commission.[47] D finally retracted his story and claimed that he had dreamed up the incident as a way of gaining entry to the United States so that he could participate in anti-Castro activities there. When the State Department continued to be interested in his story— perhaps in light of his less-than-persuasive account of why he had perpetrated the hoax—Alvarado retracted his retraction, only to be judged a liar by a polygraph machine.[48] The FBI (which had primary investigative responsibility in the assassination) was by this time understandably curious about who, in fact, Alvarado was and what lay at the bottom of his multilayered deceit. The Bureau did not have a chance to find out. The Agency thwarted the Bureau's repeated attempts to interrogate D.[49] The FBI was frozen out; the bizarre incident was finished.

The machinations of intelligence-related intrigue and deception that surrounded Oswald in life from Moscow to New Orleans to Mexico to Dallas continued after his death. On a long trail of rather crudely executed fabrications from Sylvia Odio's living room to the shabby, stucco Cuban consulate in Mexico City to the sixth floor of the Texas School Book Depository, the legend of a violent, unstable pro-Castroite was built on a foundation created by Oswald himself, in his role as agent-provocateur.

10

Cover-Ups

And ye shall know the truth and the truth shall make you free.
John: XXIII, inscribed on the marble wall of the
lobby at CIA headquarters in Langley, Virginia

CIA Inspector General Lyman Kirkpatrick described the ideal covert operation as one that would remain secret "from inception to eternity."[1]

The CIA has continuously obstructed pursuit of the truth about Oswald. In its dealings with the Warren Commission, the Rockefeller Commission, and the House Assassinations Committee, it has been both deceptive and recalcitrant in answering the questions posed about Oswald's links to U.S. intelligence and his associations and activities at the time of the assassination.

In 1963–64 the Agency tried to squelch what the Warren Commission had termed the "dirty rumor," that Oswald worked for U.S. intelligence. The Commission worried about the rumor, only to be told by one of its members that inquiries into this matter were likely to go nowhere because it was "a terribly hard thing to disprove. . . . How do you disprove it?"[2]

These were the words of Commissioner Allen Dulles, and his expertise on this matter was indisputable. Dulles was one of the CIA's founding fathers. He was consulted in 1947 when the Agency was created by Congress. The following year President Truman appointed him to a three-man commission whose task was to monitor the progress of the fledgling intelligence agency. Truman made Dulles deputy director of the CIA in 1951; Eisenhower made him director in 1953.[3] Dulles's 11-year reign came to an abrupt and rancorous end in 1961 when President Kennedy fired him during the post Bay of Pigs shake-up of the Agency.

In what must surely rank as one of the more historically significant conflicts of interest, Dulles was appointed by President Johnson to the commission responsible for assessing whether Oswald was linked to the CIA and whether the CIA was linked to the assassination. During most of a crucial period concerning Oswald's possible relationship to the Agency (when he defected to the Soviet Union), Dulles was serving as CIA director. Thus he was in the position of investigating events that occurred under his own stewardship.

Dulles admonished his commission colleagues that proving that Oswald was not a CIA agent was all but impossible because of the Agency's characteristics. It compartmentalized its activities, did not keep paper records of all of its work, coded much of its data in "hieroglyphics," and sometimes would not reveal the identity of its agents even when its officers were put under oath.[4] After arguing that a definitive conclusion was not possible, Dulles did a complete turnabout and offered to provide one. In order to assuage the continuing concerns of his fellow commissioners, he said he could produce an affidavit that Oswald was not an Agency employee:

> Depending as of the time we are talking about, I might have a little problem on that—having been Director until November 1961, it would depend upon as of what time he was supposed to have been an agent of the CIA. The only problem—there is no problem so far as making an affidavit to the period up to November 26, 1961, if you want me to.[5]

If the Commission needed sworn affidavits to forget the dirty rumor, the Agency was prepared to provide a bevy of them, surely at Dulles's suggestion. In direct conflict with what Dulles had told the Commission about the impossibility of a definitive conclusion, the CIA prepared four draft affidavits that stated that Oswald had never been connected with the Agency, either directly or indirectly. These documents were never signed, notarized, or forwarded to the Commission. Four identical affidavits were prepared for four of the CIA's top administrators: Deputy Director Marshall Carter, Deputy Director for Intelligence Ray Cline, Director of Security Robert Bannerman, and Deputy Director for Plans Richard Helms. The statements asserted the following:

Lee Harvey Oswald was not an agent, employee, or informant of the Central Intelligence Agency;

the Agency never contacted him, interviewed him, talked with him, or received or solicited any reports or information from him, or communicated with him, directly or indirectly, in any other manner;

the Agency never furnished him any funds or money, or compensated him, directly or indirectly, in any fashion;

Lee Harvey Oswald was never associated or connected, directly or indirectly, in any way whatsoever with the Agency.[6]

This denial would later be used, almost verbatim, by CIA Director John McCone in his testimony before the Warren Commission.

A CIA internal memorandum declassified in 1976 reveals that Dulles met with a CIA administrator (probably James Jesus Angleton) who was sent by Deputy Director Richard Helms to discuss "certain questions which Mr. Dulles feels the Warren Commission may pose to CIA."[7] First on the agenda, not surprisingly, was the dirty rumor. Dulles counseled that the allegation that Oswald was connected with the CIA should be met with a reply that was "straightforward and to the point." The reply should contain language "which made it clear that Lee Harvey Oswald was never an employee or agent of CIA." Furthermore, Dulles instructed, the response should state that "neither CIA nor anyone acting on CIA's behalf was ever in contact or communication with Oswald." The memo concludes by expressing agreement with Dulles that "a carefully phrased denial of the charges of involvement with Oswald seemed most appropriate."

Dulles's helpful suggestions to his Commission colleagues were not confined to intelligence matters. At an executive session early on in the Commission's deliberations, Dulles sought to relieve the group of much of its investigative burden before any witnesses had been heard. He wanted to put the Kennedy assassination in what he offered as historical context— that it fit the pattern of U.S. history in which assassinations were perpetrated by lone gunmen.[8]

Allen Dulles: I've got a few extra copies of a book that I passed out to our Counsel. Did I give it to you, Mr. Chief Justice?

Chief Justice Earl Warren: I don't think so.

Dulles: It's a book written about ten years ago giving the background of seven attempts on the lives of presidents.

Warren: I have not seen it.

> *Dulles*: It's a fascinating book, but you'll find a pattern running through here that I think we'll find in this present case. I hate to give you a paperback, but that's all there is.
>
> *Rep. Gerald Ford (Rep. MI)*: When was the book written?
>
> *Dulles*: 1952. The last one is the attack on Truman. There you have a plot, but these other cases are all habitual going back to the attack on Jackson in 1835. I found it very interesting.
>
> *John J. McCloy*: The Lincoln assassination was a plot?
>
> *Dulles*: Yes, but one man was so dominant that it almost wasn't a plot.

Dulles's conflict of interest edged toward obstruction of justice when he maintained close contact with his former colleagues at the Agency throughout the Commission's investigation. James Jesus Angleton, the CIA counterintelligence chief who, for a time, served as liaison officer for the Agency dealings with the Commission, told Congress in 1976 that he "informally discussed the assassination with Dulles while the investigation was in progress."[9] In fact, Dulles saw fit to coach CIA officers concerning their testimony before the Commission. A heavily censored document obtained from the CIA under the Freedom of Information Act reveals that Dulles coached his former colleagues on dealing effectively with the dirty rumor when confronting the Commission.[10]

Angleton, who was in contact with Dulles, in turn coached the FBI as to how the Bureau might look out for CIA interests. The Bureau functioned as the Commission's primary investigative arm and provided it with most of the information used to write its final report. Angleton passed information to the Bureau concerning the Commission's investigation.[11] He also wrote a memo instructing the FBI as to how it should respond when queried about the dirty rumor. To avoid different replies from the two agencies (FBI and CIA) Angleton offered the CIA's response in writing so that Director Hoover would be sure to respond as follows:

1. Q: Was Oswald ever an agent of the CIA?

   A: No.

2. Q: Does the CIA have any evidence showing that a conspiracy existed to assassinate President Kennedy?

   A: No.[12]

Dulles had two routes of influence: direct influence, from within the Commission; and indirect influence, from himself to Angleton (and other of his former colleagues), and then from Angleton to the FBI back to the Commission. All channels carried the same message: Oswald was a lone assassin with no Agency affiliation.

The CIA not only insisted that Oswald was not their agent but also that he was not even a subject of continuing interest. Despite his defection to the Soviet Union and its possible links to the U–2, the Agency claimed to have no interest in him when he returned to the United States, to the extent that the CIA claimed never to have contacted him.

Dulles's successor as CIA director, John McCone, testified before the Commission using the same broad denial that had appeared in the unused affidavits:

> My examination has resulted in the conclusion that Lee Harvey Oswald was not an agent, employee, or informant of the Central Intelligence Agency. The Agency never contacted him, interviewed him, or talked with him, or received or solicited any reports from him, or communicated with him directly or in any other manner. . . . Oswald was never associated or connected directly or indirectly in any way whatsoever with the Agency.[13]

McCone, who had been a Wall Street lawyer before Kennedy brought him in to head the Agency, provided this iron-clad guarantee based on the expertise of his deputies, who were more knowledgeable than he. Outsider McCone's track record for keeping tabs on the clandestine careerists was not good; he was fired by President Johnson, in part, for not knowing about his own Agency's assassination attempts on Castro.[14]

Richard Helms, who in 1963 was the CIA's Deputy Director for Plans, extended McCone's guarantee of disassociation from Oswald even further, to include the minds of CIA personnel. He told the Commission, under oath, that the Agency had nothing on Oswald, "either in records or in the mind of any individuals that there was any contact had, or even contemplated with him."[15] Such extreme assurances now ring hollow, if not suspicious, because their absolute nature is in conflict with the Agency's own claims (from Dulles as well as others) concerning the impossibility of such assurances, given the CIA's complex internal security procedures and its convoluted chains of command. Moreover, a CIA document previously described directly refutes Helms's claim. The November 25, 1963 memo refers to events in 1960 and states that Helms had discussed "the laying on of interviews with Lee Harvey Oswald."

Despite the steadfast denials there were hints of an Agency interest in Oswald. A photo of him taken in· 1961 in a public square in Minsk happened to turn up in Warren Commission materials. The source of the photo was the CIA, even though it claimed that it had never monitored Oswald's defection. The Commission noted that the picture was allegedly taken by a "tourist" who did not know Oswald. It concluded that the photo represented nothing more than coincidence.[16]

The CIA's explanation was that the picture was one of a batch of photos routinely obtained from tourists traveling abroad.[17] There were, the Agency claimed, 160 pictures in this batch, and Oswald by chance happened to appear in one of them. It is a startling coincidence: out of millions of people in the Soviet Union and tens of thousands in Minsk, Oswald is accidentally, but clearly, photographed. Then, out of the 160 photos, the Agency again just happens to pick Oswald's as one of five selected to be retained. Why, if the Agency had no interest in him whatsoever? The two CIA employees who handled the photos testified before the House Select Committee on Assassinations and provided two less than compelling explanations. One stated that the Oswald photo was retained because it also included the picture of a Soviet Intourist Guide; the other stated that the picture was kept because it showed a crane in the background.[18]

In accepting these explanations we are asked to believe that CIA data gathering is so detailed, so catholic that it finds Intourist Guides and cranes to be subjects of inherent interest, while defectors to the USSR who possess knowledge about the Agency's spy plane are not subjects of interest.

In 1977 the House Assassinations Committee was interested in Richard E. Snyder, the consular official in the U.S. Embassy in Moscow who handled Oswald's defection and return. Some researchers suspected that Snyder was a CIA agent using diplomatic cover.[19] Snyder testified to the House Committee that he had worked for the CIA for only 11 months in 1949–50, and that he had no contact with the Agency between 1950 and 1970, when he wrote to inquire about employment.

The Committee requested Snyder's CIA file. They discovered that it had been "red flagged," and maintained on a "segregated" basis, because of a "DCI [Director of Central Intelligence] statement" and a "matter of cover" concerning Snyder.[20] The Committee pursued this and discovered that the DCI statement in question "presumably" referred to comments made about the Oswald case in 1974 by then Deputy Director for Plans Richard Helms.

Snyder's file had been red flagged so that all inquiries about him would be referred to a particular office—the Directorate of Operations. This would seem to be very sensitive treatment for the dossier of a pure diplomat whose only relationship to the Oswald case was to process a defection in which the Agency claimed to have no interest. The Agency was unable to explain the reference to "cover" because, said the Committee, "according to its [CIA] records, Snyder had never been assigned any cover while employed [by the CIA]."[21] Regardless of Snyder's status, the reference to cover could have another meaning which the Committee never considered: it could have referred to Oswald's cover.

The Committee did not regard the Agency's explanations about Snyder's file as "satisfactory." For one thing, the file revealed that he had been working for the Agency as a "spotter" for the year 1956–57, after his contact with the Agency was supposed to have ended. As a spotter Snyder worked at a university campus in the United States where his role was to obtain "access to others who might be going to the Soviet Union."[22]

A March 17, 1964 internal CIA memorandum, obtained by the author from the Agency's Kennedy-assassination file, has a paragraph describing Snyder's CIA service. The two page document is entitled "Comment Regarding Article Alleging Oswald was interviewed by CIA Employees." It states the following:

> He [Snyder] entered on duty with CIA on 8 November 1949 as a GS–9 ($4600.00 per annum). According to his personnel file he was assigned to OPC [Office of Policy Coordination] and was slated to serve in Tokyo (the file contains no entry showing that he actually served in Tokyo). He did, however, serve in Heidelberg beginning in March 1950. While in Germany he apparently resigned effective 26 September 1950 in order to assume a position with HICOG [United States High Commissioner's Office in Germany]. There are no further entries in his personnel file.

The Office of Policy Coordination (OPC) was created in 1948 as the covert action arm of the U.S. government. Its mandate included paramilitary operations and political and economic warfare. OPC's budget and personnel were drawn from the CIA, but it was headed by the Secretary of State and it reported to the State and Defense Departments, bypassing the Director of the CIA. OPC was abolished in 1952 when Allen Dulles brought covert action more firmly under the stewardship of the Director of Central Intelligence. OPC conducted extensive operations in Germany and carried on some of the most secret covert actions of the Cold War. In 1949 it had only 300–400 employees.

Snyder's "apparent" resignation from OPC to join HICOG would not necessarily place him outside the context of intelligence operations. For example, CIA officer Michael Burke is described in U.S. foreign service listings as HICOG's "chief of plans and policy development" within its "office of intelligence" from 1951–54. But he also was appointed as a CIA European station chief in early 1951 and worked on both covert action and espionage activities, such as the formation of a U.S. spy ring within the Soviet bloc.

The 1964 CIA memo summarizing Snyder's work for the Agency contains no reference to his stint as a "spotter" in 1956–57. This involvement was discovered by HSCA based on the Snyder file that the Committee obtained from the Agency. Snyder did work for the State Department in Tokyo. According to the department's biographic register, he was at the U.S. embassy there from 1954–56 and went back two months after returning Oswald's passport to him. Snyder had arrived in Moscow four months before Oswald's defection. Oswald's 1957 service at Atsugi Airbase (only a few miles southwest of Tokyo) did not coincide with Snyder's tenure at the U.S. Embassy in Tokyo.

The 1964 CIA memo also states that "In March 1959 (probably just before Snyder's departure for Moscow), State requested that he be given two weeks of the OBS course (probably ORR's training in the Soviet Order of Battle)."

ORR was the CIA's Office of Research and Reports. "Order of battle" refers to patterns and practices of deploying military forces. Most likely, "OBS" was a course in estimating and understanding Soviet military deployment. One wonders if Oswald took the same course. He certainly had a rather singular interest in Soviet military patterns.

Regarding Oswald's file, HSCA further discovered an apparent shortfall of documents. A 1964 internal CIA memorandum (stamped "Secret, Eyes Only") stated that no fewer than 37 documents, including 25 cables, were missing from the file. The Agency explained that the documents were not really "missing" but had been checked out of the file at the time the memo was written in 1964. This explanation might have carried more weight if the CIA had proved that the papers were returned, by producing them for the Committee. But the documents were never provided.[23]

The Agency's sensitivity concerning Oswald's case as it related to other defectors is manifested in another internal memo dated April 5, 1972, found by the author in the CIA's general file on the JFK assassination. It states, "Today the [deleted] staff advised me that the Director had relayed via the DDP [Deputy Director for Plans] the instruction that the agency was not, under any circumstances, to make inquiries or ask questions of any source or defector about Oswald."[24]

With regard to mail being sent to and from the Soviet Union by Americans, the Agency was interested in everyone's mail—except, of course, Oswald's. In 1976, during hearings unconnected with the assassination, the Senate Intelligence Committee discovered that a massive CIA project to intercept mail to and from the Soviet Union had been in operation during Oswald's defection (1959–62).[25] Under this program thousands of letters were routinely opened and photographed over a period of years. A special laboratory was set up at LaGuardia Airport in New York. CIA agents opened bags of Soviet-bound mail and tested for secret coding and invisible ink.[26] Yet the CIA's mail-intercept file contains only a single Oswald letter, written to his mother in 1961. Oswald's family kept copies of more than 50 letters exchanged during his stay in Russia.

Why did the Agency have only one Oswald letter? The explanation to the House Committee was that the mail intercept "only operated four days a week, and even then proceeded on a sampling basis."[27] We are asked to believe the implausible: that letters from ordinary tourists were of interest while 49 letters to and from a defector were missed because he was of no special interest. For its domestic mail-intercept program the Agency developed a lengthy list of individuals and organizations to be targeted. The number of Soviet defector was small and, logically, their mail should have been of particular interest.

The CIA's vaunted data-gathering network was a sieve when it came to Oswald. He would trip through organizations, buildings, and political contexts in a variety of geographic locations in the United States and abroad, and extensive CIA surveillance would always miss him. Cameras would malfunction when Oswald passed through; huge networks of Agency spies and informers would miss him while he was in their presence; data-gathering efforts would produce extensive files concerning Cuban politics in the United States (both pro- and anti-Castro), but would never produce a jot concerning Oswald's protracted involvements in these arenas.

Among the artifacts discovered after the assassination was Oswald's "historic diary," found among his effects. It is purportedly his account of life in the Soviet Union during his defection. While the House Committee's experts certified the authenticity of the handwriting, they also concluded that the "diary" was written in one or two sittings rather than over the span of two and a half years that Oswald spent in Russia.[28] The diary's pidgin-English style conflicts sharply with the quite articulate way in which Oswald spoke, and with other examples of his writing.

In this letter written in 1963, for example, he expresses himself quite well, although by no means flawlessly (there are spelling and syntactical errors):

As you will notice on the membership blank there is a place for those who *do* wish to subscribe to the national mailings for a fee of $5.00, that fee will go directly to you in New York.

As soon as any member *has* paid dues adding up to five dollars in any year, I will forward that fee to you and then you may handle it as if it was a usual application for membership in the national F.P.C.C.[29]

In marked contrast, here is a description from the "historic diary" of Lee and Marina's wedding, replete with horrendous errors of spelling and syntax:

We are married. At her aunts home we have a dinner reception for about 20 friends and neboribos who wish us happiness (in spite of my origin and accept which was in general rather disquiting to any Russian since for. are very rare in the soviet Union even tourist. After an evening of eating and drinking in which . . . started a fright and the fuse blow on an overload circite we take our leave and walk the 15 minutes to our home.[30]

It has not been established when and where this "diary" was written, much less why. One would imagine that the strikingly odd syntax would have raised some eyebrows at our nation's premier spy agency. Not so. In fact, the CIA used the diary to analyze the time, motion, and events of Oswald's defection. It became the Agency's baseline for scrutinizing whether he had been recruited by the Soviets as a spy.[31] Based partly on the diary, Deputy Director Richard Helms assured the Warren Commission that there was nothing unusual about Oswald's defection.[32]

The authenticity of the diary was never questioned by the Agency. Even if Oswald did write it, choosing the style of a Russian struggling through elementary English, it is not an authentic document. It was used as a contemporaneous record but was concocted in two or more sittings. Was the Agency especially trusting of the Soviets, especially incompetent in analyzing the diary, or did it have a level of knowledge concerning Oswald, his defection, and even his diary that precluded the question of authenticity—a question that seemed so obvious to those less informed about what Oswald was really doing in the Soviet Union.

There was plenty of cause for concern. The U.S. Embassy in Moscow notified the State Department that Oswald had left his Moscow hotel and his whereabouts were unknown. This disappearance lasted for nearly six weeks. Was he being debriefed? Attending a Soviet spy school? Despite the embassy's concern, the Warren Commission decided that he "probably" did not leave Moscow and was really hole up in his hotel room—a conclusion based largely on his diary.[33] But, as Sylvia Meagher perceptively noted, the "diary" had only one blanket entry dated November 16 to December 30. Meagher asks why Oswald made more detailed, daily entries before this period but could not find time to "record his meals and emotions during a six week period of being hole up in his hotel room."[34] This question apparently never troubled the Agency.

In 1975 President Gerald Ford (a member of the Warren Commission) appointed the Rockefeller Commission to investigate domestic spying abuses by the CIA. The Commission also looked into possible CIA involvement in the assassination. Its chief counsel was David Belin, who had been a counsel for the Warren Commission and had written a book defending its conclusions.[35] In 1975 one subject of intense curiosity among researchers was the Dallas chapter of the anti-Castro commando group Alpha–66, headquartered on Harlendale Street at the time of the assassination. As previously described, the CIA-sponsored group was well armed and its leader had been mistaken for Oswald. Paul Hoch, one of the most scholarly and respected assassination researchers, brought this matter to the attention of the Rockefeller Commission.

It was not until 1982, with the release of CIA documents to researchers using the Freedom of Information Act, that the Agency's response to the Rockefeller Commission was made public. The terse, nonsensical reply was that Agency files contained "no record of any CIA contact with an anti-Castro group in Dallas. No Cuban organization is listed in the 1963 Dallas telephone directory. Dallas city map and 1963 criss-cross directory reveal no street named Harlendale."[36]

Beyond the ludicrous notion that the way to find Alpha–66 is to check the phone book—presumably in the Yellow Pages under "commandos"—there is, and was in 1963, a Harlendale street in Dallas. It is a long one, nearly impossible to miss.

In 1984 I initiated a Freedom of Information Act request to obtain Rockefeller Commission documents dealing with CIA activities in Dallas in 1963. The Commission's papers are held by the Ford Presidential Library in Ann Arbor, Michigan. Don W. Wilson, then director of the library, denied my request, claiming that the documents are part of President Ford's papers and "did not originate as Federal records". Thus the Freedom of Information Act did not apply.[37]

What is perhaps more disturbing than the CIA's protracted record of cover-up concerning Lee Harvey Oswald is that in 25 years of being queried by various commissions and committees, all possessing official standing, the Agency has never been compelled to account for its actions or inactions regarding Oswald, his file, or matters of central relevance to him.

11

Beyond Disinformation

It [the CIA] would agree with historian David Hackett Fisher that history is not what happened but what the surviving evidence says happened. If you can hide the evidence and keep the secrets, then you can write the history.

Thomas Powers,
The Man Who Kept the Secrets:
Richard Helms and the CIA[1]

It is a complex and arcane matriculation: from the U–2 base to Moscow to New Orleans to Clinton, then to Mexico and to the Texas School Book Depository. Always there are mysteries: unexplained activities in Mexico, disappearances in Russia and Dallas, unknown routes to and from the Soviet Union. There is favorable treatment from the U.S. government: loans, quick passports, an early discharge from the Marines. Always the government fails to treat Oswald in the usual manner: it conducts no damage assessment, posts no lookout cards, conducts no debriefings, dispenses no punishments. At the same time, CIA-related programs, people, and projects are a constant presence in Oswald's life, as are the Agency's opportunities to monitor him.

There is Oswald's veneer of leftism behind which his interactions are just the opposite. The pinko Marine retains his security clearance and perhaps even studies at the government's Monterey School. The defector who may have peddled secrets is given swift and friendly treatment by some of the most staunchly anti-communist bastions of our government. The FPCC chapter president is enmeshed in the "Cuban Grand Central Station" of anti-Castroism at Camp Street. The civil rights observer goes to Clinton with communist-hater David Ferrie. Back in Dallas, the Soviet defector settles into the anti-communist, Russian exile community under the wing of George de Mohrenschildt. To trip through all of these arenas of clandestine activity and to do what Oswald did cannot be explained as the innocent sojourn of a confused ideologue.

To conclude that he was a Soviet agent one must presuppose total incompetence in our national security apparatus, which missed numerous chances to discover him at the time of most obvious suspicion (when he recanted and returned to the United States). One must also try to imagine what the Soviets would have had in mind. Did the KGB really want to spy on the FPCC or CORE? Did it believe that Oswald could discover U.S. secrets or assassinate our president by becoming a conspicuous pro-Communist who purposely brought his activities to the attention of the FBI by requesting to see an agent and regaling him with tales of FPCC activity?

Still, the mainstream media remains captive to decades of secrecy and disinformation regarding Oswald, much of it emanating from the CIA. Intimations by CIA officers that the only missing pieces of the Oswald puzzle and the only valid questions of conspiracy relate to the Soviet Union was endorsed on January 7, 1990, by the *New York Times*. (See the testimony of former CIA director Richard Helms before the HSCA, Appendix B, where he asserts that without access to the files of communist intelligence agencies, it will be difficult to finalize conclusively the JFK case.) In an editorial in its Sunday edition, entitled "Mysteries That Matter," the paper urged that with the dramatic thaw in the Cold War, "Eastern Europe's new governments have a rare chance to serve both justice and history by unlocking the secret archives of their former communist masters." Among the mysteries that matter to the *Times* is, "Who Was Lee Harvey Oswald?"

> According to the Warren Commission, the man who killed John F. Kennedy in 1963 was a psychotic, acting alone. Not so, according to tireless conspiracy theorists, who speculate that Oswald, who had visited Moscow, was a KGB "asset" in Dallas. Perhaps East European archives can finally resolve conflicting stories from various Soviet defectors about Oswald's ties, or lack of them, with Soviet intelligence.

The editorial concludes with the democratic imperative that "an honest reckoning of the past is a crucial step to a more open society." It apparently has never occurred to the *Times'* editors that in Oswald's case, this applies to U.S. intelligence as well (and, in fact, more so).

The Agency has waged a propaganda campaign abroad—surely at home as well—designed to prop up the Warren Commission's conclusions and discredit Commission critics while seeking to preserve the illusion of CIA distance from Oswald. A 1967 "dispatch" from CIA headquarters to "chiefs, certain stations and bases" is entitled "Countering Criticisms of the Warren Report." It laments the new wave of books and articles challenging the Commission and points with alarm to a poll indicating that 46 percent of the public believes that Oswald did not act alone. This situation is perceived as a direct threat to Agency credibility because, "Our organization itself is directly involved: among other facts, we contributed information to the investigation [Warren Commission]. Conspiracy theories have frequently thrown suspicion on our organization; for example, by falsely alleging that Lee Harvey Oswald worked for us." How should CIA offices deal with this threat to "the whole reputation of the American government"? The dispatch seeks to "provide material for countering and discrediting the claims of the conspiracy theorists."

Here is a sampling of the strategic wisdom and substantive argument set forth in the document.

To discuss the publicity problem with friendly elite contacts (especially politicians and editors), pointing out that the Warren Commission made as thorough an investigation as humanly possible, that the charges of the critics are without serious foundation, and that further speculative discussion only plays into the hands of the opposition. Point out also that parts of the conspiracy talk appear to be generated by Communist propagandists. Urge them to use their influence to discourage unfounded and irresponsible speculation.

To employ propaganda asserts to answer and refute the attacks of the critics. Book reviews and feature articles are particularly appropriate for this purpose. The unclassified attachments to this guidance should provide useful background material for passage to assets. Our play should point out, as applicable, that the critics are (I) wedded to theories adopted before the evidence was in, (II) politically interested, (III) financially interested, (IV) hasty and inaccurate in their research, or (V) infatuated with their own theories.

Conspiracy on the large scale often suggested would be impossible to conceal in the United States, esp. since informants could expect to receive large royalties, etc. Note that Robert Kennedy, Attorney General at the time and John F. Kennedy's brother, would be the last man to overlook or conceal a conspiracy. And as one reviewer pointed out, congressman Gerald R. Ford would hardly have held his tongue for the sake of the

Democratic administration, and Senator Russell would have had every political interest in exposing any misdeeds on the part of Chief Justice Warren. A conspirator moreover would hardly choose a location for a shooting where so much depended on conditions beyond his control: the route, the speed of the cars, the moving target, the risk that the assassin would be discovered. A group of wealthy conspirators could have arranged much more secure conditions.

Oswald would not have been any sensible person's choice for a co-conspirator. He was a "loner," mixed-up, of questionable reliability and an unknown quantity to any professional intelligence service.

In 1975 CIA Director William Colby met with newsperson Dan Rather and producer Les Midgley of CBS News to discuss a forthcoming documentary on assassinations. According to a September 6, 1975 "Memorandum of Conversation" authored by Colby (obtained by the author from the Agency's Kennedy assassination file), the meeting covered "a variety of matters," but the topic of Oswald's possible connection to the CIA seems clearly to have been the central concern. "I referred to Dick Gregory's paranoia on the subject of CIA connections with the Kennedy death," Colby reports. He then describes how he assured the news people that Oswald never had any contact with the Agency. The memo concludes on a hopeful note but refuses to leave things to chance.

The two gentlemen expressed appreciation for our discussion. . . . From their attitude, I believe there is a chance that the program will indicate that there is no CIA connection with Oswald beyond that noted above. This could make a contribution to knocking down the paranoiac belief to the contrary. We must, however, insure that Mr. Rather does not learn anything which would cause the slightest doubt on the above account before he produces the program in November.

The only variable as salient and consistent as the CIA's presence in the contexts in which Oswald appeared is the Agency's alleged disinterest in monitoring him—as a defector who might be returning to the United States as a Soviet spy, or as a pro-Castro activist who might be trying to infiltrate the Agency's anti-Castro network. The best explanation for all this is that the "dirty rumor" is true: Lee Harvey Oswald was a U.S. intelligence agent.

Such a role does not, *ipso facto*, mean that elements of U.S. intelligence were involved in the assassination, any more than John W. Hinckley, Jr.'s attempted assassination of President Reagan can be laid at the doorstep of the Colorado college he attended. Spies can become deranged and commit individual acts of violence, like persons in any other oc-cupation. But Oswald was framed to appear leftist and guilty, whatever his role in the assassination. This occurred while he was still doing intelligence work in Dallas (tinting the left Kremlin-red). His intelligence milieu was populated with characters whose animosity toward President Kennedy was venomous: Ferrie, anti-Castro Cubans, and surely Guy Banister.

The shadowy figures who surrounded him (de Mohrenschildt, Ferrie, Banister, and some of the anti-Castro Cubans) were CIA-connected. This does not mean that the Agency as an institution conspired to assassinate the president. In the convoluted, compartmentalized world of covert action, certain networks and their activities may be only loosely account-able to CIA headquarters. The impetus for an operation may come from a deputy director's office in Langley, Virginia, but it may then be im-plemented by CIA agents in the field who hire contract agents, such as David Ferrie was alleged to have been. As former CIA Director Allen Dulles told his Warren Commission colleagues, someone in the field might not tell his own superior that he had hired someone. One of the things we learned from the Iran–Contra affair is that in the clandestine world it is difficult to determine who is really working for the government, as opposed to those who pretend they are or who think they are.

Elements of the CIA's anti-Castro network (including the Cubans and their CIA case officers) could easily have conspired to assassinate the president, using Oswald as the centerpiece of the operation. It is clear that Oswald was framed, whether he was a gunman or a patsy. He was also moved by his handlers along a path leading to the assassination as he quit his job and moved to Dallas, traveled to Mexico City, and perhaps mail-ordered the rifle to his left-wing post office box.

The conspiracy may have been a renegade one involving between a half dozen to a dozen men who had control of Oswald and of the shadowy network that surrounded him.[2] Given the nature of this arena, one would not have to look very far to find trained killers. Such a renegade element may have acted on its own in assassinating the president. Or it may have had the overt or tacit support of persons further up the shadowy chain of allegiance and deception, a chain stretching from New Orleans and Dallas back to Washington.

One of the characteristics of intelligence work is that some operatives are accustomed to acting on instructions from their controllers in the field with little or no knowledge of where in the chain of command and accountability (if there is one) the order originated. Therefore, it is pos-sible for someone with control over a network to misappropriate it. The men impersonating Oswald may have been performing a task, as per instructions, with no idea who Oswald really was or what plan of action was unfolding. The conspiracy would not have to be massive, institutionally sponsored, or involve only witting participants—not on this turf.

Investigative journalist Seymour Hersh said in 1975, "I've read a lot of stuff about Jack Kennedy's assassination. . . . My feeling about the conspiracy theory is this: that if after the statute of limitations is up, if somebody doesn't write a book for a million dollars, then there was no conspiracy."[3] But Mr. Hersh would probably not dispute a conspiracy in the murder of former Teamsters' Union President James Hoffa, despite the absence of a book or a valid confession. It was former CIA Inspector General Lyman Kirkpatrick who asserted that the ideal clandestine operation was one that remained secret "from inception to eternity." In 1976 the CIA admitted to a congressional committee that since 1961 it had conducted some 900 covert operations of various kinds. Some of these, or some additional ones that have not been admitted, have remained secret from the press, the public, and probably Congress itself. Only within the last few years it came to light that the CIA and military intelligence were relocating suspected Nazi war criminals to the United States. These fugitives from justice were provided with new identities by their patron agencies, who deemed them useful for one purpose or another. The secret was kept for almost half a century.

One of the ways that criminal and clandestine organizations keep secrets is to murder those who might reveal them. Some of the people who knew the most about Oswald's links to U.S. intelligence, and may have had important information about the assassination, died violent deaths: Oswald himself was murdered; Ferrie and de Mohrenschildt allegedly perished by their own hand, before they could be thoroughly questioned. There may be others. Every assassination is not, as some are wont to believe, a conspiracy; however, successful conspiracies to commit murder do occur. Even outside of the clandestine arena of covert action and spying, some murder conspiracies remain unsolved.

Many journalists, politicians, and analysts reject a conspiracy in this assassination because, they assert, it would require too many people—agencies, commissions, and individuals throughout government joining in a massive, coordinated effort to hide the truth. Such a cover-up would be impossible, it is asserted, because someone would blow the whistle. This argument neglects the fact that there are a variety of reasons why agencies or individuals engage in a cover-up. Knowingly trying to ensure the success of an assassination conspiracy is only one. Very likely, much of the cover-up in the Kennedy case was perpetrated for self-protection or to preserve other secrets; it was done by people having no direct knowledge of the conspiracy.

For example, it is unlikely that Oswald was being groomed as a pawn or hit man when he posed as a defector to spy on the Soviets. After the assassination, those who orchestrated his defection would be desperate to cover it up to protect the larger program(s) of which it was a part, to protect the covers of those involved, to avoid being in the unenviable, if not untenable, position of saying, "Yes, Oswald was our agent in his Soviet days but that was then; we had nothing to do with the assassination."

The CIA's handling of the Mexico City episode may be another example of a cover-up spawned by self-protection rather than conspiratorial design. Agency personnel who had knowledge of the photos and audio tapes of an Oswald impostor would not have to be privy to the assassination plot to want to suppress the data. Proof of an impostor would point to the conclusion that Oswald was framed. This would create a firestorm of investigation and suspicion, engulfing vital Agency projects and assets. It would also raise questions about the credibility of the Agency's assertions that he had been an ordinary defector, and not someone special or sinister.

If some office or officers within the CIA had a picture of the impostor, they had photographed a conspirator, or conspirator's agent, at work. What if it were someone known to the Agency or someone whom its massive, computerized database at Langley could identify? If it turned out to be an anti-Castroite who was Agency-sponsored, the CIA would have evidence implicating its own assets in the president's murder. The choice of whether to inflict extensive, perhaps permanent, damage on the organization or to suppress the evidence was probably a very clear one for those involved.

Someone who knew Oswald's background in U.S. intelligence might have perceived him as the perfect centerpiece for the plot precisely because of this. It could easily have been predicted that, in the aftermath of the president's murder, agencies with information on Oswald's spooky past (especially the CIA) would immediately cover up, to insulate themselves from suspicion and scrutiny. The morning after the assassination an untold number of intelligence officers in various agencies or branches must have panicked about their Oswald file(s) and the problems it could cause them. Conspirators could have correctly calculated that the possessors of such files would attempt to freeze out or stonewall any official investigators who inquired about Oswald. Thus the cover-up could be quite extensive while the conspiracy could be rather small and tight-knit.

Despite the passage of time, the cover-ups, and the inadequacy of official investigations, there is more that we can learn about Oswald and the crime with which he is so intimately associated. First, withheld files should be released. Approximately 5 percent of the Warren Commission's papers remain secret after nearly three decades. In 1985 there was supposed to be a legally mandated review of these documents in order to determine which of them could be released. There was no further disclosure and the next such review will be in 1995. Numerous CIA documents are among the still-classified Commission records. The Agency also refuses to release most of the data it provided to the House Assassinations Committee between 1976 and 1978.

As of this writing, the FBI is still withholding an estimated 15 percent of its original case file on the assassination. Researchers have noted that the Bureau is particularly resistant to disclosing documents relating to Mexico City: Oswald's alleged activities, the story put forth by CIA source "D" (that Oswald was paid by Castro's agents to shoot the president), "Oswald" photos and tapes, and so on.

In addition to public disclosure, the CIA should also be required to find or account for what is known to be missing from Oswald's file and for what data it clearly should have on him but professes not to have. This could be accomplished by a congressional oversight committee and does not require a full-blown reinvestigation of the case.

As for Congress, it should begin by passing the long-overdue legislation that would eliminate its own secrecy cloak. After the House Select Committee on Assassinations disbanded in 1978, it declared its voluminous records to be "congressional materials," a status that allows them to be withheld from the public until the year 2028.[4] Unlike most government records, "congressional materials" are sealed for 50 years and cannot be accessed through the Freedom of Information Act (FOIA). Public disclosure through FOIA applies to all executive-branch agencies (including the CIA) but does not apply to Congress, which decided to exempt itself when passing this landmark legislation for the public right to know. Many CIA and intelligence-related documents long sought by serious students of the case were obtained by the House Committee from various agencies, only to end up in a black hole of legislative secrecy, sealed more tightly now than when the agencies possessed them.

Unlike many events that cry out for valid explanation, for historical clarity, those involving what Allen Dulles termed "the craft of intelligence" are more difficult to fathom. The document that might be the Rosetta Stone of accurate understanding may not simply be locked in someone's vault awaiting posthumous exposure: it may be nonexistent. Moreover, the impetus for secrecy and disinformation does not fade completely with the passing decades, as demonstrated by the CIA's interactions with the House Committee in 1978.

In 1963 Alpha–66 was one of the most violent CIA-backed Cuban exile groups. Its members were in Dallas and well armed at the time of the assassination. It had openly defied President Kennedy's ban against launching raids on Cuba from the United States. The group continued its activities and was still conducting strikes against Castro in the early 1980s. In the summer of that year a five-man assassination squad, allegedly sent from the United States to kill Castro, was captured in Cuba. Alpha–66 not only took credit for the foiled attempt but did so at a press conference in Miami. Said one Cuban diplomat, "What got Castro mad was not just that the hit squad was sent after him, but that Alpha–66 was allowed to hold a press conference in Florida promising to try again, all without any sign of concern from the U.S. government."[5] If Alpha–66 and its offshoots still enjoyed Agency patronage in the 1980s, any incriminating secrets involving the Kennedy assassination would most likely be perceived by the CIA as a potential threat to its ongoing operations. The cover-up would continue.

All of this notwithstanding, there is more we can learn, and need to learn, about Oswald and about this crime against U.S. democracy. Like presidential elections, the darker side of our political process, assassinations, profoundly alter not only the succession of leadership and the distribution of political power but the course of public policy and history. If the U.S. Secret Service is to effectively protect our political leaders, it must understand the various root causes of these assaults: lumping Oswald with Squeaky Fromme and John W. Hinckley, Jr. as fitting "the profile" of U.S. assassins (lone, deranged drifters) is too simplistic for effective protective research.[6] It is also essential in a democracy that institutions and agencies of government be held publicly accountable for their performance and actions, an accountability that should not be voided by official secrecy and disinformation.

Finally, if some cabal successfully conspired to subvert the democratic process by disenfranchising citizens' ballots with bullets, this fact must be confronted. Doing so will serve history and democracy well, even if criminal justice cannot now be achieved. We can begin to comprehend a great deal more about the assassination of President John F. Kennedy, about the sources of violence that threaten our political system, and about the nature of covert power and politics when we know the truth about Lee Harvey Oswald: U.S. intelligence agent-provocateur.

Appendix A: Selected Chronology of Lee Harvey Oswald

October 18, 1939	Born in New Orleans, Louisiana
October 18, 1955	Joins New Orleans chapter, Civil Air Patrol, allegedly headed by David Ferrie
October 24, 1956	Joins United States Marine Corps
September 11, 1959	Released from active duty
October 15, 1959	Crosses Finnish–Soviet border en route to Moscow
October 31, 1959	Visits U.S. Embassy in Moscow and announces his intention to defect to the USSR
April 30, 1960	Marries Marina Prusakova
May 1, 1960	Francis Gary Powers's U–2 spy plane is shot down in the USSR
February 15, 1962	Daughter June is born
May 1962	Arranges return to United States with help of State Department
June 1, 1962	Leaves USSR by train to Holland
June 2, 1962	Leaves Holland via liner for United States
June 14, 1962	Arrives Fort Worth and lives with brother Robert
October 10, 1962	First day at Jaggers-Chiles-Stovall photo-optics firm
November 3, 1962	Rents apartment at 602 Elsbeth St., Dallas
March 3, 1963	Moves to apartment at 214 W. Neely St., Dallas
April 6, 1963	Last day of work at Jaggers-Chiles-Stovall

April 24, 1963	Leaves Dallas. Family moves to Irving, TX to live with Michael and Ruth Paine
April 25, 1963	Arrives in New Orleans
May 9, 1963	Takes job at Reily Coffee Co.
May 11, 1963	Family joins him in New Orleans
mid-June, 1963	Hands out FPCC leaflets at Dumaine St. wharf where *U.S.S. Wasp* is docked
July 19, 1963	"Fired" from Reily Coffee Co.
August 9, 1963	Arrested for disturbing the peace during leafletting (Bringuier scuffle)
August 16, 1963	Passes out FPCC leaflets outside Trade Mart, New Orleans
late August to early September 1963	Oswald and Ferrie visit Clinton, Louisiana during CORE voter-registration campaign
September 27, 1963	Travels to Mexico. Family stays at Paines' home in Irving, TX
October 3, 1963	Returns to Dallas and registers at YMCA
October 4–6, 1963	Visits Irving, TX where wife and child are living
October 14, 1963	Rents apartment at 1026 N. Beckley, Dallas
October 15, 1963	Takes job at Texas School Book Depository
October 20, 1963	Second daughter, Rachel, is born
November 1, 1963	Rents a new post office box at Terminal Annex Post Office, Dallas. Authorizes mail for the ACLU and the FPCC to be received
November 22, 1963	Goes to work at Depository. President Kennedy is shot at 12:30 P.M. Arrested in Texas Theater at 1:50 P.M.
November 24, 1963	Murdered in basement of Dallas police station by Jack Ruby

Appendix B: Excerpts from the Testimony of Former CIA Director Richard Helms before the House Select Committee on Assassinations

Richard Helms testified in August 1978. In these first excerpts he hints that there was Agency concern about who might have been behind Oswald, but that the most relevant data reside in foreign intelligence files (and, by implication, not in CIA files):

> There is hardly any question there was more discussed during those days as to who was behind Lee Harvey Oswald, if indeed he was the man who was responsible, what had affected his life, why had he done the things he had done, and so forth.
>
>   *   *   *
>
>   I think if the Chair would indulge me a minute, I would like to make a comment about the various investigations into the assassination of President Kennedy based on the long years I have spent in the intelligence business, and that is, until the day that the KGB in Moscow or the Cuban intelligence in Havana is prepared to turn over their files to the United States as to what their relationships to these various people were, it is going to be extraordinarily difficult to tidy up this case, finally and conclusively.[1]

The CIA had denied that it had any interest in or data on Oswald beyond his rather meager "201 file." A 201 file was described by the Agency as an expression of routine interest in a person—nothing extraordinary. The House Committee was interested in the question of why such a routine file was not opened on Oswald in the fall of 1959 when he defected rather than waiting until December 1960. Moreover, Helms's testimony appears to have been inconsistent on this point. [2]

Committee Counsel Michael Goldsmith: Mr. Helms, what is a 201 file?

Director Richard Helms: I believe the 201 file, if memory serves, is simply the number given to a type of file at the Agency in which personality information is placed. In other words, if you open a 201 file on the chairman of this committee, for example, it would simply be information that had come into the Agency which involved that gentleman.

Goldsmith: Why would the Agency have opened a 201 file on Oswald?

Helms: Why would it have?

Goldsmith: Yes, sir.

Helms: I believe at some point a decision must have been made that Oswald was perhaps a matter of continuing interest and therefore the information which we held on him should be put in the file.

I would like to suggest to the committee that when a Government agency receives mail it has to do something with it, and one of the things that you do with it is to try to categorize the type of information it is and where it would best be filed so that if you need it at some future date you can get it back.

Goldsmith: I would ask that Mr. Helms be shown JFK exhibit F–534. For the record, that is a Department of State telegram dated October 31, 1959. Would you please read to yourself that telegram.

Helms: Yes, Mr. Goldsmith, I have read it now.

Goldsmith: This telegram makes reference to Oswald, indicating his intention or desire to defect, and it says that Oswald has offered the Soviets any information he has acquired as an enlisted radar operator. My question to you is whether information contained in this particular telegram would normally lead to the opening of a 201 file?

Helms: I just don't know how to answer the question. I would have thought so but, on the other hand, maybe a decision would be made that this was something that involved the Marine Corps and that this was their concern. After all, the Department of Defense has a very large Defense Intelligence Agency and then it has intelligence units in the Army, Navy, and Air Force and they do have jurisdiction over their people and their security.

Goldsmith: Mr. Helms, I would ask you to refer to your previous testimony to this committee on page 75, specifically to line 15, your response to the question posed by me.

Goldsmith: Would the information contained in this telegram normally lead to the opening of a 201 file?

We are referring to the same telegram. Would you please read the response that you gave that day?

Helms: "Mr. Helms. I would have thought so, an American who was defecting to the Soviet Union would have been of counterintelligence interest and that would have been quite sufficient to have caused the Agency to open a file."

Goldsmith: Mr. Chairman, I move for the admission of this exhibit.

Cong. Richardson Preyer (Dem. NC): Without objection, the exhibit is ordered into the record at this point.

Former Director Helms expressed profound skepticism regarding the claim made by Soviet sources, such as defector Yuri Nosenko, that the KGB had absolutely no interest in Oswald and never debriefed him. Many analysts, including the author, greet the CIA's denials of interest in Oswald with similar skepticism, based on the mirror image of Helms's reasoning to the Committee:[3]

I simply do not understand that assertion. I would have thought, to begin with, that any American who went to the Russian government and said, "I want to defect to the Soviet Union" would have immediately been taken over by the KGB to find out what his game was because, after all, the KGB's charter is to protect the Soviet state against infiltration.

How would they know that he was serious about this? How would they know that the CIA had not sent him to make a fake defection and to try to get into Soviet society through this device?

So, for that reason, if not for many others, I find it quite incredible, the assertion by Nosenko that Oswald was never interrogated or was never in touch with the KGB while he was in the Soviet Union. This really stretches one's credulity. It goes back to the testimony this morning that this is the hardest thing about the whole Nosenko case to swallow, and I have not been able to swallow it in all these years.

Congressman Floyd J. Fithian (Dem., IN) raised the question of damage assessment regarding Oswald's possible U–2 secrets.[4]

Congressman Fithian: Would you, would the Agency then not have— as a matter of practice—not have inquired of DOD or someone as to how much damage to our U–2 operation, let's say, theorized, that Oswald might be able to do by the defecting?

Helms: I don't know. We might have, but I would have thought that the feeling would be that that was the Navy Department's responsibility.

Fithian: Is it your best assessment that in all probability the Agency did not make any effort to assess the potential damage of Oswald's . . .

Helms: I think that is right. In other words, he was another Marine, but what specialty he had or what he had been involved with, I don't think we would have gone into that unless it were volunteered to us in some form.

Under rather sharp, lengthy questioning, an acerbic Helms was asked whether Oswald had been "connected" with the CIA.[5]

Committee Counsel Michael Goldsmith: Did the Agency ever conduct an investigation to determine whether Lee Harvey Oswald had been connected with the CIA?

Helms: Yes, and I believe that [then CIA Director] Mr. McCone presented to the Warren Commission a sworn affidavit saying that he had no formal connection with the CIA of any kind. I gather that through the years a couple of people have been identified who had once thought that maybe the Agency should have some kind of a contact with Lee Harvey Oswald, but to the best of my knowledge no contact was ever made.

In any event, he was not an agent of the CIA and I was horrified this morning to have Mr. Blakey [the committee's chief counsel], as a part of this committee's work coming out with the allegation at this late date that he had some identification with the Agency. Can't this ever be put to rest? What does it take to put it to rest?

Excuse me, I am asking you a question. I will rephrase it. I would hope that at some juncture someone would find some means of putting this allegation to rest.

Goldsmith: Mr. Helms, what did the Agency's investigation involve when it was looking into this matter?

Helms: We have records for one thing in the Agency, and then on top of that, I have the recollection that various people were asked whether they knew anything about Oswald or had any connection with him, people like the officers in the contact division, did you ever interview Oswald; people in the CE staff, etc.

I don't remember the exact details. Fifteen years later it would be implausible for me to remember exactly what, but I can assure you that we would not have asked or suggested or allowed Mr. McCone to swear out an affidavit, present it to the Warren Commission, unless we believed the affidavit to be truthful.

Goldsmith: Was there a written report summarizing the Agency's investigation?

Helms: I don't know.

Goldsmith: Do you think one should have been filed?

Helms: I don't know.

Goldsmith: Why not?

Helms: I don't have any idea why it should have. If it manifested itself in the affidavit sworn by Mr. McCone, isn't that evidence enough?

Goldsmith: Are the Agency's files sufficiently accurate to resolve that issue?

Helms: I don't know. You know, after this inquiry today, I am reminded of the fact that back in the days of the Continental Congress that intelligence, espionage, and counter-espionage were conducted by committees of the Continental Congress. I think maybe the best thing to do would be to return secret intelligence to the aegis of the U.S. Congress and let you fellows run it.

Goldsmith: Mr. Helms, did the Agency ever have an operational interest in Lee Harvey Oswald?

Helms: Not that I am aware of.

Goldsmith: I would ask that the witness be shown JFK F–526. I would ask that you read that.

For the record, this is a memorandum dated November 25, 1963.

Helms: I have glanced at this memorandum. I have not read it in great detail. Who wrote it?

Goldsmith: You are asking me who wrote it?

Helms: Oh, I am sorry. I am supposed to take an anonymous memorandum and make judgments on it. I'll do the best I can.

Goldsmith: I might add that this is a sanitized document and I would hope you would not want me to indicate who wrote it.

Referring you to the first paragraph that makes reference to the laying on of interviews.

Helms: The first paragraph makes reference to the laying on of interviews with Lee Harvey Oswald.

Goldsmith: Does the language of this memorandum suggest that the possibility of a contact with Oswald was contemplated?

Helms: The memorandum does not say anything about a contact.

Goldsmith: Does the memorandum make reference to the laying on of interviews?

Helms: It says I had discussed—some time in summer 1960—with almost a whole line blank, the laying on of interviews through blank or other suitable channels. At the moment, I don't recall if this was discussed while Oswald and his family were en route to this country or was after his arrival.

Goldsmith: I am sorry. I didn't ask you to read the document. I simply asked you to . . .

Helms: I am sorry. I didn't know I was disobeying.

Goldsmith: I simply asked you whether the document makes reference to the laying on of interviews?

Helms: Yes, it says someone thought about laying on an interview.

Goldsmith: In light of that, does it suggest that at the very least a contact with Oswald was contemplated by the Agency?

Helms: Not by the Agency, by some individuals in the Agency. For a lawyer, I think you ought to be more precise.

Goldsmith: Mr. Helms, I am not in a position here today to respond to your criticism.

Helms: I am sorry. That was not criticism.

Goldsmith: Mr. Helms, have you testified before at a congressional hearing?

Helms: At any time?

Goldsmith: Yes.

Helms: Do you mean in my life?

Goldsmith: Yes, sir.

Helms: On more than one occasion, yes.

Goldsmith: And during those occasions, sir, was the standard operating procedure for the attorney to ask the questions and for the witness to answer them?

Helms: I must confess during my life, Mr. Goldsmith, that I was usually asked questions by the Senators or the Congressmen involved.

Goldsmith: Very well, Mr. Helms. Under those circumstances again, was the procedure for the member of the committee or its staff to ask the questions and to have the witness answer the questions?

Helms: Yes.

Goldsmith: Did anyone tell you before you came to testify here today that standard operating procedure would not be followed?

Helms: I don't recall discussing it with anyone.

Goldsmith: Fine. Let's follow the standard operating procedure, Mr. Helms.

Helms: Certainly, Mr. Goldsmith.

Goldsmith: Do you know what follow-up there was to this memorandum dated November 25, 1963? [The memo refers to CIA discussions about Oswald that occurred in 1960.]

Helms: I have no idea.

Goldsmith: I would like to draw your attention to the last line of this memorandum. It makes reference to the Harvey story.

Helms: Yes.

Goldsmith: Do you know what Harvey story that is referring to?

Helms: No, I do not.

Goldsmith: Did the Agency debrief Lee Harvey Oswald upon his return from the Soviet Union?

Helms: I was not aware that it did. I don't believe it would.

Goldsmith: Would standard operating procedure have called for Oswald to have been debriefed?

Helms: I would not have thought so, Mr. Goldsmith. I think that the standard operating procedure after he returned to the United States would have been for the Navy to debrief him.

Goldsmith: Why is that, sir?

Helms: Because he had been a member of the Marine Corps, and I believe he stayed in the Marine Reserve, if I am not mistaken. But in any event, the understandings were that military officers were handled by the intelligence organs of the defense establishment.

Goldsmith: So I take it, then, that the Agency had no interest in finding out whatever information Oswald may have picked up during his work at a radio factory in Minsk?

Helms: I don't know.

Goldsmith: Again, Mr. Helms, would you agree that a memorandum that makes reference to the possibility of the laying on of interviews on Oswald is contemplating a contact with Oswald? I am not suggesting a contact necessarily occurred, sir, but that it is contemplating a contact.

Helms: Apparently someone, and I am sorry but the memorandum is so sanitized that I don't know who it was nor do I know in what part of the Agency he was, apparently had an idea at some point it might be a good idea to interview Oswald. To the best of my knowledge, his thought never came to anything.

Goldsmith: Did the Agency ever interview the author of this memorandum to determine whether there was any follow-up?

Helms: I don't know. I don't know who wrote the memorandum.

Goldsmith: Do you think if there were a written report summarizing what the Agency had done in its investigation of the Oswald allegation, perhaps issues like this might more readily be resolved?

Helms: I don't know. I think these issues are very difficult to resolve, particularly 15 years later when I don't even know what I am dealing with.

Goldsmith: Do you think the availability of a written report summarizing the steps that the Agency went through would facilitate resolving this issue today?

Helms: Yes, I think probably it would have been, in light of hindsight, might have been very useful if we had had a memorandum for the record of everybody in the Agency who was talked to about Oswald. We should have kept that going for several years.

After discussing Oswald's 201 file, Helms was questioned about the possibility that the CIA doctored 201 files for covert purposes. One document in the Committee's possession referred to a "forged and backdated" 201 file to be used in connection with political assassinations (the "ZR Rifle" project).[6]

Committee Counsel Michael Goldsmith: Are 201 files ever maintained on a covert basis or is there ever such a thing as a fake 201 file?

Helms: I don't know. You brought to my attention the fact that you had discovered one in the Agency. I was not aware of the phenomenon myself prior to your having brought it to my attention. Since you did find one, then I concede that I guess there was such a thing, but I was not aware of the one that you brought to my attention and I am not aware of any others.

Goldsmith: Let's examine that particular one at this point. I would ask Mr. Helms be given JFK F–522.

What was the ZR Rifle project?

Helms: My understanding from the hearings of the Church committee, I believe the ZR Rifle originally started out as an indicator for a project which was supposed to cover a man who in turn had been taken on to have available an operational capability to kill people. This man was hired before I was aware of these things. I have this in hindsight but I believe that is what the ZR rifle was supposed to be and then I believe later it metamorphosed into something else. But anyway, after I became Deputy Director for Plans, I put on the shelf for good any and all use of this capacity for killing people. We didn't need that, so that was the end of that.

If the ZR rifle continued after that, it was in another context and I don't remember precisely what the context was. I can read what you have given me here, that it was to spot, develop, and use agent assets for Division D operations. My recollection of Division D was that it was the operational staff in the Agency which attempted to procure code and cipher materials overseas for use by the National Security Agency.

Goldsmith: In fact, that form which you were just reading, the reference to Division D, has no bearing at all upon any executive action-type problem, any type of assassination program?

Helms: I would not have thought so. If that was in Division D, maybe it was there for convenience. Maybe they didn't know where else to put it, and I can't blame them.

Goldsmith: Is it also possible the person writing these notes was writing that aspect of it to mislead people to cover the fact that this was assassination activity?

Helms: I don't know whether that was the idea or not, Mr. Goldsmith.

Goldsmith: Let's take a closer look at this particular document. This document consists of handwritten notes. The notes are in the handwriting of two different individuals.

Helms: Yes, I notice here on one of the pages, "It should have a phony 201 to backstop this."

Goldsmith: You are reading from which page, sir?

Helms: I am sorry, they are not numbered, Mr. Goldsmith. I am not trying to be difficult. It is 1, 2, 3—this is page 4.

Goldsmith: You are referring to the bottom of the page where it says, "should have phony 201 in RI"?

Helms: That is it.

Goldsmith: This document indicates, "should have phony 201 in RI to backstop this. All documents therein forged and backdated. Should look like"—I believe that says a "CE file."

Helms: I think that must be what it means.

Goldsmith: Let's refer your attention now to page 6, two pages further.

Helms: Right.

Goldsmith: At the bottom right-hand portion of the page approximately five or six lines up, the person wrote in, "Never mention the word assassination." Is that true?

Helms: Yes, that is what it says.

Goldsmith: Would you turn to the next page. Does that page say "No projects or papers except for cover"? Does it also say "cover file create from RIS"—the rest of it not really legible? Does it contain that language?

Helms: Yes. I don't know, I can't read it either. It is so cut up and excised, and so forth, it really doesn't make much sense.

Goldsmith: In any event, Mr. Helms, do these handwritten notes contain any indication that this particular project contemplated the use of fake files?

Helms: That is what is says here. I don't know any more about it than that if this is the item I mentioned a moment ago that you had brought to my attention and I concede that is what this says. But I find it awfully difficult to deal with these matters so totally out of context and excised and sanitized, and so forth. My recollection is as I have told you, that the ZR Rifle project was an individual who was supposed to kill people. He never killed anybody and he was never used for that purpose after I had anything to do with it, and any further business the ZR Rifle was involved in was something else's entirely.

Goldsmith: Mr. Helms, I would ask you to refer to page 86 of your prior testimony which is given at a time when you had access to the complete document.

Helms: Is the top of that page supposed to have been censored by the Agency or is that somebody else's lining?

Goldsmith: No, sir, that was not intended to be sanitized by the Agency. I believe your lawyer will confirm that.

[Witness conferring with counsel.]

Helms: Excuse me, Mr. Goldsmith, I was confused by what I was looking at here.

[Witness reading from prior testimony.]

Goldsmith: The question to you: "In any event, would you agree that here is a case where at the very least Agency personnel were contemplating the use of a fake 201 file and possibly a fake operational file?"

Would you please read your answer?

Helms: [reading] "Yes, it looks like that. But then his boss would have known about this. He would have had to get permission to do that. Somebody would have known about it."

Notes

The 26 volumes of testimony, documents, and exhibits that accompany the *Report of the President's Commission on the Assassination of President John F. Kennedy* (Washington, DC: U.S. Government Printing Office, 1964) are cited by volume and page—for example, XXI, p. 76. The single volume summary is referred to as the *Warren Report*. Throughout the 26 volumes, material is often designated as a numbered Commission Document (hereafter referred to as CD) or Commission Exhibit (hereafter referred to as CE).

Regarding the *Report of the Select Committee on Assassinations*, U.S. House of Representatives (Washington, DC: U.S. Government Printing Office, 1979), the final report is hereafter referred to as *HSCA Report*. The accompanying twelve volumes are cited by volume and page—for example, *HSCA* VI, p. 10.

INTRODUCTION

1. VI, p. 270.
2. *Warren Report*, p. 334.
3. "The Evolution of an Assassin: A Clinical Study of Lee Harvey Oswald," *Life*, Feb. 21, 1964, p. 72.

CHAPTER 1

1. Henry Hurt, *Reasonable Doubt: An Investigation into the Assassination of John F. Kennedy* (New York: Holt Rinehart and Winston, 1985), p. 193.
2. *HSCA Report*, p. 197.
3. "Additional Notes and Comments on the Oswald Case," Dec. 11, 1963 (CIA 376–154), quoted in Henry Hurt, *Reasonable Doubt*, p. 226.
4. Michael Eddowes, *The Oswald File* (New York: Clarkson N. Potter, 1977).

5. Robert Sam Anson, *"They've Killed the President"* (New York: Bantam, 1975), p. 283.

6. *Transcript*, Warren Commission Executive Session, January 22, 1964. Warren Commission members: Chief Justice Earl Warren, Rep. Hale Boggs (Dem., LA), John J. McCloy (coordinator of disarmament activities in the Kennedy administration), Sen. John Sherman Cooper (Rep., KY), Allen W. Dulles, Sen. Richard B. Russell (Dem., GA), Rep. Gerald Ford (Rep., MI).

7. Philip Agee, *Inside the Company: CIA Diary* (New York: Bantam, 1975), p. 85.

8. David Belin, *Final Disclosure* (New York: Charles Scribners & Sons, 1988), p. 212.

9. Executive Session *Transcript*, January 27, 1964.

CHAPTER 2

1. V, p. 301.

2. XIX, p. 665.

3. Details of Oswald's experience, as described here, are taken from J. Edward Epstein's *Legend* (New York: Bantam, 1966), unless otherwise specified.

4. Hearings, "Events Incident to the Summit Conference," p. 124, Senate Foreign Relations Committee, 86th Congress, 2nd Session. Testimony by Secretary of Defense Thomas S. Gates, June 2, 1960.

5. Epstein and/or Henry Hurt interviewed several of the men who worked with Oswald in the Atsugi radar bubble (Epstein, *Legend*).

6. *Warren Report*, p. 609.

7. FBI document MI 62–1178, DL 89–43. November 30, 1963 interview with Daniel Powers, Oswald's Atsugi squadron leader, p. 3.

8. VIII, p. 298.

9. Epstein, *Legend*, p. 280.

10. Ibid., p. 69.

11. Hurt, *Reasonable Doubt*, p. 200.

12. Anson, *"They've Killed the President,"* p. 157.

13. Anthony Summers, *Conspiracy* (New York: McGraw Hill, 1978), pp. 156–57.

14. Anson, *"They've Killed the President,"* p. 157.

15. David Wise and Thomas B. Ross, *The Invisible Government* (New York: Vintage Books, 1964), p. 122.

16. Ibid., p. 11.

17. Ibid.

18. William R. Corson, *The Armies of Ignorance* (New York: Dial Press, 1977), pp. 374–75.

19. Final Report of the Senate Select Committee to Study Government Operations with Respect to Intelligence, *Investigation into the Assassination of*

President John F. Kennedy, Book V (Washington, DC: U.S. Government Printing Office, 1976), pp. 58–59.

20. Wise and Ross, *Invisible Government*, pp. 122–24.

21. *HSCA Report*, p. 220.

22. Summers, *Conspiracy*, p 156; *HSCA IX*, p. 603; *HSCA VIII*, pp. 313–15; *HSCA XIX*, p. 601.

23. Summers too notes this possibility; Summers, *Conspiracy*, p. 156. His own research confirmed the use of such a ploy by British intelligence, as far back as World War I.

24. *HSCA Report*, p. 220.

25. VIII, p. 298.

26. VIII, p. 232.

27. *HSCA XI*, p. 84.

28. XXIII, p. 796.

29. *Warren Report*, p. 685.

30. Ibid., p. 611.

31. Ibid., p. 612. According to the Commission, Oswald manifested some interest in Marxism in high school and occasionally extolled Communism and debunked capitalism (*Report*, pp. 362, 381, 383, 385–86, 690; XXII, p. 812). Yet he became possessed by an urgent desire to join the Marines at age sixteen. As will be described in Chapter 4, he was a member of the Civil Air Patrol squadron in New Orleans headed by anti-Communist zealot David Ferrie, who encouraged the youths to join the Marines. Implicitly, the Commission seemed to view Oswald's Marxism as a linear development from his high school days. But this alleged high school interest may have been rechannelled in the Civil Air Patrol toward the Marine Corps and from there, toward a life of intrigue. Moreover, the assertions of Oswald's high school Marxism were described by his former school friend Edward Voebel as "baloney." (See Summers, *Conspiracy* p. 143. Says Summers, Voebel's statement "recalls the plethora of incidents which have somehow rung false [about Oswald]."

32. Epstein, *Legend*, pp. 86–89.

33. Ibid.

34. Interview with Professor James Weeks, Department of Modern Languages, Southeastern Massachusetts University, February 18, 1981.

35. Summers, *Conspiracy*, p. 155.

36. *Transcript*, Warren Commission Executive Session, January 27, 1964.

37. Telephone inquiry, Public information Office, Defense Language Institute, Monterey, CA, Feb. 18, 1981.

38. *Warren Report*, pp. 613–14.

39. Ibid., p. 614.

40. VIII, p. 257.

41. XVI, p. 337; CD 107, p. 37.

42. *Warren Report*, p. 367.

43. XVIII, p. 162. See Sylvia Meagher, *Accessories After the Fact* (New York: Bobbs-Merrill, 1967), p. 331.

44. CE 2676; XXVI, p. 32. See also *HSCA Report*, p. 211. The Committee could not explain the timing of the arrival in Helsinki.

45. *Warren Report*, p. 692.

46. On defectors generally, see *The Dallas Conspiracy*, Peter Dale Scott (unpublished manuscript). On Oswald's defection, see *Warren Report*, pp. 616–17.

47. *Warren Report*, pp. 617–18.

48. Ibid. Richard E. Snyder, the diplomat who dealt with Oswald at the U.S. Embassy, later asserted that the would-be defector told him that

> he [Oswald] had told Soviet officials that as a Soviet citizen he would make known to them whatever he knew about the Marine Corps and his specialty in radar. He intimated that he might know something of special interest.

Snyder also said that Oswald might have "thought he was establishing credibility with Russian ears-in-the-wall [electronic surveillance of the U.S. Embassy by the KGB]." See Richard E. Snyder, "The Soviet Sojourn of Citizen Oswald," *Washington Post* Magazine, April 1, 1979, p. 29.

49. *Warren Report*, p. 367.

50. See CD 434 and 451; *HSCA Report*, pp. 101–3; *HSCA XII*, p. 475.

51. CE 941; XVIII, p. 155.

52. II, p. 162.

53. Curry interview with Anthony Summers (Summers, *Conspiracy*, p. 128).

54. Alexander interview with Summers (Summers, *Conspiracy*, p. 128).

55. Patrolman Warren Roberts' statement to FBI, 11/30/63 file 89–69, p. 1.

56. *Warren Report*, pp. 747–50; Anson, *"They've Killed the President,"* p. 161.

57. Jim Marrs, *Crossfire: The Plot That Killed Kennedy* (New York: Carroll & Graf, 1989), p. 114. Marrs describes Snyder as "a CIA intelligence operative serving as senior consular officer at the Moscow embassy." It has been established that Snyder worked for the Agency prior to his Moscow diplomatic assignment. It has not been established that he worked for the Agency while dealing with Oswald. Marrs's book is devoid of footnotes. In an introductory note he states that "any statements without attribution indicates historical fact or issues which are undisputed among the majority of credible assassination researchers." This seems a rather ephemeral baseline since interpretations of historical fact in this case differ markedly, as do perceptions of who is or is not a credible researcher. Conversely, the fact that a majority of mainstream historical descriptions of the case accept Oswald's guilt does not make it true.

58. *HSCA Report*, p. 215—HSCA quotes concerning Snyder are from this page unless otherwise specified; see also David C. Martin, *Wilderness of Mirrors* (New York: Ballantine, 1980), p. 117, on CIA officers under diplomatic cover in Moscow.

59. Anson, *"They've Killed The President,"* p. 161 (on Snyder's reaction); also Meagher, *Accessories*, p. 339.

60. CE 909; VII, p. 2.
61. VIII, p. 298.
62. VIII, p. 298, discussed in Meagher, *Accessories*, p. 339.
63. Epstein, *Legend*, pp. 102, 366.
64. Ibid.
65. Ross and Wise, *Invisible Government*, p. 123.
66. Summers, *Conspiracy*, p. 204. Summers and Dick Fontaine interviewed Prouty in 1978 and Summers corresponded with Prouty in 1979.
67. See Gary Powers with Curt Gentry, *Operation Overflight* (New York: Holt, Rinehart and Winston, 1970); also Summers, *Conspiracy*, pp. 204, 206.
68. Powers interview, *The Times*, April 20, 1971.
69. The following discussion of the Soviets' interrogation of Powers is taken from Epstein, *Legend*, pp. 120, 300n.2.
70. Oswald's letter and possible presence in Moscow when Powers was there: Epstein, *Legend*, p. 121.
71. XVIII, p. 131; XVI, pp. 705–6.
72. XVIII, p. 137.
73. V, p. 284; XVIII, pp. 160–2; Marina visa: XVIII, p. 158.
74. The Davison incident is taken from: *Warren Report*, p. 634; CD 87 SS 569; CD 235; CD 409, p. 3; CD 1115 section XIII; XIII, item 104.
75. XVI, p. 616; XVIII, p. 16.
76. Robert Oswald with Myrick and Barbara Land, *Lee: A Portrait of Lee Harvey Oswald* (New York: Coward McCann, 1967), p. 117.
77. CE 18; XVI, p. 50.
78. *HSCA* XII, p. 250.
79. Penkovsky, Oleg *The Penkovsky Papers* (New York: Avon Books, 1966), p. 24.
80. Ibid., pp. 360, 366.
81. CD 87; CD 235; CD 409, p. 3; CD 1115, section XIII, item 103.
82. *HSCA Report*, pp. 215–17.
83. *Warren Report*, p. 671; cf. p. 669.
84. Ibid., p. 674.
85. Ibid., pp. 671–73.
86. Ibid., pp. 722, 750.
87. Ibid., p. 667.
88. Ibid.
89. XXII, p. 12; XXIV, p. 509.
90. Anson, *"They've Killed The President,"* p. 167.
91. Ibid.
92. Ibid., p. 59; *Warren Report*, pp. 370, 626, 674–75.
93. CE 29; XVI, p. 144.
94. CE 9.
95. *Transcript*, Warren Commission Executive Session, January 27, 1964.
96. *Warren Report*, p. 173.

97. *Free China and Asia* (Taipei), August 1959 (cited by Scott, *The Dallas Conspiracy*, Ch. 2, p. 23).

98. Wise and Ross, *Invisible Government*, p. 241; on emigrés: Morton Halperin et al., *The Lawless State* (New York: Penguin Books, 1976), pp. 137–38.

99. CBS Television, "The American Assassins," November 26, 1975.

100. Ibid.

101. Senate Select Committee, *Investigation into the Assassination of JFK*, Book V, p. 88.

102. IV, pp. 417–20.

103. Senate Select Committee, *Investigation into the Assassination of JFK*, Book V, p. 87.

104. IV, p. 417.

105. *HSCA Report*, p. 209.

106. Epstein, *Legend*, p. 312; *HSCA Report*, p. 207–9; *HSCA* XII, pp. 463–65.

107. Victor Marchetti and John D. Marks, *The CIA and the Cult of Intelligence* (New York: Dell Publishing Co., 1975), pp. 219–21; Wise and Ross, *Invisible Government*, pp. 4, 5, 199, 201–4, 249.

Two months after the assassination, a KGB intelligence officer named Yuri Nosenko defected to the United States. Among other things, he claimed to have been the officer who, as a routine part of his duties, personally handled Oswald's case while the young defector was in the Soviet Union. He asserted that the Soviets had no involvement in the assassination because there had been no Soviet intelligence contact with Oswald: he had never been interviewed by the KGB, Nosenko claimed, because he was of no interest and was simply regarded as "unstable." Needless to say, there was considerable skepticism within the CIA, concerning this assertion as well as others involving Soviet–U.S. espionage. A debate raged as to whether Nosenko was a plant proffering disinformation. This complex espionage puzzle eventually led to Nosenko being placed in isolation in a vault-like room for four years of interrogation. HSCA condemned this as inhumane treatment but also concluded that Nosenko had lied about Oswald to the FBI, the CIA, and the Committee as well. See *HSCA Report*, pp. 101–2; Summers, *Conspiracy*, pp. 194–99.

108. Halperin, *The Lawless State*, p. 137.

109. XVIII, p. 367 (March 31, 1961 memo of State Department).

110. Summers, *Conspiracy*, pp. 219–20.

111. Ibid.

112. *New York Times*, June 30, 1959 (cited by Scott, *The Dallas Conspiracy*).

113. Ibid.

114. Scott, *Dallas Conspiracy*, Ch. 2, p. 2.

115. Ibid.

116. Summers, *Conspiracy*, pp. 177–78; Scott, *Dallas Conspiracy*, Ch. 2, p. 2.

117. Sources cited in note 112.

118. Summers, *Conspiracy*, pp. 177–78.

119. Ibid.

120. Ibid., p. 178.

121. Priscilla Johnson McMillan, *Marina and Lee* (New York: Harper & Row, 1978), p. 107.

122. Prouty letter to Anthony Summers, June 25, 1979 (Summers, *Conspiracy*, p. 168, n.168).

123. CIA document 1004–400, declassified in 1976.

124. Bernard Fensterwald and Michael Ewing, *Coincidence or Conspiracy?* (New York: Zebra Books, 1977), p. 230.

125. Employment aptitude tests: X, pp. 121–27, 144, 155; XI, pp. 475–78; *Warren Report*, pp. 402–3. Cunningham quotes: X, pp. 123–24, 127. On Oswald's IQ and general intelligence, see VIII, pp. 247, 290, 300.

126. Testimony of Jaggars-Chiles-Stovall employee Dennis Ofstein, X, p. 202.

127. XVI, p. 155.

128. XVII, p. 801.

129. *Warren Report*, pp. 386–87.

130. CD 75, pp. 461–62; CD 1209; CD 1211, 1218, 1226, 1230, 1241. It is not clear whether the source of this claim was Oswald's recorded assertion or some other source.

131. Senate Select Committee, *Investigation Into the Assassination of JFK*, p. 54, cited in Hurt, *Reasonable Doubt*, p. 242.

CHAPTER 3

1. *Denver Post*, May 2, 1976.

2. See Anson, *"They've Killed The President,"* pp. 178–81; Summers, *Conspiracy*, Ch. 16; CE 1409.

3. Lee (V.T.) Exhibit I; XX, p. 511.

4. XX, pp. 514–18.

5. Oswald's two visits to Bringuier: XIX, p. 240; XXV, p. 773; X, p. 37; XXVI, p. 768. See also Summers' interview with Bringuier, 1978 (Summers, *Conspiracy*, pp. 300–1.).

6. Summers, *Conspiracy*, pp. 300–1.

7. *Warren Report*, p. 383.

8. HSCA X, p. 81n.

9. Summers, *Conspiracy*, pp. 307–8.,

10. Rosemary James and Jack Wardlaw, *Plot or Politics: The Garrison Case and Its Cast* (New Orleans: Pelican, 1967), p. 12.

11. For FBI Agent Quigley and Oswald interview, see Quigley FBI report, August 23, 1963 (FBI document N.O. 100–16601–18); XVII, pp. 758–62.

12. IV, p. 437; XVII, pp. 758–62; HSCA X, p. 123.

13. X, pp. 41, 61, 68; XVI, p. 342; XXV, p. 771. See also CD 206, pp. 216–18; CD 114, p. 629; CD 75, pp. 69–70.

14. This trend is described by Senate Committee to Study Government Intelligence. Senate Select Committee, *Investigation into the Assassination of JFK*, Book V.

15. Halperin, *Lawless State*, pp. 135–40.

16. Senate Select Committee, *Investigation into the Assassination of JFK*, Book, V, p. 60.

17. Ibid.

18. Memo from FBI Director J. Edgar Hoover to Warren Commission Chief Counsel J. Lee Rankin, June 11, 1964.

19. Senate Select Committee, *Investigation into the Assassination of JFK*, Book V, p. 64.

20. Ibid.

21. XXVI, p. 783; CE 3120.

22. XXIV, pp. 332, 337.

23. XX, p. 512; XX, p. 518; XX, p. 524.

24. Sources used for this portrait of Banister include: HSCA X, pp. 123–27; Harold Weisberg, *Oswald in New Orleans—Case for Conspiracy with the CIA* (New York: Canyon Books, 1967), pp. 51–52, 327–29, 337–40, 364, 391, 410; Summers, *Conspiracy*, pp. 319–26.

25. Hurt, *Reasonable Doubt*, p. 289. See also Jim Garrison, *On The Trail of the Assassins: My Investigation and Prosecution of the Murder of President Kennedy* (New York: Sheridan Square Press, 1988), p. 5. Garrison states that this incident occurred at sunset on the day of the assassination. He cites a New Orleans police report (K12634–63). Garrison has generally implied a CIA-based conspiracy. *On the Trail* incorporates much of the material from his 1970 book *A Heritage of Stone* and adds a memoir concerning his 1967–69 probe (as New Orleans District Attorney) into a possible conspiracy involving New Orleans businessman Clay Shaw, a probe that focused intensely on Ferrie and Banister as well. Shaw was acquitted in March 1969 of conspiracy to kill the president. Garrison's investigation and methods came under sharp criticism, which his latest book seeks to refute with a spirited defense.

26. Summers, *Conspiracy*, p. 321.

27. State of Louisiana, Secretary of State, May 17, 1967. Friends of Democratic Cuba, Inc., Articles of Incorporation cited in Jim Garrison, *Heritage of Stone* (New York: G. P. Putnam & Sons, 1970), p. 97.

28. Summers, *Conspiracy*, p. 321.

29. Ibid., p. 320.

30. E. Howard Hunt, *Give Us this Day* (New York: Arlington House, 1973), pp. 40–51, 181–89. For front organization see HSCA X, p. 57.

31. Summers, *Conspiracy*, p. 319.

32. Ibid.

33. Milton E. Brener, *The Garrison Case: A Study in the Abuse of Power* (New York: Clarkson N. Potter, 1969), p. 47.

34. Summers, *Conspiracy*, pp. 318–19.

35. *Warren Report*, pp. 407–09.

36. Summers, *Conspiracy*, p. 326.

37. Ibid.

38. Ibid.

39. *HSCA* X, pp. 130–31.

40. *HSCA Report*, p. 144.

41. Summers, *Conspiracy*, p. 257. Summers interview of Kohly, 1978.

42. Ibid., pp. 427–28. Summers obtained a copy of an audio tape made by a Dallas policeman at a John Birch Society meeting.

43. William Manchester, *Death of a President* (New York: Harper & Row, 1967), p. 53.

44. Garrison, *Heritage*, pp. 98–100; *Trail of the Assassins*, p. 37.

45. Summers, *Conspiracy*, p. 324.

46. Summers, *Conspiracy*, p. 325.

47. XVI, p. 67.

48. Weisberg, *Oswald in New Orleans*, pp. 78–80.

49. Wise and Ross, *Invisible Government*, pp. 26, 42; Anson, *"They've Killed The President,"* p. 250.

50. XXII, p. 828; Weisberg, *Oswald in New Orleans*, p. 79.

51. George Valsky, "Cuban Exiles Recall Domestic Spying and Picketing for CIA," *New York Times*, January 4, 1975.

52. Warren Commission, Bringuier Exhibits 3 and 4.

53. Fensterwald and Ewing, *Coincidence*, pp. 468–70; telephone conversation with Bernard Fensterwald, September 21, 1981.

54. Ibid.

55. CIA document 1433–492-AB. May 8, 1967 memo, "Garrison and the Kennedy Assassination," one page.

56. Senate Select Committee to Study Government Activities with Respect to Intelligence Activities, *Supplementary Detailed Staff Reports on Intelligence Activities and the Rights of Americans* (Washington, DC: U.S. Government Printing Office, 1976), Book III, pp. 620–22. Hereafter referred to as *Rights of Americans*.

CHAPTER 4

1. The profile of David Ferrie is based on the following sources: *HSCA* X, pp. 103–11; Anson, *"They've Killed the President,"* pp. 105–6; CIA document 1359–503, February 7, 1968; *El Tiempo*, New York, March 1967; CD 75, pp. 287–90.

2. Hurt, *Reasonable Doubt*, p. 263.

3. Summers, *Conspiracy*, pp. 482–83.

4. James and Wardlaw, *Plot or Politics?* p. 45. See also *HSCA Report*, p. 143 note.

5. J. Edward Epstein, *Counterplot* (New York: Viking Press, 1969), p. 37.

6. Ibid.

7. Ibid.; William Turner, "The Garrison Commission on the Assassination of President Kennedy," *Ramparts*, January 1968, p. 48.

8. Summers, *Conspiracy*, p. 329.

9. Richard H. Popkin, "Garrison Case," *New York Review of Books*, September 14, 1967, p. 28.

10. James and Wardlaw, *Plot or Politics?* p. 72; *El Tiempo*, New York, March 1967.

11. James and Wardlaw, *Plot or Politics?* p. 131.

12. Senate Select Committee, *Investigation Into the Assassination of JFK*, Book V, pp. 12–15; *New Orleans States-Item*, May 5, 1963.

13. Summers, *Conspiracy*, p. 329.

14. CD 87, p. 3.

15. HSCA X, p. 132n.

16. Summers, *Conspiracy*, p. 329.

17. Ibid.

18. CIA document 1326–1042.

19. CD 75, pp. 285–97; HSCA IX, pp. 103–5; Hurt, *Reasonable Doubt*, p. 284.

20. Summers, *Conspiracy*, pp. 477–78, pp. 601 n.3; HSCA IV, pp. 499, 567; HSCA IX, p. 806.

21. Hurt, *Reasonable Doubt*, p. 286, citing CD 75, pp. 285–87.

22. Weisberg, *Oswald in New Orleans*, p. 184.

23. Ibid.

24. FBI Report, November 26, 1963, no. 89–68, National Archives—"David Ferrie" file, p. 4 (CR7593).

25. Epstein, *Counterplot*, p. 37.

26. Turner, "Garrison Commission," p. 46; FBI Report, November 26, 1963.

27. CD 301, p. 87 (Secret Service Report).

28. Ibid.

29. FBI Report, November 26, 1963 (CR7593), p. 4.

30. CD 301, p. 85.

31. Ibid.

32. CD 301, p. 86 (National Archives).

33. Turner, "Garrison Commission," p. 46.

34. HSCA X, pp. 108–9.

35. HSCA XI, p. 103; VIII, p. 14; XXII, p. 826.

36. HSCA IX, p. 104.

37. HSCA X, pp. 102–4, 108–9; VIII, p. 14.

38. Summers, *Conspiracy*, p. 339.

39. HSCA X, pp. 108–9.

40. XXV, p. 140.

41. Ibid.

42. Delphine Roberts' interview with Anthony Summers (Summers, *Conspiracy*, pp. 323–26, 335–36, 579–80n).

43. Garrison, *Heritage*, p. 129.

44. This description of the Clinton incident draws on the following sources: *HSCA Report*, pp. 142–45, *HSCA IV*, pp. 482–85; Summers, *Conspiracy*, pp. 332–37; *HSCA X*, pp. 114, 132, 203.

45. Summers, *Conspiracy*, p. 335.

46. James W. Clarke, *American Assassins: The Darker Side of Politics* (Princeton, NJ: Princeton University Press, 1982), p. 118.

47. Summers, *Conspiracy*, p. 336, speculates on a possible FBI link to the Clinton incident, specifically to Cointelpro. State agencies were also known to have an interest in surveillance of civil rights activities.

48. Halperin, *Lawless State*, p. 136.

49. Ibid., p. 137.

50. Ibid., p. 138.

51. Ibid., pp. 142–43.

52. Ibid. Only a small fraction of these were actually opened.

53. Ibid., p. 153.

54. *Report to the President by the Commission on CIA Activities within the United States* (Rockefeller Commission Report), U.S. Government Printing Office, June 1975, pp. 152–55; Halperin, *Lawless State*, pp. 146–47.

55. Senate Select Committee, *Rights of Americans*, Book III, p. 725.

56. Halperin, *Lawless State*, p. 146.

57. Ibid.

58. *Rockefeller Commission Report*, p. 1153; Senate Select Committee, *Rights of Americans*, Book III, pp. 723–26.

59. Marchetti and Marks, *CIA and the Cult*, p. 217.

60. Ibid.

61. *Rockefeller Commission Report*, p. 153.

62. "CIA Infiltrated Black Groups Here in 60s," *Washington Post*, March 30, 1978.

63. Ibid.

64. Ibid.

65. CR 75, FBI Report, November 11, 1963, p. 3.

66. National Archives, record group 272. Statement of David W. Ferrie, witnessed by FBI Agent Regis L. Kennedy, New Orleans, December 10,1963 (CD 205, p. 588).

67. *HSCA X*, p. 114.

68. Ibid., p. 113.

69. Summers, *Conspiracy*, p. 497.

70. FBI Report, November 27, 1963 (File no. 89–69), Special Agents Wall and Viater.

71. Garrison, *Heritage*, p. 111.

72. Hurt, *Reasonable Doubt*, p. 265, citing Weisberg, *Oswald in New Orleans* and *New York World Journal Tribune*, February 28, 1967.

73. Garrison, *Heritage*, p. 111; *Trail of the Assassins*, p. 141.

74. Hurt, *Reasonable Doubt*, p. 264; March 1, 1967 statement of George Lardner, Jr. to New Orleans District Attorney's Office.

75. Fensterwald and Ewing, *Coincidence*, pp. 304–5.

76. *HSCA Report*, p. 147.

CHAPTER 5

1. *Rockefeller Commission Report*, p. 152.

2. II, pp. 407–12.

3. Sylvia Meagher and Gary Owens, *Master Index to the JFK Assassination Investigations* (Metuchen, NJ: Scarecrow Press, 1980). See *HSCA* witness and contact lists, pp. 307–12.

4. II, p. 408.

5. Ibid., pp. 408–12.

6. Ibid., p. 409.

7. Ibid.

8. Ibid.

9. Ibid.

10. Ibid.

11. Summers, *Conspiracy*, p. 399.

12. XX, pp. 271–73.

13. CE 1145, pp. 17–18.

14. See Meagher's perceptive analysis in *Accessories*, pp. 220–22. For FBI to Warren Commission see CE 2718.

15. See Hurt, *Reasonable Doubt*, pp. 300–2. Researcher Fred Newcomb made the initial discovery of this dimension regarding the Dodd Committee.

16. Ibid. on Kleins; Hurt, *Reasonable Doubt*, p. 300 on Seaport Traders.

17. Meagher, *Accessories*, pp. 312–13. See also testimony of Communist Party official Arnold Johnson, X, pp. 103–5.

18. Halperin, *Lawless State*, p. 153. The ACLU's Dallas chapter was listed by the Dallas police as one of the "known subversive and extremist groups" in the city, some of which police claimed to have "successfully infiltrated" (CE 710). It seems likely that cold warriors in the intelligence community would hold a similar view of the organization.

19. Marchetti and Marks, *CIA and the Cult*, p. 217.

20. Ibid., pp. 216–18.

21. *Rockefeller Commission Report*, p. 152.

22. Senate Select Committee, *Rights of Americans*, Book III, p. 702.

23. Ibid., p. 692.

24. Ibid.

25. This mentality is described in Wise and Ross, *Invisible Government*, Chs. 16 and 17; Marchetti and Marks, *CIA and the Cult*, Ch. 8.

26. XX, p. 511.

27. CE 1409 (XX, p. 796).

28. Summers, *Conspiracy*, pp. 297–98, implies that it was Oswald.

29. CE 1409.

30. May 26, 1963 letter to the FPCC in XX, p. 512.

31. *HSCA* X, p. 127.

32. FPCC reply to Oswald, May 29, 1963 (XX, p. 514).

33. Senate Select Committee, *Investigation Into the Assassination of JFK*, Book V, pp. 66–67.

34. Ibid., p. 65.

35. Ibid.

36. XX, p. 800; XXV, pp. 770–75.

37. June 17, 1964 memo from Richard M. Mosk to Wesley J. Liebeler, "Oswald's Reading," 6 pages.

38. Ibid., p. 4. A copy of this memo was published in CE 1117.

39. Oswald letter to *The Worker*, CE 1145 (XXII, p. 166).

40. CE 1145 (XXII, p. 167).

41. James and Wardlaw, *Plot or Politics?* p. 12.

42. Summers, *Conspiracy*, p. 303.

43. Oswald letter of August 4, 1963 (XX, p. 524).

44. CE 1145 (XX, p. 167), Oswald letter of August 13, 1963 to Arnold Johnson.

45. CE 826, FBI file no. 100–16601, August 15, 1963 report of interview with Lee Harvey Oswald on August 10, 1963.

46. Martello's statement to FBI, November 29, 1963 (file no. 89–69), pp. 3–5.

47. XXI, p. 626.

48. Summers, *Conspiracy*, p. 301.

49. X, pp. 41, 61, 68; XXV, p. 771; XXVI, p. 342; CD 206, pp. 216–18; CD 114, p. 629; CD 75, pp. 69–72.

50. X, p. 49; XI, pp. 160–63.

51. Summers, *Conspiracy*, p. 308.

52. X, p. 42; XI, p. 171; XVII, p. 763.

53. IX, p. 166.

54. CBS Television, "The American Assassins," November 26, 1975.

55. *HSCA* X, p. 81n.

56. CD 205.

57. Ibid., p. 647.

58. XVI, p. 67; Harold Weisberg, *Oswald in New Orleans*, p. 79.

59. XXII, p. 826.

60. X, pp. 41–42.

61. Ibid.

62. XI, pp. 167–68.

63. Ibid., p. 168.

64. CIA document 590–252: March 6, 1964 memo from the CIA to the Warren Commission. The House Un-American Activities Committee (HUAC) also had a clipping on Oswald's defection in its files.

65. "Conversation Carte Blanche" broadcast on WDSU Radio, August 21, 1963, at 6:05 PM. Transcript obtained from XXI, pp. 633–41 (Stuckey Exhibit 3), "Oswald—New Orleans."

66. XIX, p. 175.

67. XXII, p. 172; CD 1145, p. 11 (letter of August 28, Oswald to American Communist Party Central Committee).

68. November 5, 1962 letter from Socialist Workers Party National Secretary Farrell Dobbs to Oswald.

69. Reply to Oswald's offer came from Mr. Bob Chester, SWP.

70. FBI memorandum "FPCC Activities," p. 4.

71. II, p. 408.

72. IV, p. 426.

73. Ibid.

74. CE 826, p. 12 (FBI document NO100–16601/CV).

75. Senate Select Committee, *Rights of Americans*, Book III, p. 728.

76. Halperin, *Lawless State*, pp. 148–52 (on the paradigm of operation CHAOS).

77. Senate Select Committee, *Investigation Into the Assassination of JFK*, Book V, p. 65.

CHAPTER 6

1. X, pp. 273–74.

2. IX, p. 217.

3. FBI document DL–105–1766, "Relationship between the Oswalds and the de Mohrenschildts," p. 17.

4. CD 777a; CE 538; IX, pp. 184–86.

5. See Wise and Ross, *Invisible Government*, pp. 125–26. The most famous case described by Wise and Ross was that of former Nazi General Reinhard Gehlen and his spy network known as "The Gehlen Organization."

6. FBI document DL–105–1766, p. 22.

7. Ibid., p. 18.

8. IX, p. 170.

9. FBI document DL–105–1766, statement of Igor Voshinin, p. 18.

10. Ibid.

11. IX, p. 187.

12. Ibid.

13. "Who Was George de Mohrenschildt?" *Clandestine America*, Fall 1977.

14. Ibid.

15. Ibid.
16. Summers, *Conspiracy*, p. 226.
17. CD 777a; CE 538; IX, pp. 184–86.
18. *Clandestine America*, Fall 1977; Summers, *Conspiracy*, pp. 225–26, 560 (n. 61).
19. CIA document 18–522.
20. Summers, *Conspiracy*, p. 226.
21. *Warren Report*, p. 262.
22. Summers, *Conspiracy*, p. 225.
23. *HSCA* XII, pp. 55–58; CIA document 431–154B.
24. Ibid., p. 60.
25. Summers, *Conspiracy*, p. 249.
26. *HSCA* XII, pp. 60–61.
27. Summers, *Conspiracy*, p. 249.
28. FBI document DL–105–1766, p. 19. Statement of Gary E. Taylor.
29. Ibid.
30. Ibid.
31. Ibid., p. 22, statement of Ilya Mamantov.
32. *HSCA* XII, pp. 60–61; Summers, *Conspiracy*, p. 607 n.28.
33. Hurt, *Reasonable Doubt*, p. 223; *HSCA* XII, p. 57.
34. Cogswell, *New York Daily News*, April 12, 1977. This information on de Mohrenschildt was used by the HSCA (*HSCA* XII, p. 60).
35. VIII, p. 358; IX, pp. 3, 5.
36. Scott, *Dallas Conspiracy*, Ch. 3, p. 9.
37. Summers, *Conspiracy*, 225.
38. *HSCA* XII, p. 61; Garrison, *Heritage*, p. 80.
39. Ibid.
40. *HSCA* XII, p. 61.
41. Ibid.
42. Garrison, *Heritage*, p. 114; II, p. 386.
43. CD 206, p. 66.
44. Summers, *Conspiracy*, p. 225.
45. Telephone call to Mary Ferrell, July 7, 1981.
46. IX, p. 96.
47. FBI document DL–105–1766, p. 13.
48. Ibid., p. 14. Statement of Samuel B. Ballen.
49. Summers, *Conspiracy*, p. 229.
50. Ibid., p. 230.
51. Ibid.
52. Ibid.
53. Ibid.
54. Ibid., p. 231.
55. Ibid.
56. X, p. 202.

57. Hurt, *Reasonable Doubt*, p. 222.

58. Summers, *Conspiracy*, p. 231.

59. X, p. 201.

60. IV, p. 388.

61. *Warren Report*, p. 603.

62. Garrison (*Heritage*, p. 81) alleges that the Dallas police also found what they described as "an unknown electronic device." If true, this would certainly be intriguing. Garrison cites XXI, pp. 596–97 but those pages contain no such reference.

63. FBI document DL 89–43, December 4, 1963, FBI laboratory to New York field office. This memo indicates that the Bureau compared the film found in Oswald's Minox to Minox film relating to another case (designated "LOCFAB, ESP-R"). The two films were not produced by the same camera, said the Bureau. It would be interesting to discover with what other case the FBI was cross-checking Oswald's film.

64. *HSCA* XII, pp. 390, 397; Earl Golz, *Dallas Morning News*, August 7, 1978; Anthony Summers' interview with Dallas District Attorney Bill Alexander (Summers, *Conspiracy*, pp. 231–32).

65. XVI, p. 53.

66. Telephone conversation with Steven Baker of Jaggars-Chiles-Stovall, May 14, 1981.

67. See also X, pp. 184–85 (Graef testimony).

68. Epstein, *Legend*, p. 142; on words and sentences: Ofstein, X, p. 197.

69. X, pp. 175–76 (Graef).

70. Ibid., pp. 167–212, testimonies of Robert L. Stovall, John G. Graef, Dennis Ofstein.

71. Ibid., Stovall and Ofstein.

72. Ibid., p. 204 (Ofstein).

73. Ibid., p. 194.

74. Ibid., pp. 194–212 (Ofstein).

75. Ibid., p. 208.

76. Ibid., p. 198.

77. Ibid., p. 202.

78. Ibid., pp. 207–8.

79. Ibid., p. 208.

80. Ibid., pp. 202–3.

81. Ibid., p. 206.

82. Oswald's letters were responded to by Mr. Robert Chester, Socialist Workers Party, Dec. 9, 1962; Mr. James J. Torney, Hall-Davis Defense Committee, Dec. 13, 1962; Mr. Louis Weinstock, *The Worker*, Dec. 19, 1962.

83. Summers, *Conspiracy*, pp. 312–13.

84. CE 1940.

85. Garrison, *Heritage*, p. 129. Garrison's office obtained an application form containing this information.

86. CE 1941; Marachini: Garrison, *Heritage*, p. 129.

87. Garrison, *Heritage*, p. 129

88. Ibid., p. 130, based on interview of John P. Voltz, New Orleans District Attorney's Office, conducted with Melvin Coffee, February 18, 1967.

89. Ibid., based on interview of James Lewallen with Alcock and Ivon, New Orleans District Attorney's Office, February 19, 1967.

90. The information concerning Coffee and the CAP is taken from his November 30, 1963 FBI interview by Agent Ernest C. Wall; Lewallen and the CAP: Lewallen's November 27, 1963 FBI interview by Agents Wall and Viater (Bureau File NO 89–69).

91. Hurt, *Reasonable Doubt*, p. 219.

92. IX, p. 237.

93. *HSCA Report*, p. 217.

94. Ibid.

95. Ibid.

96. Ibid.

97. Summers' interview with Jeanne de Mohrenschildt (Summers, *Conspiracy*, p. 228).

98. Ibid., p. 227.

99. Ibid.

100. For account of Moore see 1976 interview by a reporter, appearing in "Three Witnesses," Dick Russell, *New Times*, June 24, 1977.

101. Summers' interview with Jean de Mohrenschildt (Summers, *Conspiracy*, p. 227).

102. Epstein, *Legend*, p. 314.

103. VIII, p. 355.

104. FBI document DL–105–1766, p. 14.

105. Ibid.

106. *Dallas Morning News*, March 30, 1978. It has been alleged that at this point in his life, de Mohrenschildt was suffering from psychological problems that made his assertions unreliable.

107. *Boston Globe*, Associated Press article, March 27, 1977, "Assassination Probe Witness Found Dead," p. 8.

108. Summers, *Conspiracy*, Chapter 7, p. 499.

CHAPTER 7

1. The "sensitive source" was most likely the CIA's audio and visual surveillance.

2. FBI report, November 30, 1963, Laredo, Texas, File no. 5A 89–67.

3. CD 75, pp. 588, 613, 652; Anson, *"They've Killed the President,"* p. 181.

4. Gaudet's statements concerning his role and activities have come from three interviews: with Allen Stone in 1975, Bernard Fensterwald in 1975, Sum-

mers in 1977 and 1978; see also Gaudet's HSCA deposition (*HSCA Report*, pp. 218–19).

5. Fensterwald interview of May 13, 1975.

6. Summers' interviews, Summers, *Conspiracy*, p. 364.

7. Ibid., pp. 364–65.

8. Ibid., p. 365.

9. *HSCA Report*, pp. 218–19; Summers, *Conspiracy*, p. 365.

10. XXVI, p. 337; also FBI 44–2064.

11. *HSCA Report*, pp. 218–19.

12. Summers, *Conspiracy*, pp. 584–85, n.89; CD 963 (24 pages), pp. 17–19.

13. XXV, pp. 30, 35, 39; Fensterwald and Ewing, *Coincidence*, pp. 233–35. See also XI, p. 220; XXIV, p. 576, XXV, pp. 42, 45, 75; *Warren Report*, p. 733.

14. XXV, pp. 25, 44–47.

15. *Warren Report*, p. 305.

16. Fensterwald and Ewing, *Coincidence*, p. 234.

17. Ibid.

18. Summers, *Conspiracy*, p. 370.

19. *Warren Report*, p. 733; XXV, pp. 42, 45, 76; XXIV, p. 576.

20. Fensterwald and Ewing, *Coincidence*, p. 234.

21. Ibid.

22. Ibid., XXIV, p. 642.

23. XI, p. 214; Summers, *Conspiracy*, p. 369.

24. XI, p. 215; Summers, *Conspiracy*, p. 369.

25. Meagher, *Accessories*, pp. 334–36.

26. Ibid., p. 337.

27. XVI, p. 33; XXIV, p. 590; XXV, pp. 586, 634–35; *HSCA* III, pp. 6–8.

28. *Warren Report*, p. 299; *HSCA Report*, pp. 123–25, 248–55.

29. Testimony of Azcue to House Assassinations Committee, *HSCA* III, pp. 126–58; *HSCA Report*, pp. 123–26; Azcue's formal statement made during public hearings in Havana, conducted by the Committee, July 29, 1978.

30. Sylvia Duran's interview with Anthony Summers, May 13, 1979 (Summers, *Conspiracy*, p. 376).

31. Also, Mrs. Duran wrote to Summers, June 22, 1979, regarding her observations about the film.

32. CD 1216.

33. *HSCA* III, p. 103.

34. Ibid. For Oswald's height see *Autopsy Report*, FBI file; New Orleans police arrest record.

35. *HSCA* III, p. 69.

36. See *HSCA Report*, pp. 124–25. Summers' 1978 interview with Contreras in Summers, *Conspiracy*, pp. 377–78.

37. *HSCA* III, p. 172; *HSCA Report*, p. 251.

38. *HSCA* III, pp. 142, 155, 176.

39. The FBI monitored Oswald for links with the American Communist Party from the time he returned to the United States after his defection to the Soviet Union. He never joined the Party.

40. Summers' interview with Duran (Summers, *Conspiracy*, p. 370). Neither the Warren Commission, the House Assassinations Committee, nor the New Orleans police possessed such a photo, and there is no indication that the real Oswald ever possessed it either.

41. CD 631.

42. Colby's interview with Dan Rather, CBS TV special "The American Assassins," November 26, 1975.

43. On the mystery-man photograph see *Warren Report*, p. 364; XI, p. 469; CD 1287; CD 631; CD 674; CIA internal memorandum, May 5, 1967; Summers, *Conspiracy*, pp. 380–82.

44. David Phillips, *The Night Watch* (New York: Atheneum, 1977), p. 142.

45. *HSCA* IV, p. 215; XI, p. 63; see also Central Intelligence Agency document 579250.

46. XXVI, p. 149 (CE 2764).

47. XI, p. 469; CD 1287; CD 631; CD 674.

48. CIA memorandum to Warren Commission, July 1964 (CD 1287).

49. Summers, *Conspiracy*, p. 382.

50. CIA memorandum, July 1964 (CD 1287).

51. Agee, *Inside the Company*, p. 528.

52. Phillips, *Night Watch*, p. 142.

53. Summers, *Conspiracy*, p. 384.

54. Phillips, *Night Watch*, p. 142.

55. Summers, *Conspiracy*, p. 383.

56. Ibid. Summers' interview with former House Committee chief counsel Richard Sprague, 1978.

A key figure in the Mexico city affair and the impostor question is the late David Phillips, the CIA officer who was chief of Cuban Operations in Mexico City during Oswald's visit. Phillips became embroiled in a complex controversy regarding whether he had been operating under the cover name "Maurice Bishop." In a series of testimonies and interviews, Cuban exile leader Antonio Veciana, the founder of the violent anti-Castro group Alpha–66, told how his CIA case officer "Maurice Bishop" had orchestrated raids against Castro in defiance of President Kennedy's ban on such activity. Veciana claims that in late August or early September 1963 he was called to Dallas to meet Bishop. At the meeting, says Veciana, Bishop was accompanied by a quiet, strangely preoccupied young man whom Veciana would later recognize as Lee Harvey Oswald. Phillips vehemently denied being "Bishop" or meeting Oswald.

The HSCA took the Bishop matter quite seriously. Building on the work of HSCA investigator Gaeton Fonzi, journalist Anthony Summers has unearthed a rich trail of evidence that confirms the existence of a "Maurice Bishop" such as Veciana described. There is also a striking series of parallels between Phillips and Bishop in terms of physical appearance, CIA assignments, and activities.

Fonzi said in 1989 "that Antonio Veciana should produce, in describing the role and character of Maurice Bishop, a figure so specifically identical to David Phillips, and that Phillips' history should have so many relevant and interconnected facets bearing on the Kennedy assassination breaches the bounds of coincidence." See Summers, *Conspiracy* (Paragon House ed, 1989), pp. 324–35, 504–19. Fonzi published a lengthy article on Phillips/Bishop in the November 1980 issue of *Washingtonian Magazine*.

57. Summers, *Conspiracy* (New York: Paragon House, 1989), pp. 519–23, 535.

58. Summers, *Conspiracy*, pp. 373–74.

59. CBS-TV, "The American Assassins," November 25, 1975.

60. *Washington Post*, May 6, 1977.

61. Letterhead memorandum from J. Edgar Hoover to James J. Rowley, Secret Service, November 23, 1963 (JFK Classified Document 000169).

62. *HSCA Report*, p. 251.

63. FBI agent-in-charge in Dallas, Gordon Shanklin, claimed no knowledge of the tapes. However, Shanklin suffered "serious impairment of credibility" in the view of the House Committee because he had been involved in destroying a note allegedly given to the FBI by Oswald before the assassination: *HSCA Report*, pp. 195–96.

64. CD 1084D, p. 5; CD 1084d, p. 4; Slawson memo, February 14, 1964; State Department telegram, November 28, 1963 (U.S. Ambassador Mann to Secretary of State Rusk).

65. Ron Kessler, *Washington Post*, November 26, 1976.

66. Ibid.

67. LWT Productions, London, England. Shown on Showtime cable channels in the United States.

CHAPTER 8

1. *Warren Report*, p. 609. (The Warren Commission rejected this story and also the general notion of an Oswald impostor.)

2. XXIV, pp. 729–34.

3. Hurt, *Reasonable Doubt*, p. 395.

4. X, p. 353; XXVI, p. 685.

5. X, p. 353.

6. XXVI, p. 685.

7. *Warren Report*, p. 298.

8. Ibid.

9. XVI, pp. 178–79; X, pp. 327–40; *Warren Report*, p. 331.

10. X, p. 311.

11. The account of this incident is taken from X, pp. 309–27; quotation at p. 312.

12. The description of this incident is taken from XXIV, pp. 704–5.

13. Ibid.
14. *Warren Report*, p. 295.
15. Ibid.
16. Hurt, *Reasonable Doubt*, p. 346, citing: XXVI, p. 406; CD 1, pp. 267–68; Gary Shaw and Larry Harris, *Cover-Up* (Cleburne, TX: 1976), p. 111 (privately published manuscript).
17. For Odio incident see *HSCA Report*, pp. 137–39; XI, pp. 327–86; XXVI, pp. 362, 472; XVI, p. 834; CD 1553; Summers' interviews with Odio, 1978 and 1979 (Summers, *Conspiracy*, pp. 411–17).
18. Summers, *Conspiracy*, p. 413.
19. XX, pp. 688–91.
20. Summers, *Conspiracy*, p. 414.
21. *Warren Report*, p. 324.
22. Summers, *Conspiracy*, p. 411.
23. Ibid., p. 416.
24. XXVI, p. 595.
25. *Warren Report*, p. 324.
26. Edward J. Epstein, *Inquest* (New York: Bantam, 1966), p. 103.
27. Meagher, *Accessories*, p. 387.
28. Peter Noyes, *Legacy of Doubt* (New York: Pinnacle Books, 1973), p. 29.
29. Weisberg, *Oswald in New Orleans*, pp. 161, 273–76.
30. XVI, p. 436; CD 294.
31. Weisberg, *Oswald in New Orleans*, pp. 161, 273–76.
32. CD 1553, p. 9; William Turner, *Power on The Right* (Berkeley: Ramparts Press, 1971), p. 106.
33. Memo from William Scott Malone to C. Fenton, House Assassination Committee chief investigator, June 3, 1977.
34. For Craig incident see XIX, p. 524; *HSCA* XIII, pp. 17–18; *Warren Report*, pp. 52, 446; Shaw and Harris, *Cover-Up*, pp. 15–17.
35. James P. Kelly and N. C. Livingston, "Could the President Survive a Real-Life James Bond Movie?" *Washingtonian Magazine*, September 1981.
36. The role of federal agencies in presidential protection is described in a memo from Secret Service Chief Rowley to Secretary of the Treasury Douglas Dillon, December 18, 1963. Part 1A, "Identification of Individuals Believed to be Dangerous to the President," Records group 272, National Archives, record subgroup 22, "Records Relating to the Protection of the President."
37. Summers, *Conspiracy*, pp. 417, 418.
38. For CIA response to Secret Service see Warren Commission Document 853B, from Protective Research Office of Secret Service to Dallas field office, March 18, 1964 (SS–3670), item no. 9.
39. FBI report of Wallace R. Heitman, May 26, 1964 (FBI document no. DL 105–1740).
40. For FBI interviews of Ruiz see CD 1085, part U, p. 5.
41. Dallas Sheriff's Office, report of Deputy Sheriff Eddy Walthers, November 23, 1963; CE 5323, p. 534.

42. For FBI report on "Oswald" see. FBI document 1085U, p. 1.

43. For physical description of Ruiz see CD 835B. FBI profile of Ruiz, March 9, 1964, signed by J. Edgar Hoover.

44. For ATFB agent and gun shop see Warren Commission Document 853A, no. 2, p. 2 (Protective Research Section analysis of Ruiz, Jan. 14–17, 1964).

45. CE 2694; CD 778, pp. 13–14.

46. For FBI memo on ammunition see Agent Jevons to Agent Conrad, December 2, 1963; subject: "Assassination of President John F. Kennedy."

47. For Russell and gun shop owner see "Is the 'Second Oswald' Alive in Dallas?" *Village Voice*, August 23, 1976, pp. 23–27; telephone conversation with Russell, July 21, 1981.

48. Anson, *"They've Killed the President,"* p. 200. Anson cites the *New York Times*, February 23, 1975.

49. Ibid.

50. Ibid.

51. At one point, Oswald was unaccounted for by U.S. officials for a period of six weeks during his stay in Russia.

CHAPTER 9

1. *Life*, February 21, 1964.

2. *Warren Report*, pp. 608–9.

3. Meagher, *Accessories*, p. 208.

4. Summers, *Conspiracy*, p. 96; Anson, *"They've Killed the President,"* p. 79.

5. Anson, *"They've Killed the President,"* p. 79.

6. Meagher, *Accessories*, p. 208.

7. Summers, *Conspiracy*, p. 99. Summers also asserts (p. 96) that one of the publications held by Oswald in the photograph contained a letter from Dallas signed "L. H." Some researchers who credit the photos as genuine posit they they may have been an artifact of Oswald's activities as a provocateur or monitor of left-wing groups, just as his letters seemed to be.

8. Stated on CBS-TV, December 1977; see also Pickard interview with Anthony Summers, January 1978 (Summers, *Conspiracy*, p. 95).

9. Thompson, *HSCA* VI, pp. 219–20; Thompson interview for the BBC filmed January 1978 (see Summers, *Conspiracy*, p. 95).

10. *HSCA* II, p. 430; VI, p. 215.

11. Priscilla Johnson McMillan, *Marina and Lee* (New York: Harper & Row, 1978), p. 489, note 9.

12. *HSCA* VI, p. 151, shows the original inscription. For translation see *HSCA* II, p. 388.

13. *HSCA* II, p. 386.

14. *HSCA* II, p. 321; *HSCA* IV, p. 141.

15. Hester was interviewed by Earl Golz of the *Dallas Morning News* in 1978

and by Jim Marrs, *Fort Worth Star-Telegram*, September 21, 1978 (cited by Summers, *Conspiracy*, p. 97).

16. For Dillard and Powell photos see *HSCA* IV, pp. 109–10, 115.

17. *HSCA* IV, p. 115.

18. Ibid.

19. *HSCA Report*, p. 42.

20. For the palmprint see *Warren Report*, pp. 122–23; IV, pp. 261–62; CE 3145; Meagher, *Accessories*, pp. 120–24. Evidentiary conflicts and problems also plague the other crime attributed to Oswald—the murder of Dallas Police Officer J. D. Tippit. Tippit was shot dead within 45 minutes of the president's assassination, supposedly by Oswald (while en route from his Dallas apartment to the Texas Theater where he would be arrested). Excellent analyses of the flaws and controversies attending the official conclusions in the Tippit case are provided by Henry Hurt (*Reasonable Doubt*, pp. 139–69) and Sylvia Meagher (*Accessories*, pp. 253–82); Summers, *Conspiracy* (1989 Paragon House ed), pp. 487–88.

Problems include timing—whether Oswald could have gotten to the Tippit scene in time to do the shooting—and *modus operandi*. Tippit was seen summoning his eventual murderer to the patrol car. The man walked to the vehicle and bent down to converse with the officer through the passenger-side window. Tippit got out and was walking toward the front of his car when he was gunned down (Hurt, *Reasonable Doubt*, p. 142). Although an all-points-bulletin was issued for the president's assassin, neither Tippit's casual behavior nor the assailant's calm approach seem compatible with the scenario of the officer stopping a desperately fleeing suspect for questioning.

Moreover, as Hurt describes, "accounts of Tippit's murder and the descriptions of his assailant are as contradictory as any aspect of the assassination story" (*Reasonable Doubt*, p. 141). Several witnesses would ultimately identify Oswald as the assailant, but the witness who had perhaps the best view of the crime, Domingo Benavides, could not identify Oswald. Mrs. Helen Markham, the Warren Commission's star witness, had picked Oswald out of a seriously flawed line-up, but she also stated that the murderer had black hair (unlike Oswald) and that she talked with Tippit as he lay dying (by all evidence, he was killed instantly). One witness said there was another man with the gunman; another claimed that the killer fled in a car. However, Oswald was alone, and on foot. Witnesses said the gunman approached from the west (early police and Secret Service reports also state this). Oswald's route between his apartment and the movie theater would have brought him toward Tippit from the east end of Patton Street.

Tippit's assailant allegedly discarded four spent shells at the crime scene before fleeing. These have been conclusively matched to the .38 revolver Oswald was carrying when arrested. This means that at some undetermined point in time, the four shells allegedly found near Tippit's body were fired from Oswald's gun. But when? The bullets recovered from the victim's body did not manifest sufficient markings for the FBI laboratory to perform ballistics tests. Thus there is no established link between the murder bullets and Oswald's gun, only between the discarded cartridge and Oswald's gun. In addition, of the bullets removed from Tippit, three were manufactured by Winchester-Western and one by Remington-Peters; the cartridges allegedly found at the crime scene were two Remington-Peters and two Winchester-Western. The cartridges were the last items of evidence to be turned over to the FBI by the Dallas police, a full six days after the murder. This lagged significantly behind the rest of the evidence, leading some to suspect that the shells might have been produced *ex post facto*.

Tippit's own behavior further fuels the controversy surrounding his death. He was three miles out of his assigned district when he was killed. Just before the shooting he had rushed into a store and brushed customers aside to make a phone call. Five witnesses saw him sitting in his parked cruiser in a gas station lot before speeding away. These events occurred not far from where he was killed.

Henry Hurt has provided a possible explanation for Tippit's behavior (*Reasonable Doubt*, pp. 165–68, drawing on the work of researchers Larry Harris and Gary Shaw and journalist Earl Golz). The officer had been involved in a romantic triangle with a woman who lived within a few minutes of the area where his strange actions occurred just before the shooting. Hurt asserts: "The woman's confirmation of the affair supported the original speculation that Tippit's presence far from his own patrol district, his peculiar movements and activities, even his murder, could all be laid to an intensely emotional and explosive set of personal circumstances" (*Reasonable Doubt*, p. 165). The woman's husband had reportedly been greatly upset by the affair and had followed his wife late at night while she was in Tippit's company (Summers, p. 488, drawing on the research of Larry Harris and Ken Holmes, Jr.).

Had Oswald lived to receive a fair trial for Tippit's murder, it is clear that the widely assumed historical "fact" of his killing the policeman while trying to escape after the president's assassination would have been called into serious doubt.

21. The matter of the magazines in Alba's garage is analyzed by Henry Hurt, *Reasonable Doubt*, pp. 296–99. Hurt credits Paul Hoch's 1970 memo to critics. See XXIII, pp. 227–28; XXVI, p. 764; X, pp. 220, 227.

22. XXVI, p. 764; XXIII, p. 728.

23. Hoch memo to critics, 1970, cited in Hurt, *Reasonable Doubt*, p. 298.

24. Truly's FBI statement, November 23, 1963.

25. VII, p. 382.

26. VI, p. 385.

27. Fritz statement INV–2, National Archives documents.

28. VII, p. 383.

29. Meagher, *Accessories*, p. 93; III, pp. 228–32.

30. Anson, *"They've Killed the President,"* p. 349. Anson cites no source for this conclusion and the author was unable to verify it.

31. CE 2003, p. 127.

32. CD 3, Part 1, December 18, 1963 memo from Treasury Secretary Douglas Dillon to Earl Warren, Part III.

33. Meagher, *Accessories*, p. 96.

34. IV, p. 463; *HSCA* XII, pp. 600–8, especially p. 604.

35. *HSCA Report*, pp. 221–23.

36. Robert Sam Anson (*"They've Killed the President,"* p. 175n) asserts that the name "Harvey Lee Oswald" appeared in a 1960 list of defectors requested from the CIA by the White House. The names of other defectors were correct, says Anson. He offers no source for this claim and no specific citation for the "list." A page in CD 275, which may be the document Anson was referring to, cites Oswald as "Lee Henry Oswald."

37. *HSCA* IV, p. 184.

38. Anson, *"They've Killed the President,"* p. 285, citing Peter Dale Scott, "Government Documents and the JFK Assassination" (unpublished monograph).

39. Anson citing Scott as described in Note 38.

40. Philip H. Melanson, "The CIA's Secret Ties to Local Police," *The Nation*, March 26, 1983. Through the Freedom of Information Act, the author obtained 362 pages of heavily deleted documents from the Agency's "Domestic Police Training File." The relationship far exceeded the CIA's euphemism of "training." In some cases police intelligence squads conducted surveillance and even break-ins for the Agency and extracted agents from run-ins with the law. CIA agents were provided with police IDs. In return the Agency dispensed largesse, explosives, and exotic equipment—in some cases, unknown to administrative higher-ups (beyond the intelligence squads) in the departments involved.

41. *Warren Report*, p. 284.

42. Summers, *Conspiracy*, p. 442.

43. Senate Select Committee to Study Intelligence, "Investigation of the Assassination of President John F. Kennedy," Book V, pp. 28–31.

44. Summers, *Conspiracy*, p. 440. Summers interviewed U.S. Ambassador to Mexico Thomas Mann, who had dealt with the "D" affair.

45. *Warren Report*, p. 285.

46. CD 1084.

47. *Warren Report*, p. 285.

48. Ibid.

49. Senate Select Committee to Study Intelligence, "Investigation of the Assassination of President Kennedy," Book V, pp. 42–43.

CHAPTER 10

1. Thomas Powers, *The Man Who Kept the Secrets: Richard Helms and the CIA* (New York: Knopf, 1979), p. 82.

2. *Transcript*, Warren Commission Executive Session, December 5, 1963.

3. Wise and Ross, *Invisible Government*, p. 98.

4. *Transcript*, December 5, 1963.

5. David Lifton, *Document Addendum to the Warren Report* (El Segundo, CA: Sightext Publications, 1968), p. 263.

6. CIA document 155–422B.

7. CIA document 657–831.

8. Lifton, *Document Addendum*, p. 110.

9. Senate Select Committee, *Investigation into the Assassination of JFK*, Book V, p. 69.

10. CIA document 657–831, April 13, 1964 (author and addressee deleted).

11. Senate Select Committee, *Investigation into the Assassination of JFK*, Book V, p. 49.

12. Ibid.

13. V, p. 120.

14. William R. Corson, *The Armies of Ignorance: The Rise of American Intelligence Agencies* (New York: Dial Press, 1977), p. 35.

15. V, p. 120.

16. *Warren Report*, pp. 267–68 (Kramer Exhibit 1); XX, p. 474 (Kramer Exhibit 2).

17. *HSCA Report*, pp. 204–5.

18. Ibid., p. 205.

19. *Who's Who in CIA* (published by Julius Mader, Berlin, 1968) identifies Snyder as a CIA operative.

20. *HSCA Report*, p. 215.

21. Ibid., pp. 214–15.

22. Ibid., p. 215.

23. Ibid., pp. 203–4.

24. CIA document 1562–115B, April 5, 1972, two pages, at p. 1.

25. Senate Select Committee, *Rights of Americans*, Book III, pp. 566–68.

26. Halperin et al., *Lawless State*, p. 140.

27. *HSCA Report*, pp. 206–7; Senate Committee to Study Government Intelligence, Book III, pp. 566–68.

28. *HSCA XII*, p. 236.

29. Lee (V.T.) Exhibit 4.

30. *Warren Report*, p. 704.

31. CE 2762; XXVI, p. 146.

32. Ibid.

33. *Warren Report*, pp. 696, 750.

34. Meagher, *Accessories*, pp. 331–32.

35. David Belin, *November 22, 1963: You're the Jury* (New York: Quadrangle Books, 1973). On the twenty-fifth anniversary of the assassination Charles Scribner's Sons published Belin's *Final Disclosure: The Full Truth about the Assassination of President Kennedy* (1988). The book is based on Belin's work for the Warren and Rockefeller Commissions as described in his personal notes. It is far more interesting for what it doesn't disclose than for what it does. There are

11 chapters dealing with the CIA and its domestic spying, but there is not a single mention of the FPCC, Alpha–66, CORE, David Ferrie, project MER-RIMAC, or any anti-Castro Cuban groups or individuals. Belin baldly asserts that "there is no evidence to show there were any specific contacts between anti-Castro Cubans and Oswald in the U.S. much less Mexico" (p. 215). There is no mention of the U–2. Oswald's entire Soviet experience is dealt with in a single page.

36. CIA document 1636–1086, "Addendum to Comments on Paul Hoch Memorandum regarding CIA and the Warren Commission Investigation," p. 1.

37. June 1, 1984 letter to the author from Don W. Wilson.

CHAPTER 11

1. Thomas Powers, *The Man Who Kept the Secrets: Richard Helms and the CIA* (New York: Knopf, 1979), p. 297.

2. An example of a much broader, more encompassing conspiracy is the one recently posited by Jim Marrs (*Crossfire*, pp. 581–82): "So the decision was made at the highest level of the American business-banking-politics-military-crime power structure—should anything happen to Kennedy it would be viewed as a blessing for the nation." Voting him out would not work, Marrs asserts, because there were two more Kennedy's waiting to become president.

> Therefore the decision was made to eliminate John F. Kennedy by means of a public execution for the same reason criminals are publicly executed—to serve as a deterrent to anyone considering following in his footsteps. . . . Once the consensus was reached among the nation's top business-crime-military leadership, the assassination conspiracy went into action.

While "operational orders probably originated with organized crime chieftains" already working with the CIA, the mobsters recruited a "world-class assassin" from an international crime syndicate who "was then given entrée to the conspiracy groups within U.S. intelligence, the anti-Castro Cubans, right-wing hate groups and the military."

3. *Rolling Stone*, April 11, 1975. Quoted in Anson, *"They've Killed the President,"* p. 151.

4. For a fuller discussion of this matter see Philip H. Melanson, *The MURKIN Conspiracy: An Investigation into the Assassination of Dr. Martin Luther King, Jr.* (New York: Praeger, 1989), Appendix C, pp. 169–71. The Committee investigated both the King and Kennedy cases and similarly sealed its records in both cases.

5. Stephen Kinzer, "Cubans see U.S. Administration as Barking Dog that Won't Bite," *Boston Globe*, December 22, 1981, p. 10.

6. Philip H. Melanson, *The Politics of Protection: The U.S. Secret Service in the Terrorist Age* (New York: Praeger, 1984). The inadequacies of this alleged "profile" are discussed on pp. 76–81.

APPENDIX B

1. *HSCA*, IV, p. 157.
2. Ibid., pp. 185–86.
3. Ibid., pp. 178–79.
4. Ibid., p. 178.
5. Ibid., pp. 182–85.
6. Ibid., pp. 189–91.

Selected Bibliography

ON LEE HARVEY OSWALD AND THE KENNEDY ASSASSINATION

Books

Anson, Robert Sam *"They've Killed the President."* New York: Bantam, 1975.

Belin, David. *Final Disclosure: The Full Truth about the Assassination of President Kennedy.* New York: Charles Scribner's Sons, 1988.

Bringuier, Carlos. *Red Friday: November 22, 1963.* Chicago: C. Hallberg, 1969.

Curry, Jesse. *JFK Assassination File: Retired Dallas Police Chief Jesse Curry Reveals His Personal File.* Dallas: American Poster & Pub. Co., 1969.

Eddowes, Michael. *The Oswald File.* New York: Clarkson N. Potter, 1977.

Epstein, Edward J. *Counterplot.* New York: Viking, 1969.

————. *Legend: The Secret World of Lee Harvey Oswald.* New York: McGraw-Hill, 1979.

Fensterwald, Bernard, Jr., with Michael Ewing. *Coincidence or Conspiracy?* New York: Zebra Books, 1977.

Garrison, Jim. *Heritage of Stone.* New York: Berkeley, 1972.

————. *On the Trail of the Assassins: My Investigation and Prosecution of the Murder of President Kennedy.* New York: Sheridan Square Press, 1988.

Guth, DeLloyd J., and David R. Wrone. *The Assassination of John F. Kennedy: A Comprehensive Historical and Legal Bibliography, 1963–1979.* Westport, CT: Greenwood Press, 1980.

Hurt, Henry. *Reasonable Doubt: An Investigation into the Assassination of John F. Kennedy.* New York: Holt, Rinehart & Winston, 1986.

James, Rosemary and Jack Wardlaw. *Plot or Politics?: the Garrison Case and Its Cast.* New Orleans: Pelican, 1967.

Lane, Mark. *Rush to Judgement*. New York: Holt, Rinehart & Winston, 1966.

Manchester, William. *The Death of a President: November 20–25, 1963*. New York: Harper & Row, 1967.

McKinley, James. *Assassination in America*. New York: Harper & Row, 1977.

Meagher, Sylvia. *Accessories after the Fact: The Warren Commission, the Authorities, and the Report*. New York: Vintage, 1967.

————. and Gary Owens. *Master Index to the JFK Assassination Investigations*. Metuchen, NJ and London: Scarecrow Press, 1980.

Oltmans, Willem. *Reportage over de Moordenaars*. Utrecht, Holland: Bruna & Zoon, 1977.

Oswald, Robert L, with Myrick Land and Barbara Land. *Lee: A Portrait of Lee Harvey Oswald*. New York: Coward-McCann, 1967.

Popkin, Richard H. *The Second Oswald*. New York: Coward-McCann, 1975.

Scott, Peter Dale, *The Dallas Conspiracy*, privately published (widely used by serious researchers).

————, Paul L. Hoch, and Russell Stetler. *The Assassinations: Dallas and Beyond—A Guide to Cover-Ups and Investigations*. New York: Vintage Press, 1977.

Summers, Anthony. *Conspiracy*. New York: McGraw-Hill, 1980; New York: Paragon House, 1989.

Thornley, Kerry. *Oswald*. Chicago: New Classics House, 1965.

Weisberg, Harold. *Oswald in New Orleans—Case for Conspiracy with the CIA*. New York: Canyon Books, 1967.

————. *Whitewash*. Hyattstown, MD, 1965, 1967 (vols. 1–4, self-published); and New York: Dell, 1966–67 (vols. 1 and 2).

Articles

Melanson, Philip H. "Lee Harvey Oswald and the Black Lady of Espionage." Syndicated by the Independent News Alliance, March 31, 1983.

————. "Spy Saga." *L'Actualité* (Montreal, Canada), March 1983.

Government Reports

Report of the President's Commission on the Assassination of President John F. Kennedy (Warren Report), 26 vols. of hearings and exhibits. Washington, DC: U.S. Government Printing Office, 1964.

Report to the President on CIA Activities within the United States (Rockefeller Commission Report). New York: Manor Books, 1976.

U.S. Congress, House. *Report of the Select Committee on Assassinations* (and 12 accompanying volumes of hearings and exhibits). Washington, DC: U.S. Government Printing Office, 1979.

U.S. Congress, Senate. *Investigation of the Assassination of President John F. Kennedy*, Book V: *Final Report of the Select Committee to Study Gov-*

ernment Operations with Respect to Intelligence. Washington, DC: U.S. Government Printing Office, 1976; Book III: *Supplementary Detailed Staff Reports on Intelligence Activities and the Rights of Americans*.

————. *Alleged Assassination Plots Involving Foreign Leaders: Interim Report of the Select Committee to Study Government Operations with Respect to Intelligence*. Washington, DC: U.S. Government Printing Office, 1975.

Television Documentaries

CBS-TV special, "The American Assassins," November 26, 1975.
CBS-TV documentary, "The CIA's Secret Army," June 10, 1977.

ON THE CIA, THE INTELLIGENCE COMMUNITY, AND RELATED TOPICS

Books

Agee, Philip. *Inside the Company: CIA Diary*. New York: Bantam, 1976.

Attwood, William. *The Reds and the Blacks*. New York: Harper & Row, 1967.

Barron, John. *KGB*. New York: Readers Digest Press, 1974.

Clarke, James W. *American Assassins: The Darker Side of Politics*. Princeton, NJ: Princeton University Press, 1982.

Corson, William R. *The Armies of Ignorance: The Rise of American Intelligence Agencies*. New York: Dial Press, 1977.

Donner, Frank J. *The Age of Surveillance*. New York: Vintage Books, 1981.

Dulles, Allen. *The Craft of Intelligence*. New York: Harper & Row, 1963.

Halperin, Morton et al. *The Lawless State: The Crimes of U.S. Intelligence Agencies*. New York: Penguin Books, 1976.

Hougan, Jim. *Spooks*. New York: William Morrow, 1978.

Hunt, E. Howard. *Give Us This Day*. New York: Arlington House, 1973.

Johnson, Haynes. *The Bay of Pigs: The Leader's Story of Brigade 2506*. New York: W. W. Norton, 1964.

Kirkpatrick, Lyman B. *The Real CIA*. New York: Macmillan, 1968.

Marchetti, Victor and John Marks. *The CIA and the Cult of Intelligence*. New York: Dell, 1975.

Martin, David C. *Wilderness of Mirrors*. New York: Ballantine, 1980.

Melanson, Philip H. *The Politics of Protection: The U.S. Secret Service in the Terrorist Age*. New York: Praeger, 1984.

Penkovsky, Oleg. *The Penkovsky Papers*. New York: Avon Books, 1966.

Phillips, David. *The Night Watch*. New York: Atheneum, 1977.

Powers, Gary, with Curt Gentry. *Operation Overflight*. New York: Holt, Rinehart & Winston, 1970.

Powers, Thomas. *The Man Who Kept the Secrets: Richard Helms and the CIA*. New York: Alfred A. Knopf, 1979.

Prouty, Fletcher L. *The Secret Team*. Englewood Cliffs, NJ: Prentice Hall, 1973.

Ranelagh, John. *The Rise and Fall of the CIA*. New York: Simon and Schuster, 1986.

Rositzke, Harry. *The CIA's Secret Operations*. New York: Readers Digest Press, 1977.

Schlesinger, Arthur. *A Thousand Days: John F. Kennedy in the White House*. Boston: Houghton Mifflin Co., 1965.

Wise, David. *The American Police State: Government Against the People*. New York: Vintage Books, 1976.

——— and Thomas B. Ross. *The Invisible Government*. New York: Random House, 1964.

Wright, Peter. *Spycatcher: The Candid Autobiography of a Senior Intelligence Officer*. New York: Irving, 1987.

Articles

Branch, Taylor and George Crile. "The Kennedy Vendetta." *Harpers*, August 1975.

Salisbury, Harrison. "The Gentlemen Killers of the CIA." *Penthouse*, May 1975.

Turner, William. "Garrison Case." *New York Review of Books*, September 14, 1967.

Index

ABOUT THE AUTHOR

PHILIP H. MELANSON is Professor of Political Science at Southeastern Massachusetts University, where he is chair of the Robert F. Kennedy Assassination Archives.

Dr. Melanson has published widely in the area of political science. His articles and reviews have appeared in the *American Political Science Review, Comparative Political Studies, Politics and Society, Polity, Public Policy, Transaction/Society,* as well as in *The Nation,* and in various newspapers and magazines. He is the author of *Political Science and Political Knowledge, The Politics of Protection: The U.S. Secret Service in the Terrorist Age* (Praeger, 1984), *The MURKIN Conspiracy: An Investigation into the Assassination of Dr. Martin Luther King, Jr.* (Praeger, 1989), and is the editor of *Knowledge, Politics and Public Policy.* He has appeared widely on radio and television and has served as a consultant to several documentaries dealing with political assassinations.

Dr. Melanson holds a B.A., M.A., and Ph.D. from the University of Connecticut.